10% DISCOUNT
on a Talend Training Session

Talend training courses provide all required skills to take full advantage of the tools, regardless of the scope of the user's needs. In order to receive the 10% discount, please provide the Promo Code indicated below to your Talend Representative.

PROMO CODE: UM41DI11TR

Good until Dec. 31, 2011 on all training sessions organized by Talend.

To contact Talend: info@talend.com or www.talend.com/contact

10% DISCOUNT
on Talend Integration Suite
Team Edition or Professional Edition

Talend Integration Suite is provided as a subscription and includes value-added features, support and services. It leverages the same development environment as Talend Open Studio.
In order to receive the 10% discount, please provide the Promo Code indicated below to your Talend Representative.

PROMO CODE: UM41DI11TIS

Good until Dec. 31, 2011. Applies only to a one-year subscription to one seat of Talend Integration Suite Team Edition or Professional Edition. Only one coupon per company. Cannot be used in conjunction with any other offer.

To contact Talend: info@talend.com or www.talend.com/contact

Intentionally Blank

Version 4.1_b

Adapted for Talend Open Studio v4.1.x. Supersedes previous User Guide releases.

Copyleft

This documentation is provided under the terms of the Creative Commons Public License (CCPL).

For more information about what you can and cannot do with this documentation in accordance with the CCPL, please read: http://creativecommons.org/licenses/by-nc-sa/2.0/

Talend Open Studio User Guide i

Preface ix
   Purpose ix
   Audience ix
   Typographical conventions ix
History of changes ix
Feedback and Support x

CHAPTER 1
Data integration and Talend Open Studio 1
1.1 Data analytics 2
1.2 Operational integration 2
1.3 Execution monitoring 3

CHAPTER 2
Getting started with Talend Open Studio .. 5
2.1 Important concepts in Talend Open Studio 6
2.2 Launching Talend Open Studio 6
   2.2.1 How to access one or multiple Repositories 10
      How to connect to a local repository 10
   2.2.2 How to set up a project in the repository 11
2.3 Working with different workspace directories 11
   2.3.1 How to create a new workspace directory 12
   2.3.2 How to connect to a different workspace directory 12
2.4 Working with projects 13
   2.4.1 How to create a project 14
   2.4.2 How to import the Demo project 16
   2.4.3 How to import a project 17
   2.4.4 How to open a project 18
   2.4.5 How to delete a project 18
   2.4.6 How to export a project 19
   2.4.7 Migration tasks 20
2.5 Setting Talend Open Studio preferences 21
   2.5.1 Perl/Java Interpreter path 21
   2.5.2 External or User components 22
   2.5.3 Language preferences 23
   2.5.4 Debug and job execution preferences 23
   2.5.5 Designer preferences 25
   2.5.6 Adding code by default 25
   2.5.7 Performance preferences 26
   2.5.8 Documentation preferences 27
   2.5.9 Displaying special characters for schema columns 27
   2.5.10 SQL Builder preferences 28
   2.5.11 Schema preferences 28
   2.5.12 Libraries preferences 29
   2.5.13 Type conversion 30
2.6 Customizing project settings 31

   2.6.1 Palette Settings 31
   2.6.2 Version management 33
   2.6.3 Status management 34
   2.6.4 Job Settings 36
   2.6.5 Stats & Logs 36
   2.6.6 Context settings 37
   2.6.7 Project Settings use 38
   2.6.8 Status settings 39
   2.6.9 Security settings 41

CHAPTER 3
Designing a Business Model 43
3.1 What is a Business Model 44
3.2 Opening or creating a Business Model 44
   3.2.1 How to open a Business Model 44
   3.2.2 How to create a Business Model 45
3.3 Modeling a Business Model 46
   3.3.1 Shapes 46
   3.3.2 Connecting shapes 47
   3.3.3 How to comment and arrange a model 49
      How to add a note or free text 49
      How to arrange the model view 49
   3.3.4 Business Models 50
      Appearance tab 50
      Rulers and Grid tab 51
      Assignment tab 51
3.4 Assigning repository elements to a Business Model 52
3.5 Editing a Business Model 53
   3.5.1 How to rename a Business Model 54
   3.5.2 How to copy and paste a Business Model 54
   3.5.3 How to move a Business Model 54
   3.5.4 How to delete a Business Model 54
3.6 Saving a Business Model 54

CHAPTER 4
Designing a data integration Job 57
4.1 What is a job design 58
4.2 Getting started with a basic job design 58
   4.2.1 How to create a Job 58
   4.2.2 How to drop components to the workspace .. 61
      How to drop components from the Palette 61
      How to drop components from the Metadata node 62
   4.2.3 How to search components in the Palette 63
   4.2.4 How to connect components together 64
   4.2.5 How to define component properties 65
      Basic Settings tab 65
      Advanced settings tab 68
      Dynamic settings tab 68
      View tab 70
      Documentation tab 70
   4.2.6 How to run a Job 71
      How to run a Job in normal mode 71

How to run a Job in Java Debug mode 72
How to run a Job in Traces Debug mode 73
How to set advanced execution settings 75
4.2.7 How to customize your workspace 77
How to change the Palette layout and settings ... 77
How to change panels positions 80
How to display job configuration tabs/views 81
4.3 Using connections 81
4.3.1 Connection types 81
Row connection 82
Iterate connection 84
Trigger connections 84
Link connection 85
4.3.2 How to define connection settings 86
Row connection settings 86
Iterate connection settings 87
Trigger connection settings 88
4.4 Using the Metadata Manager 88
4.4.1 How to centralize the Metadata items 88
4.4.2 How to centralize contexts and variables 89
How to use variables in a Job 89
How to use variables in the Contexts view 90
How to configure contexts 93
How to define variables from the Component view 95
How to store contexts in the repository 96
How to apply context variables to a Job from the repository 98
How to run a Job in a selected context 100
4.4.3 How to use the SQL Templates 101
4.5 Handling Jobs: advanced subjects 101
4.5.1 How to map data flows 102
4.5.2 How to create queries using the SQLBuilder ... 102
How to compare database structures 103
How to build a query 104
How to store a query in the repository 106
4.5.3 How to download external community components 106
How to install community components from Talend Exchange 107
How to manage installed components 107
4.5.4 How to install external modules 108
4.5.5 How to launch a Job periodically 110
4.5.6 How to use the tPrejob and tPostjob components 112
4.6 Handling Jobs: miscellaneous subjects 113
4.6.1 How to share a database connection 113
4.6.2 How to define the Start component 114
4.6.3 How to handle error icons on components or Jobs 115
Warnings and error icons on components 115
Error icons on Jobs 115
4.6.4 How to add notes to a Job design 116
4.6.5 How to display the code or the outline of your Job 117
Outline 117

Code viewer 118
4.6.6 How to manage the subjob display 118
How to format subjobs 119
How to collapse the subjobs 119
How to remove the subjob background color ... 119
4.6.7 How to define options on the Job view 120
How to automate the use of statistics & logs ... 120
How to use the features in the Extra tab 121
4.6.8 How to find components in Jobs 122

CHAPTER 5
Managing data integration Jobs 125
5.1 Activating/Deactivating a Job or a sub-job 126
5.1.1 How to disable a Start component 126
5.1.2 How to disable a non-Start component 126
5.2 Importing/exporting items or Jobs 127
5.2.1 How to import items 127
5.2.2 How to export Jobs in Java 129
How to export Jobs as Autonomous Job 131
How to export Jobs as Webservice 132
An example of exporting a Job as a Web service ... 132
How to export Jobs as JBoss ESB 136
How to export Jobs as Petals ESB 137
5.2.3 How to export Jobs in Perl 140
5.2.4 How to export items 142
5.2.5 How to change context parameters in Jobs .144
5.3 Managing repository items 145
5.3.1 How to handle updates in repository items .145
How to modify a repository item 145
How to update impacted Jobs automatically 146
How to update impacted Jobs manually 147
5.4 Searching a Job in the repository 147
5.5 Managing Job versions 149
5.6 Documenting a Job 150
5.6.1 How to generate HTML documentation 150
5.6.2 How to update the documentation on the spot .. 151
5.7 Handling job execution 151
5.7.1 How to deploy a Job on SpagoBI server 151
How to create a SpagoBI server entry 151
How to edit or remove a SpagoBI server entry 153
How to deploy your jobs on a SpagoBI server .153

CHAPTER 6
Mapping data flows 155
6.1 tMap operation overview 156
6.2 tMap interface 157
6.3 Setting the input flow in the Map Editor 159
6.3.1 How to fill in Input tables with a schema ...159
Main and Lookup table content 159
Variables 159
6.3.2 How to use Explicit Join 160
Unique Match 162

    First Match 162
    All Matches 162
  6.3.3 How to use Inner join 162
  6.3.4 How to use the All Rows option 164
  6.3.5 How to filter an input flow 164
  6.3.6 How to remove input entries from table 164
6.4 Mapping variables 165
  6.4.1 How to access global or context variables . 166
  6.4.2 How to remove variables 166
6.5 Using the expression editor 166
  6.5.1 How to access the expression editor 166
  6.5.2 How to write code using the Expression Builder 168
6.6 Mapping the Output setting 171
  6.6.1 Building complex expressions 172
  6.6.2 Filters 172
  6.6.3 Rejections 173
  6.6.4 Inner Join Rejection 173
  6.6.5 Removing Output entries 174
  6.6.6 Handling errors 174
6.7 Describing the schema editor 175
6.8 Solving memory limitation issues in tMap use 176
6.9 Handling lookups 178

CHAPTER 7
Managing Metadata 181
7.1 Objectives 182
7.2 Setting up a DB connection 182
  7.2.1 Step 1: General properties 182
  7.2.2 Step 2: Connection 183
  7.2.3 Step 3: Table upload 185
  7.2.4 Step 4: Schema definition 188
7.3 Setting up an FTP connection 189
  7.3.1 Step 1: General properties 189
  7.3.2 Step 2: Connection 190
7.4 Setting up a JDBC schema 191
  7.4.1 Step 1: General properties 191
  7.4.2 Step 2: Connection 191
  7.4.3 Step 3: Table upload 193
  7.4.4 Step 4: Schema definition 193
7.5 Setting up a SAS connection 194
  7.5.1 Prerequisites 194
  7.5.2 Step 1: General properties 194
  7.5.3 Step 2: Connection 194
7.6 Setting up a File Delimited schema 196
  7.6.1 Step 1: General properties 196
  7.6.2 Step 2: File upload 196
  7.6.3 Step 3: Schema definition 197
  7.6.4 Step 4: Final schema 199
7.7 Setting up a File Positional schema 200
  7.7.1 Step 1: General properties 201
  7.7.2 Step 2: Connection and file upload 201
  7.7.3 Step 3: Schema refining 202
  7.7.4 Step 4: Finalising the end schema 202
7.8 Setting up a File Regex schema 203

  7.8.1 Step 1: General properties 203
  7.8.2 Step 2: File upload 203
  7.8.3 Step 3: Schema definition 204
  7.8.4 Step 4: Finalizing the end schema 204
7.9 Setting up an XML file schema 204
  7.9.1 Setting up an XML schema for an input file 205
    Step 1: General properties 205
    Step 2: Setting the type of schema (input) 206
    Step 3: Uploading the input file 207
    Step 4: Defining the schema 208
    Step 5: Finalizing the end schema 210
  7.9.2 Setting up an XML schema for an output file ... 211
    Step 1: General properties 211
    Step 2: Setting the type of schema (output) 212
    Step 3: Defining the output file 213
    Step 4:Defining the schema 215
    Step 5: Finalizing the end schema 216
7.10 Setting up a File Excel schema 217
  7.10.1 Step 1: General properties 218
  7.10.2 Step 2: File upload 218
  7.10.3 Step 3: Schema refining 219
  7.10.4 Step 4: Finalising the end schema 220
7.11 Setting up a File LDIF schema 221
  7.11.1 Step 1: General properties 221
  7.11.2 Step 2: File upload 221
  7.11.3 Step 3: Schema definition 222
  7.11.4 Step 4: Finalising the end schema 223
7.12 Setting up an LDAP schema 223
  7.12.1 Step 1: General properties 224
  7.12.2 Step 2: Server connection 224
  7.12.3 Step 3: Authentication and DN fetching ...224
  7.12.4 Step 4: Schema definition 226
  7.12.5 Step 5: Finalising the end schema 227
7.13 Setting up a Salesforce schema 228
  7.13.1 Step 1: General properties 229
  7.13.2 Step 2: Connection to a Salesforce account 229
  7.13.3 Step 3: Schema refining 229
  7.13.4 Step 4: Finalising the end schema 230
7.14 Setting up a Generic schema 231
  7.14.1 Step 1: General properties 232
  7.14.2 Step 2: Schema definition 232
7.15 Setting up a Web Service schema 232
  7.15.1 Setting up a simple schema 232
    Step 1: General properties 232
    Step 2: URI and method definition. 233
    Step 3: Finalizing the end schema 235
7.16 Setting up an MDM connection 235
  7.16.1 Step 1: Setting up the connection 236
  7.16.2 Step 2: Defining MDM schema 238
    Defining Input MDM schema 238
    Defining output MDM schema 243
    Defining Receive MDM schema 248
7.17 Exporting Metadata as context 252

CHAPTER 8
Managing routines 253

- 8.1 What are routines 254
- 8.2 Accessing the System Routines 254
- 8.3 Customizing the system routines 255
- 8.4 Managing user routines 256
  - 8.4.1 How to create user routines 257
  - 8.4.2 How to edit user routines 259
  - 8.4.3 How to edit user routine libraries 259
- 8.5 Calling a routine from a Job 260
- 8.6 Use case: Creating a file for the current date . 261

CHAPTER 9
Using SQL templates 263

- 9.1 What is ELT 264
- 9.2 Introducing Talend SQL templates 264
- 9.3 Managing Talend SQL templates 265
  - 9.3.1 Types of system SQL templates 265
  - 9.3.2 How to access a system SQL template 266
  - 9.3.3 How to create user-defined SQL templates 268
  - 9.3.4 A use case of system SQL Templates 269

APPENDIX A
Talend Open Studio GUI 275

- A.1 Main window 276
- A.2 Menu bar and Toolbar 277
  - A.2.1 Menu bar of Talend Open Studio 277
  - A.2.2 Toolbar of Talend Open Studio 279
- A.3 Repository tree view 279
- A.4 Design workspace 281
- A.5 Palette 281
- A.6 Configuration tabs 282
- A.7 Outline and code summary panel 284
- A.8 Shortcuts and aliases 284

APPENDIX B
Theory into practice: Job example 287

- B.1 Introducing the scenario 288
  - B.1.1 Input data 288
  - B.1.2 Output data 288
  - B.1.3 Reference data 289
- B.2 Translating the scenario into a Job 289
  - B.2.1 Step 1: Job creation, input definition, file reading 289
  - B.2.2 Step 2: Mapping and transformations 292
  - B.2.3 Step 3: Reference file definition, re-mapping, inner join mode selection 294
  - B.2.4 Step 4: Output to a MySQL table 296

APPENDIX C
SQL template writing rules 299

- C.1 SQL statements 300
- C.2 Comment lines 300
- C.3 The <%...%> syntax 300
- C.4 The <%=...%> syntax 301
- C.5 The </.../> syntax 301
- C.6 Code to access the component schema elements .. 302
- C.7 Code to access the component matrix properties 302

APPENDIX D
System routines 305

- D.1 Numeric Routines 306
  - D.1.1 How to create a Sequence 306
  - D.1.2 How to convert an Implied Decimal 306
- D.2 Relational Routines 307
- D.3 StringHandling Routines 307
  - D.3.1 How to store a string in alphabetical order 309
  - D.3.2 How to check whether a string is alphabetical . 309
  - D.3.3 How to replace an element in a string 309
  - D.3.4 How to check the position of a specific character or substring, within a string 309
  - D.3.5 How to calculate the length of a string 310
  - D.3.6 How to delete blank characters 310
- D.4 TalendDataGenerator Routines 310
  - D.4.1 How to generate fictitious data 311
- D.5 TalendDate Routines 312
  - D.5.1 How to format a date 313
  - D.5.2 How to check a Date 313
  - D.5.3 How to compare Dates 314
  - D.5.4 How to configure a date 314
  - D.5.5 How to parse a Date 314
  - D.5.6 How to format the Current Date 315
- D.6 TalendString Routines 315
  - D.6.1 How to format an XML string 316
  - D.6.2 How to trim a string 316
  - D.6.3 How to remove accents from a string 316

Preface

Purpose

This User Guide explains how to manage Talend Open Studio functions in a normal operational context.

Information presented in this document applies to Talend Open Studio releases beginning with **4.1.x**.

Audience

This guide is for users and administrators of Talend Open Studio.

 The layout of GUI screens provided in this document may vary slightly from your actual GUI.

Typographical conventions

This guide uses the following typographical conventions:

- text in **bold**: window and dialog box buttons and fields, keyboard keys, menus, and menu and options,
- text in **[bold]**: window, wizard, and dialog box titles,
- text in `courier`: system parameters typed in by the user,
- text in *italics*: file, schema, column, row, and variable names,

- The icon indicates an item that provides additional information about an important point. It is also used to add comments related to a table or a figure,

- The icon indicates a message that gives information about the execution requirements or recommendation type. It is also used to refer to situations or information the end-user need to be aware of or pay special attention to.

History of changes

The below table lists the changes made in the 4.x release of the Talend Open Studio User Guide.

Version	Date	History of Changes
v4.0_a	02/04/2010	Updates in Talend Open Studio User Guide include: -New chapter about routines. -New section about autogenerated documentation. -Modification in the CDC sections -Modifications in the default join in **tMap**. -Modifications in the language preferences section.

Version	Date	History of Changes
v4.0_b	28/05/2010	Updates in Talend Open Studio User Guide include: -New chapter: SQL Template. -New Appendix for SQL. -New section about exporting jobs as petals ESB.
v4.1_a	12/10/2010	Updates in Talend Open Studio User Guide include: -Update of the **Traces** feature. -Update of the **Run** view. -New login window. -Renewed MDM wizard. -New FTP wizard. -Updated content regarding **tMap** component changes.
v4.1_b	10/12/2010	Updates in Talend Open Studio User Guide include: -Reorganized Chapter 4 and added a new section to document connection settings -Added Appendix D: System routines

Feedback and Support

Your feedback is valuable. Do not hesitate to give your input, make suggestions or requests regarding this documentation or product and find support from the **Talend** team, on **Talend**'s Forum website at:

http://talendforge.org/forum

CHAPTER 1
Data integration and Talend Open Studio

There is nothing new about the fact that organizations' information systems tend to grow in complexity. The reasons for this include the "layer stackup trend" (a new solution is deployed although old systems are still maintained) and the fact that information systems need to be more and more connected to those of vendors, partners and customers.

A third reason is the multiplication of data storage formats (XML files, positional flat files, delimited flat files, multi-valued files and so on), protocols (FTP, HTTP, SOAP, SCP and so on) and database technologies.

A question arises from these statements: How to manage a proper integration of this data scattered throughout the company's information systems? Various functions lay behind the data integration principle: business intelligence or analytics integration (data warehousing) and operational integration (data capture and migration, database synchronization, inter-application data exchange and so on).

Both ETL for analytics and ETL for operational integration needs are addressed by Talend Open Studio.

1.1 Data analytics

While mostly invisible to users of the BI platform, ETL processes retrieve the data from all operational systems and pre-process it for the analysis and reporting tools.

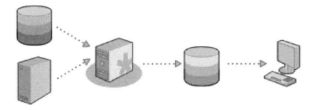

Talend Open Studio offers nearly comprehensive connectivity to:

- Packaged applications (ERP, CRM, etc.), databases, mainframes, files, Web Services, and so on to address the growing disparity of sources.
- Data warehouses, data marts, OLAP applications - for analysis, reporting, dashboarding, scorecarding, and so on.
- Built-in advanced components for ETL, including string manipulations, Slowly Changing Dimensions, automatic lookup handling, bulk loads support, and so on.

Most connectors addressing each of the above needs are detailed in the Talend Open Studio Components Reference Guide. For information about their orchestration in Talend Open Studio, see *Designing a data integration Job on page 57*. For high-level business-oriented modeling, see *Designing a Business Model on page 43*.

1.2 Operational integration

Operational data integration is often addressed by implementing custom programs or routines, completed on-demand for a specific need.

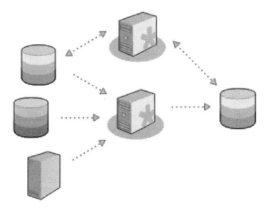

Data migration/loading and data synchronization/replication are the most common applications of operational data integration, and often require:

- Complex mappings and transformations with aggregations, calculations, and so on due to variation in data structure,

- Conflicts of data to be managed and resolved taking into account record update precedence or "record owner",

- Data synchronization in nearly real time as systems involve low latency.

Most connectors addressing each of the above needs are detailed in the Talend Open Studio Components Reference Guide. For information about their orchestration in Talend Open Studio, see *Designing a data integration Job on page 57*. For high-level business-oriented modeling, see *Designing a Business Model on page 43*.

1.3 Execution monitoring

One of the greatest challenges faced by developers of integration processes and IT Operations staff in charge of controlling their execution is to be able to control and monitor the execution of these critical processes. Indeed, failure handling and error notification can - and should - be included in data integration processes.

Furthermore, beyond on-error notification, it is often critical to monitor the overall health of the integration processes and to watch for any degradation in their performance.

The Talend Activity Monitoring Console monitors job events (successes, failures, warnings, etc.), execution times and data volumes through a single consoleavailable as a standalone environment.

For more information regarding Talend Activity Monitoring Console operation, check out the Talend Activity Monitoring Console **User Guide**.

CHAPTER 2
Getting started with Talend Open Studio

This chapter introduces Talend Open Studio. It provides basic configuration information required to get started with Talend Open Studio.

The chapter guides you through the basic steps in creating local projects. It also describes how to set preferences and customize the workspace in Talend Open Studio.

Before starting any data integration processes, you need to be familiar with Talend Open Studio Graphical User Interface (GUI). For more information, see *Talend Open Studio GUI on page 275*.

2.1 Important concepts in Talend Open Studio

When working with Talend Open Studio, you will often come across words such as repository, project, workspace, job, component and item.

Understanding the concept behind each of these words is crucial to grasping the functionality of Talend Open Studio.

What is a repository? A repository is the storage location Talend Open Studio uses to gather data related to all of the technical items that you use either to describe business models or to design Jobs. Talend Open Studio can connect to as many local repositories as needed. For more information, see *How to access one or multiple Repositories on page 10*.

What is a project? Projects are structured collections of technical items and their associated metadata. All of the Jobs and business models you design are organized in Projects.
You can create as many projects as you need in a repository. For more information about projects, see *Working with projects on page 13*.

What is a workspace? A workspace is the directory where you store all your project folders. You need to have one workspace directory per connection (repository connection). Talend Open Studio enables you to connect to different workspace directories, if you do not want to use the default one. For more information about workspaces, see *Working with different workspace directories on page 11*.

What is a job: A job is a graphical design, of one or more components connected together, that allows you to set up and run dataflow management processes. It translates business needs into code, routines and programs. Jobs address all of the different sources and targets that you need for data integration processes and all other related processes.
For detailed information about how to design data integration processes in Talend Open Studio, see *Designing a data integration Job on page 57*.

What is a component: A component is a preconfigured connector used to perform a specific data integration operation, no matter what data sources you are integrating: databases, applications, flat files, Web services, etc. A component can minimize the amount of hand-coding required to work on data from multiple, heterogeneous sources.
Components are grouped in families according to their usage and displayed in the **Palette** of the Talend Open Studio main window.
For detailed information about components types and what they can be used for, see the Talend Open Studio Reference Guide.

What is an item: An item is the fundamental technical unit in a project. Items are grouped, according to their types, as: Job Design, Business model, Context, Code, Metadata, etc. One item can include other items. For example, the business models and the Jobs you design are items, metadata and routines you use inside your Jobs are items as well.

2.2 Launching Talend Open Studio

To open Talend Open Studio, complete the following:

- Unzip the Talend Open Studio zip file and, in the folder, double-click the executable file corresponding to your operating system.
  A **[License]** window displays.

- Read and accept the terms of the license agreement to continue.
  A registration window displays.
- If required, follow the instructions provided to join **Talend** community or click **Register later** to proceed to the next step.
- If you are working behind a proxy, click **Network setting** and fill in the **Proxy Host** and **Proxy Port** fields of the **Network setting** dialog box.

 You can click the **You want to know more?** link in the registration window to open a page that explains the benefits of joining Talend community.

 Be ensured that any personal information you may provide to **Talend** will never be transmitted to third parties nor used for any other purpose other than to inform you about **Talend** and **Talend**'s products.

A Talend Open Studio main login window opens prompting you to set a connection.

- Click the three-dot button and set a connection to a local repository.
  This repository will store all the data and metadata associated with the projects and items of the project you create in Talend Open Studio. It will also store different versions of project items. For further information about connecting to a repository, see *How to access one or multiple Repositories on page 10* in Talend Open Studio User Guide.

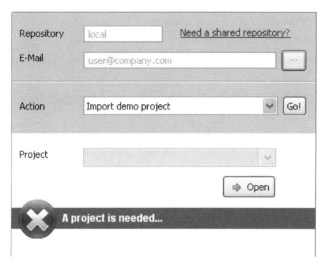

- From the **Action** field, select:

Option	To...
Import demo project	import Demo project including numerous samples of ready-to-use Jobs. This Demo project can help you understand the functionnalities of different **Talend** components. For more information, see *How to import the Demo project on page 16*.
Create a new local project	create a new local project that will hold all Jobs and Business models designed in the Studio. For more information, see *How to create a project on page 14*.
Import existing project(s) as local	import any project stored locally. For more information, see *How to import a project on page 17*.
Delete local projects	open a dialog box in which you can delete any created or imported project that you don't need anymore. For more information, see *How to delete a project on page 18*.

- Click **Go!** to proceed to the next step that varies according to the option you select. The purpose of this procedure is to create a new local project.

- In the **[New project]** dialog box, enter a name for your project, select a generation language (Perl or Java), and click **Finish** to close the dialog box. The name of the new project displays in the **Project** list.

- Click **Open**.

A progress information bar and a welcome window display consecutively. From this page you have direct links to user documentation, tutorials, **Talend** forum, **Talend Exchange** and **Talend** latest news.

- Click **Start now!** to open Talend Open Studio main window.
  For more information on how to open a project, see *How to open a project on page 18*.

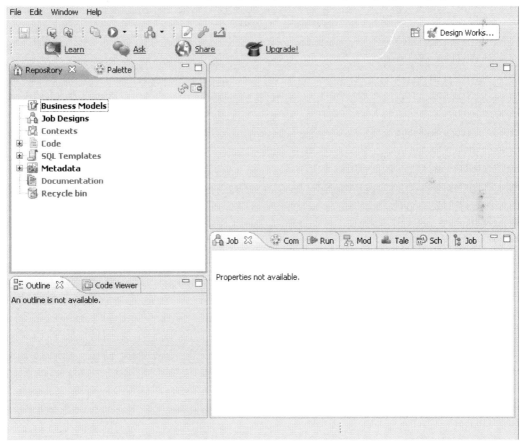

2.2.1 How to access one or multiple Repositories

On Talend Open Studio login window, you can connect to one or several local repositories where you store the data for all your projects, including Jobs and business models, metadata, routines, etc.

How to connect to a local repository

To connect to a local repository, do the following:

- On the login window of Talend Open Studio, click the three-dot button to proceed to the next step and set the connection information.

   if you have already set your user name and connection details, you can directly select the relevant entry from the **Repository** list.

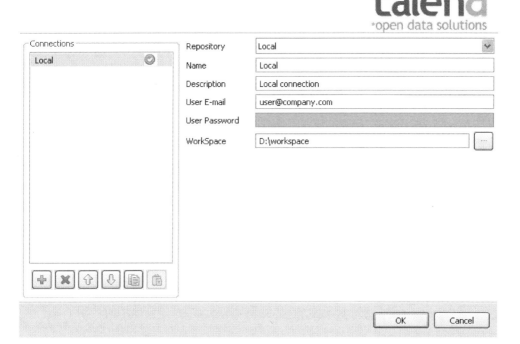

- If needed, type in a name and a description for your connection in the relevant fields.
- In the **User E-mail** field, type in the email address that will be used as your user login. This field is compulsory to be able to use Talend Open Studio.
  Be aware that the email entered is never used for another purpose other than logging in.
- If needed, click the plus [+] button in the lower left corner and set the connection information to add as many connections as needed.
- By default, the **Workspace** field shows the path to the current workspace directory which contains all of the folders belonging to the project created.
- You can still modify this path or indicate the access path to another workspace by clicking the three-dot button next to the field.

Getting started with Talend Open Studio
Working with different workspace directories

 If you modify the path to the workspace directory, a message on the login window will prompt you to restart the Studio. Click the **Restart** button on the login window to restart the Studio and access the project(s) of the indicated workspace. For more information about how to connect to a different worspace, see *Working with different workspace directories on page 11*

- Click **OK** to validate your changes and close the new view.

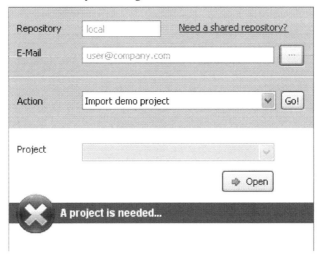

The login window displays prompting you to select a project-related option from the **Action** list.

Usually, when you connect to the Studio for the first time, you need to create a new project. For more information about how to create a project, see *How to create a project on page 14*.

For information about all other possible operations on projects, see *Managing data integration Jobs on page 125*.

2.2.2 How to set up a project in the repository

To open the Talend Open Studio main window, you must first set up a project in the repository you connected to earlier.

You can set up a project in the repository by:

- creating a new project. For more information, see *How to create a project on page 14*.
- importing one or more local projects you already created in other sessions of Talend Open Studio. For more information, see *How to import a project on page 17*.
- importing the Demo project. For more information, see *How to import the Demo project on page 16*.

2.3 Working with different workspace directories

Talend Open Studio makes it possible to create many workspace directories and connect to a workspace different from the one you are currently working on, if necessary.

This flexibility enables you to store these directories wherever you want and give the same project name to two or more different projects as long as you store the projects in different directories.

2.3.1 How to create a new workspace directory

Talend Open Studio is delivered with a default workspace directory. However, you can create as many new directories as you want and store your project folders in them according to your preferences.

To create a new workspace directory:

- On the Talend Open Studio login window, click the three-dot button next to the **Repository** field to proceed to the next step.

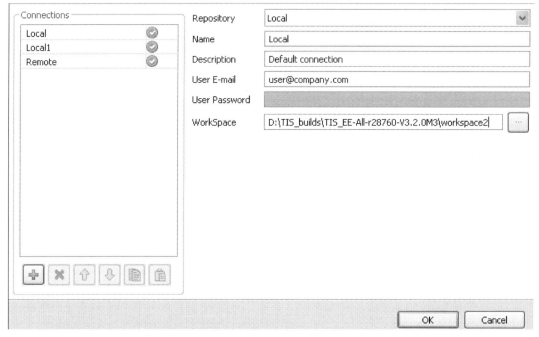

- In the **WorkSpace** field, set the path to the new workspace directory you want to create and then click **OK** to close the view.
  On the login window, a message displays prompting you to restart the Studio.

- Click **Restart** to restart the Studio.

- On the re-initiated login window, set up a project for this new workspace directory.
  For more information, see *How to set up a project in the repository on page 11*.

- Select the project from the **Project** list and click **Open** to open Talend Open Studio main window.

All business models or Jobs you design in the current instance of the Studio will be stored in the new workspace directory you created. For information on how to connect to a different workspace, see the below section.

2.3.2 How to connect to a different workspace directory

On the Talend Open Studio log-in window, you can select the workspace directory you want to store your project folders in according to your preferences.

To change the workspace directory:

- On the Talend Open Studio login window, click the three-dot button next to the **Repository** field to proceed to the next step.

- Click the three-dot button next to the **WorkSpace** field to open a dialog box where you can browse to the workspace directory you want to connect to.

- Select the workspace directory in the dialog box of your operating system and click **OK**. The dialog box closes and the path to the selected workspace directory is set in the **Workspace** field.

- Click **OK** to close the view.
  On the login window, a message displays prompting you to restart the Studio.

- Click **Restart** to restart the Studio.

- On the re-initiated login window and from the **Project** list, select a project and click **Open** to open Talend Open Studio main window.
  All business models or Jobs you design in the current instance of the Studio will be stored in the selected workspace directory.

2.4 Working with projects

In Talend Open Studio, the highest physical structure for storing all different types of data integration Jobs and business models, metadata, routines, etc. is the "project".

From the login window of Talend Open Studio, you can:

- import the Demo project to discover the features of Talend Open Studio based on samples of different ready-to-use Jobs. When you import the Demo project, it is automatically installed in the workspace directory of the current session of the Studio.
  For more information, see *How to import the Demo project on page 16*.

Getting started with Talend Open Studio
Working with projects

- create a local project. When connecting to Talend Open Studio for the first time, there are no default projects listed. You need to create a local project and open it in the Studio to store all the Jobs and business models you create in it. When creating a new project, a tree folder is automatically created in the workspace directory on your repository server. This will correspond to the **Repository** tree view displaying on Talend Open Studio main window.
  For more information, see *How to create a project on page 14*.

- If you already created projects with previous releases of Talend Open Studio, you can import them into your current Talend Open Studio workspace directory using the **Import existing project(s) as local** option.
  For more information, see *How to import a project on page 17*.

- open a project you created or imported in the Studio. For more information, see *How to open a project on page 18*.

- delete local projects that you already created or imported and that you do not need any longer.
  For more information, see *How to delete a project on page 18*.

Once you launch Talend Open Studio, you can export the resources of one or more of the created projects in the current instance of the Studio. For more information, see *How to export a project on page 19*.

2.4.1 How to create a project

When you connect to the local repository of the current Studio for the first time, there are no default projects listed. You need to create a project that will hold all data integration Jobs and business models you design in the current instance of the Studio.

To create a project:

- Launch Talend Open Studio and connect to a local repository.

- From the **Action** list in the Studio login window, select **Create a new local project** and click **Go**.
  The **[New project]** dialog box displays.

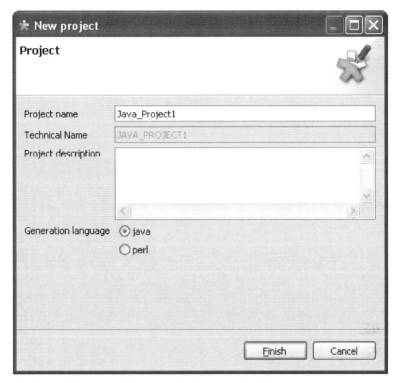

- In the **Project name** field, enter a name for the new project. This field is mandatory. A message shows at the top of the wizard, according to the location of your pointer, to inform you about the nature of data to be filled in, such as forbidden characters

     The read-only "technical name" is used by the application as file name of the actual project file. This name usually corresponds to the project name, upper-cased and concatenated with underscores if needed.

- Select the **Generation language** between **Java** and **Perl**. Later when designing Jobs and working with the different **Talend** data integration components, you have to use Perl code in Perl projects and Java code in Java projects.

- Click **Finish**. The name of the newly created project displays in the **Project** list in Talend Open Studio login window.

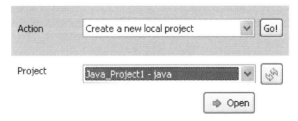

To open the newly created project in Talend Open Studio, select it from the **Project** list and then click **Open**. A generation engine initialization window displays. Wait till the initialization is complete.

Later, if you want to switch between projects, on the Studio menu bar, use the combination **File** > **Switch Project**.

> We strongly discourage having too many heterogeneous projects in both languages and switching from a
> Perl project to a Java project too often. Nevertheless, if you still want to work in both languages, we advise
> you to keep them in separate locations or even to launch two distinct instances of Talend Open Studio in
> order to avoid language conflicts.

If you already used Talend Open Studio and want to import projects from a previous release, see *How to import a project on page 17*.

2.4.2 How to import the Demo project

In Talend Open Studio, you can import the Demo project that includes numerous samples of ready to use Jobs. This Demo project can help you understand the functionalities of different **Talend** components.

- From the **Project** list on the login window of Talend Open Studio, select **Import demo project** then click **Go**. The **[Import demo project]** dialog box displays

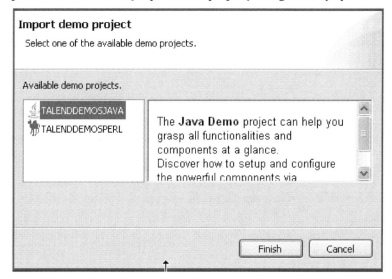

- Select your preferred language between Perl and Java and then click **Finish** to close the dialog box.

A confirmation message displays to say that the Demo project has been successfully imported in the current instance of the Studio.

- Click **Ok** to close the confirmation message. The imported Demo project displays in the **Project** list on the login window.

To open the imported Demo project in Talend Open Studio, select it from the **Project** list and then click **Open**. A generation engine initialization window displays. Wait till the initialization is complete.

The Job samples in the open Demo project are automatically imported into your workspace directory and made available in the **Repository** tree view under the **Job Designs** folder.

You can use these samples to get started with your own job design.

2.4.3 How to import a project

In Talend Open Studio, you can import projects you already created with previous releases of the Studio.

- From the **Project** list on the login window of Talend Open Studio, select **Import existing project(s) as local** then click **Go**. The **[Import]** wizard displays.

- Click **Import several projects** if you intend to import more than one project simultaneously.
- Click **Select root directory** or **Select archive file** depending on the source you want to import from.
- Click **Browse...** to select the workspace directory/archive file of the specific project folder. By default, the workspace in selection is the current release's one. Browse up to reach the previous release workspace directory or the archive file containing the projects to import.
- Select the **Copy projects into workspace** check box to make a copy of the imported project instead of moving it.

 If you want to remove the original project folders from the Talend Open Studio workspace directory you import from, clear this check box. But we strongly recommend you to keep it selected for backup purposes.

- From the **Projects** list, select the projects to import and click **Finish** to validate the operation.

In the login window, the names of the imported projects now appear on the **Project** list.

Getting started with Talend Open Studio
Working with projects

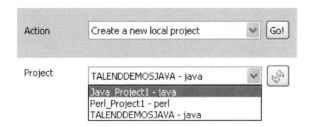

You can now select the imported project you want to open in Talend Open Studio and click **Open** to launch the Studio.

 A generation initialization window might come up when launching the application. Wait until the initialization is complete.

2.4.4 How to open a project

 *When you launch Talend Open Studio for the first time, no project name displays on the **Project** list. First you need to create a project or import a local or Demo project in order to populate the **Project** list with the corresponding project names that you can then open in the Studio*

To open a project in Talend Open Studio:

- On the Studio login window, click the refresh button to update the list of projects then choose the relevant project name and click **Open**.

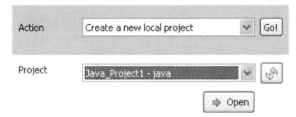

A progress bar displays then the Talend Open Studio main window opens. A generation engine initialization dialog bow displays. Wait till initialization is complete.

 When you open a project imported from a previous version of the Studio, an information window pops up to list a short description of the successful migration tasks. For more information, see *Migration tasks on page 20*.

2.4.5 How to delete a project

- From the **Project** list on the Studio login window, select **Delete local project(s)** and then click **Go** to open the **[Select Project]** dialog box.

- Select the check box(es) of the project(s) you want to delete.
- Click **OK** to validate the deletion.
  The project list on the login window is refreshed accordingly.

 *Be careful, this action is irreversible. When you click **OK**, there is no way to recuperate the deleted project(s).*

 If you select the **Do not delete projects physically** check box, you can delete the selected project(s) only from the project list and still have it/them in the *workspace* directory of Talend Open Studio. Thus, you can recuperate the deleted project(s) any time using the **Import existing project(s) as local** option on the **Project** list from the login window.

2.4.6 How to export a project

Talend Open Studio, allows you to export projects created or imported in the current instance of Talend Open Studio.

- On the toolbar of the Studio main window, click to open the **[Export Talend projects in archive file]** dialog box.

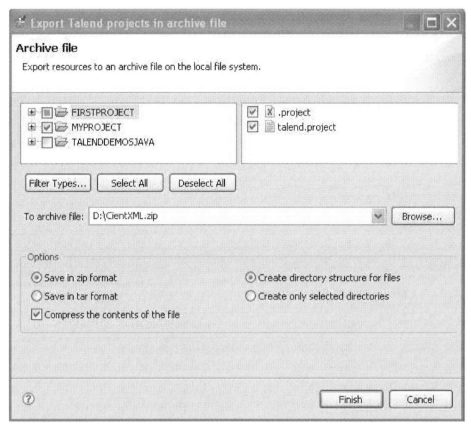

- Select the check boxes of the projects you want to export. You can select only parts of the project through the **Filter Types...** link, if need be (for advanced users).
- In the **To archive file** field, type in the name of or browse to the archive file where you want to export the selected projects.
- In the **Option** area, select the compression format and the structure type you prefer.
- Click **Finish** to validate the changes.

The archived file that holds the exported projects is created in the defined place.

2.4.7 Migration tasks

Migration tasks are performed to ensure the compatibility of the projects you created with a previous version of Talend Open Studio with the current release.

As some changes might become visible to the user, we thought we'd share these update tasks with you through an information window.

This information window pops up when you launch the project you imported (created) in a previous version of Talend Open Studio. It lists and provides a short description of the tasks which were successfully performed so that you can smoothly roll your projects.

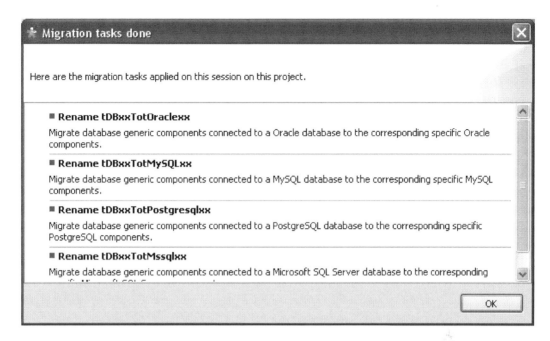

Some changes that affect the usage of Talend Open Studio include, for example:

- **tDBInput** used with a MySQL database becomes a specific **tDBMysqlInput** component the aspect of which is automatically changed in the Job where it is used.

- **tUniqRow** used to be based on the Input schema keys, whereas the current **tUniqRow** allows the user to select the column to base the unicity on.

2.5 Setting Talend Open Studio preferences

You can define various properties of Talend Open Studio main design workspace according to your needs and preferences.

Numerous settings you define can be stored in the **Preference** and thus become your default values for all new Jobs you create.

The following sections describe specific settings that you can set as preference.

First, click the **Window** menu of your Talend Open Studio, then select **Preferences**.

2.5.1 Perl/Java Interpreter path

In the preferences, you might need to let Talend Open Studio pointing to the right interpreter path, Perl or Java.

- If needed, click the **Talend** node in the tree view of the **[Preferences]** dialog box.
- Enter a path to the Perl/Java interpreter if the default directory does not display the right path.

Getting started with Talend Open Studio
Setting Talend Open Studio preferences

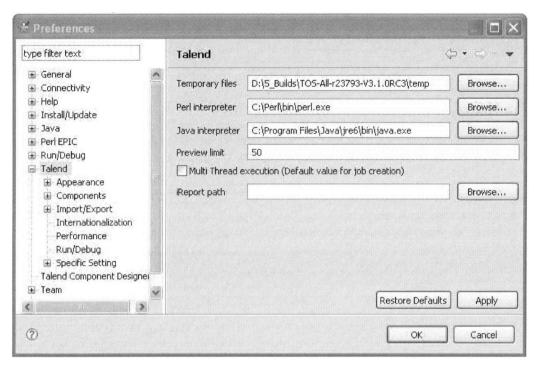

On the same view, you can also change the preview limit and the path to the temporary files or the OS language.

2.5.2 External or User components

You can create and develop your own components for use in Talend Open Studio.

For further information about the creation and development of user components refer to our wiki, *Component creation tutorial section.*

In the tree view of the **[Preferences]** dialog box, expand the **Talend** node and select **Components**.

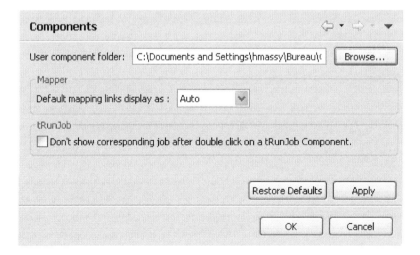

- Enter the **User components folder** path or browse to the folder that holds the components to be added to the Talend Open Studio **Palette**.

- From the **Default mapping links display as** list, select the mapping link type you want to use in the **tMap**.

- Under **tRunJob**, select the check box if you do not want the corresponding job to open upon double clicking a **tRunJob** component.

> You will still be able to open the corresponding Job by right clicking the tRunJob component and selecting **Open tRunJob Component**.

- Click **Apply** and then **OK** to validate the set preferences and close the dialog box.
  The external components are added to the **Palette**.

2.5.3 Language preferences

You can set language preferences in Talend Open Studio. To do so:

- On the menu bar, click **Window** > **Preferences** to open the **[Preferences]** dialog box.
- Expand the **Talend** node and click **Internationalization** to display the relevant view.

- From the **Local Language** list, select the language you want to use for Talend Open Studio graphical interface.
- Click **Apply** and then **OK** to validate your change and close the **[Preferences]** dialog box.
- Restart Talend Open Studio to display the graphical interface in the selected language.

2.5.4 Debug and job execution preferences

You can set your preferences for debug and job executions in Talend Open Studio. To do so:

- On the menu bar, click **Window** > **Preferences** to display the **[Preferences]** dialog box.
- Expand the **Talend** node and click **Run/Debug** to display the relevant view.

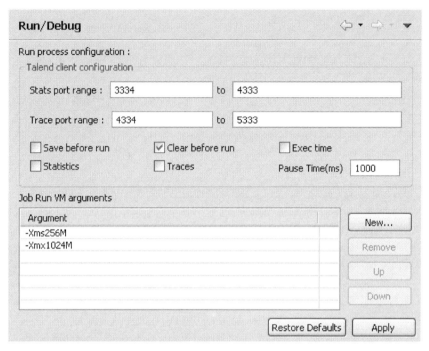

In the **Talend client configuration** area, you can define the execution options to be used by default:

- In the **Stats port range** fields, you can specify a range for the ports used for generating statistics. In particular, if the ports defined by default are used by other applications.

- In the **Trace port range** fields, you can specify a range for the ports used for generating traces. In particular, if the ports defined by default are used by other applications.

- Select the **Save before run** check box to automatically save our Job before its execution.

- Select the **Clear before run** check box to delete the results of a previous execution before re-executing the Job.

- Select the **Exec time** check box to show job execution duration.

- Select the **Statistics** check box to show the statistics measurement of data flow during job execution.

- Select the **Traces** check box to show data processing during job execution.

- In the **Pause time** field, enter the time you want to set before each data line in the traces table.

- In the **Job Run VM arguments** list, you can define the parameter of your current JVM according to your needs. The by-default parameters **-Xms256M** and **-Xmx1024M** correspond respectively to the minimal and maximal memory capacities reserved for your job executions.
  If you want to use some JVM parameters for only a specific Job execution, for example if you want to display the execution result for this specific Job in Japanese, you need open this Job's **Run** view and then in the **Run** view, configure the advanced execution settings to define the corresponding parameters.

For further information about the advanced execution settings of a specific Job, see *How to set advanced execution settings on page 75*.

For more information about possible parameters, check the site
http://java.sun.com/javase/technologies/hotspot/vmoptions.jsp.

2.5.5 Designer preferences

You can set component and job design preferences to let your settings be permanent in the Studio.

- On the menu bar, click **Window** > **Preferences** to open the **[Preferences]** dialog box.
- Expand the **Talend** > **Appearance** node.
- Click **Designer** to display the corresponding view.

On this view, you can define the way component names and hints will be displayed.

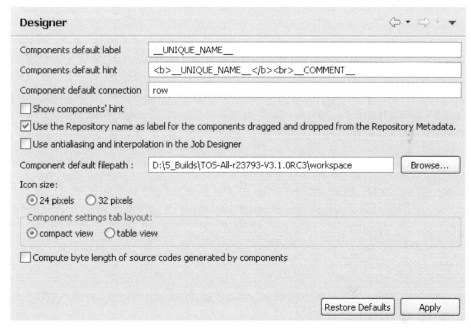

Select the relevant check boxes to customize your use of Talend Open Studio design workspace.

2.5.6 Adding code by default

You can add pieces of code by default at the beginning and at the end of the code of your Job.

- On the menu bar, click **Window** > **Preferences** to open the **[Preferences]** dialog box.
- Expand the **Talend** and **Import/Export** nodes in succession and then click **Shell Setting** to display the relevant view.

- In the **Command** field, enter your piece/pieces of code before or after %GENERATED_TOS_CALL% to display it/them before or after the code of your Job.

2.5.7 Performance preferences

You can set the **Repository** tree view preferences according to your use of Talend Open Studio. To refresh the **Repository** view:

- On the menu bar, click **Window** > **Preferences** to open the **[Preferences]** dialog box.
- Expand the **Talend** node and click **Performance** to display the repository refresh preference.

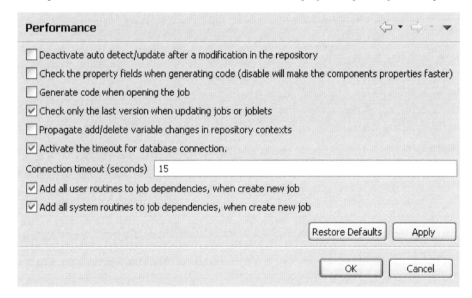

 You can improve your performance when you deactivate automatic refresh.

Set the performance preferences according to your use of Talend Open Studio:

- Select the **Deactivate auto detect/update after a modification in the repository** check box to deactivate the automatic detection and update of the repository.

- Select the **Check the property fields when generating code** check box to activate the audit of the property fields of the component. When one property filed is not correctly filled in, the component is surrounded by red on the design workspace.

   You can optimize performance if you disable property fields verification of components, i.e. if you clear the **Check the property fields when generating code** check box.

- Select the **Generate code when opening the job** check box to generate code when you open a job.

- Select the **Check only the last version when updating jobs or joblets** check box to only check the latest version when you update a job or a joblet.

- Select the **Propagate add/delete variable changes in repository contexts** to propagate variable changes in the Repository Contexts.

- Select the **Activate the timeout for database connection** check box to establish database connection time out. Then set this time out in the **Connection timeout (seconds)** field.

- Select the **Add all user routines to job dependencies, when create new job** check box to add all user routines to job dependancies upon the creation of new Jobs.

- Select the **Add all system routines to job dependencies, when create job** check box to add all system routines to job dependencies upon the creation of new Jobs.

2.5.8 Documentation preferences

You can include the source code on the generated documentation.

- On the menu bar, click **Window** > **Preferences** to open the **[Preferences]** dialog box.

- Expand the **Talend** node and click **Documentation** to display the documentation preferences.

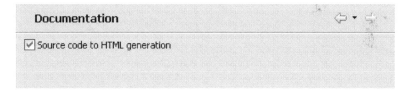

- Select the **Source code to HTML generation** check box to include the source code in the HTML documentation that you will generate.

For more information on documentation, see *How to generate HTML documentation on page 150* and *Documentation tab on page 70*.

2.5.9 Displaying special characters for schema columns

You may need to retrieve a table schema that contains columns written with special characters like Chinese, Japanese, Korean. In this case, you need to enable Talend Open Studio to read the special characters. To do so:

- On the menu bar, click **Window** > **Preferences** to open the **[Preferences]** dialog box.

- On the tree view of the opened dialog box, expand the **Talend** node.

- Click the **Specific settings** node to display the corresponding view on the right of the dialog box.
- Select the **Allow specific characters (UTF8,...) for columns of schemas** checkbox.

2.5.10 SQL Builder preferences

You can set your preferences for the SQL Builder. To do so:

- On the menu bar, click **Window** > **Preferences** to open the **[Preferences]** dialog box.
- Expand the **Talend** and **Specific Settings** nodes in succession and then click **Sql Builder** to display the relevant view.

- Select the **add quotes, when you generated sql statement** check box to precede and follow column and table names with inverted commas in your SQL queries.
- In the **AS400 SQL generation** area, select the **Standard SQL Statement** or **System SQL Statement** check boxes to use standard or system SQL statements respectively when you use an AS400 database.
- Clear the **Enable check queries in the database components (disable to avoid warnings for specific queries)** check box to deactivate the verification of queries in all database components.

2.5.11 Schema preferences

You can define the default data length and type of the schema fields of your components.

- On the menu bar, click **Window** > **Preferences** to open the **[Preferences]** dialog box.
- Expand the **Talend** node and click **Default Type and Length** to display the data length and type of your schema.

Getting started with Talend Open Studio
Setting Talend Open Studio preferences

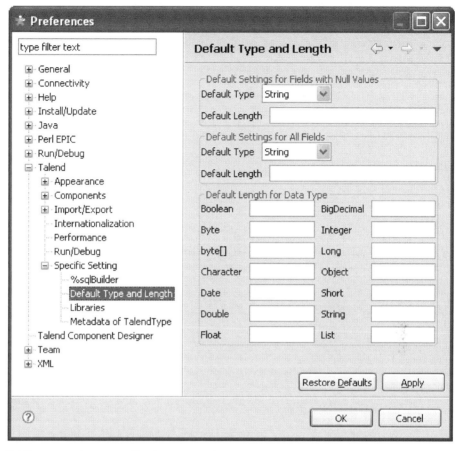

Set the parameters according to your needs:

- In the **Default Settings for Fields with Null Values** area, fill in the data type and the field length to apply to the null fields.

- In the **Default Settings for All Fields** area, fill in the data type and the field length to apply to all fields of the schema.

- In the **Default Length for Data Type** area, fill in the field length for each type of data.

2.5.12 Libraries preferences

You can define the folder where to store the different libraries used in Talend Open Studio. To do so:

- On the menu bar, click **Window** > **Preferences** to display the **[Preferences]** dialog box.

- Expand the **Talend** and **Specific Settings** nodes in succession and then click **Libraries** to display the relevant view.

Getting started with Talend Open Studio
Setting Talend Open Studio preferences

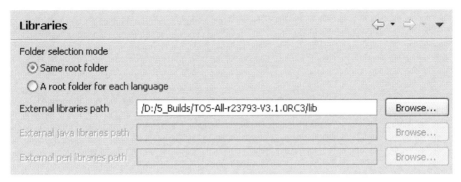

- In the **Folder selection mode** area, select the **Same root folder** check box to store the Java and Perl libraries in the same folder. You can set the access path in the **External libraries path** field through the **Browse...** button.

- If you prefer to store the Java and Perl libraries in two different folders, select the check box **A root folder for each language** and set the access paths in the **External java libraries path** and **External perl libraries path** for Java and Perl libraries respectively.

2.5.13 Type conversion

You can set the parameters for type conversion in Talend Open Studio, from Java towards databases and vice versa.

- On the menu bar, click **Window** > **Preferences** to display the **[Preferences]** dialog box.

- Expand the **Talend** and **Specific Settings** nodes in succession and then click **Metadata of Talend Type** to display the relevant view.

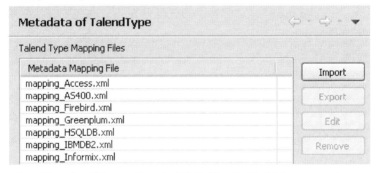

The **Metadata Mapping File** area lists the XML files that hold the conversion parameters for each database type used in Talend Open Studio.

- You can import, export, or delete any of the conversion files by clicking **Import**, **Export** or **Remove** respectively.

- You can modify any of the conversion files according to your needs by clicking the **Edit** button to open the **[Edit mapping file]** dialog box and then modify the XML code directly in the open dialog box.

2.6 Customizing project settings

Talend Open Studio enables you to customize the information and settings of the project in progress, including the **Palette**, job settings and job version management, for example.

- To access the project settings, click on [icon] on the Studio tool bar. Alternatively you can click on **File** > **Edit Project Properties** on the menu bar. The **[Project Settings]** dialog box opens.

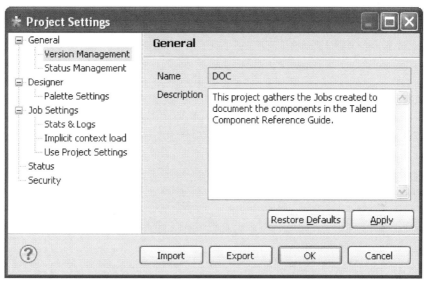

- In the tree diagram to the left of the dialog box, select the setting you wish to customize and then customize it, using the options that appear to the right of the box.

From the dialog box you can also export or import the full assemblage of settings that define a particular project.

- To export the settings, click on the **Export** button. The export will generate an XML file containing all of your project settings.

- To import settings, click on the **Import** button and select the XML file containing the parameters of the project which you want to apply to the current project.

2.6.1 Palette Settings

You can customize the settings of the **Palette** display so that only the components used in the project are loaded. This will allow you to launch the Studio more quickly:

- On the toolbar of the Studio's main window, click [icon] or click **File** > **Edit Project Properties** on the menu bar to open the **[Project Settings]** dialog box.

Getting started with Talend Open Studio
Customizing project settings

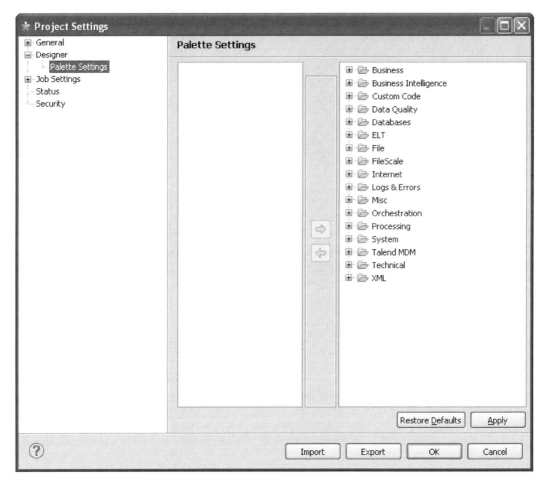

In the **General** view of the **[Project Settings]** dialog box, you can add a project description, if you did not do so when creating the project.

To customize the **Palette** display settings:

- In the tree view of the **[Project Settings]** dialog box, expand **Designer** and select **Palette Settings**. The settings of the current **Palette** are displayed in the panel to the right of the dialog box.

- Select one or several components, or even set(s) of components you want to remove from the current project's **Palette**.

- Use the left arrow button to move the selection onto the panel on the left. This will remove the selected components from the **Palette**.

- To re-display hidden components, select them in the panel on the left and use the right arrow button to restore them to the **Palette**.

- Click **Apply** to validate your changes and **OK** to close the dialog box.

To get back to the **Palette** default settings, click **Restore Defaults**.

For more information on the **Palette**, see *How to change the Palette layout and settings on page 77*.

2.6.2 Version management

You can also manage the version of each item in the **Repository** tree view through **General** > **Version Management** of the **[Project Settings]** dialog box.

- On the toolbar of the Studio main window, click [icon] or click **File** > **Edit Project Properties** from the menu bar to open the **[Project Settings]** dialog box.

- In the tree view of the dialog box, expand **General** and select **Version Management** to open the corresponding view.

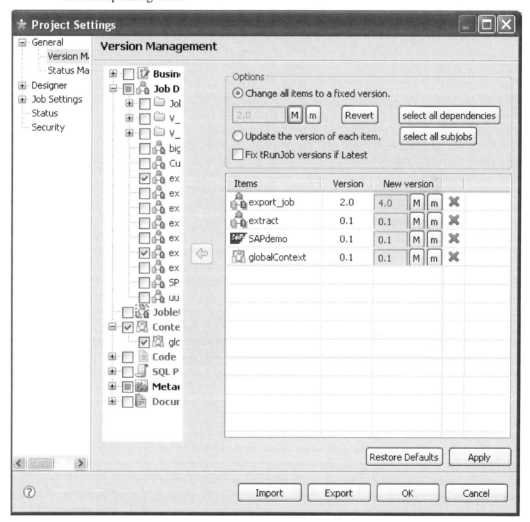

- In the **Repository** tree view, expand the node holding the items you want to manage their versions and then select the check boxes of these items.
  The selected items display in the **Items** list to the right along with their current version in the **Version** column and the new version set in the **New Version** column.

- In the **Options** area, select the **Change all items to a fixed version** check box to change the version of the selected items to the same fixed version.

- Click **Revert** if you want to undo the changes.

- Click **Select all dependencies** if you want to update all of the items dependent on the selected items at the same time.

- Click **Select all subjobs** if you want to update all of the subjobs dependent on the selected items at the same time.

- To increment each version of the items, select the **Update the version of each item** check box and change them manually.

- Select the **Fix tRunjob versions if Latest** check box, if you want the father job of current version to keep using the child Job(s) of current version in the **tRunjob** to be versioned, , regardless of how their versions will update. For example, a **tRunjob** will update from the currrent version *1.0* to *1.1* at both father and child levels. Once this check box is selected, the father Job *1.0* will continue to use the child Job *1.0* rather than the latest one as usual, say, version *1.1* when the update is done.

> *To use this check box, the father Job must be usingchild Job(s) of the latest version as current version in the tRunjob to be versioned, by having selected the Latest option from the drop-down version list in the Component view of the child Job(s). For more infomation on **tRunJob**, see the tRunJob section in the Talend Open Studio Components Reference Guide.*

- Click **Apply** to apply your changes and then **OK** to close the dialog box.

> For more information on version management, see *Managing Job versions on page 149*.

2.6.3 Status management

You can also manage the status of each item in the **Repository** tree view through **General** > **Status Management** of the **[Project Settings]** dialog box.

- On the toolbar of the Studio main window, click or click **File** > **Edit Project Properties** from the menu bar to open the **[Project Settings]** dialog box.

- In the tree view of the dialog box, expand **General** and select **Status Management** to open the corresponding view.

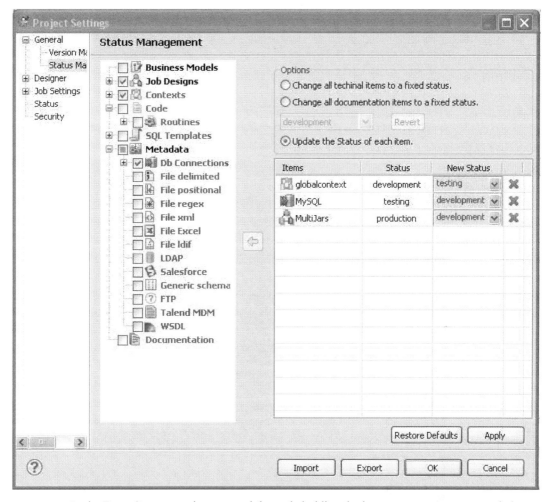

- In the **Repository** tree view, expand the node holding the items you want to manage their status and then select the check boxes of these items.
  The selected items display in the **Items** list to the right along with their current status in the **Status** column and the new status set in the **New Status** column.

- In the **Options** area, select the **Change all technical items to a fixed status** check box to change the status of the selected items to the same fixed status.

- Click **Revert** if you want to undo the changes.

- To increment each status of the items, select the **Update the version of each item** check box and change them manually.

- Click **Apply** to apply your changes and then **OK** to close the dialog box.

 For further information about Job status , see *Status settings on page 39*.

2.6.4 Job Settings

You can automatically use **Implicit Context Load** and **Stats and Logs** settings you defined in the **[Project Settings]** dialog box of the actual project when you create a new job. To do so:

- On the toolbar of the Studio main window, click [icon] or click **File** > **Edit Project Properties** from the menu bar to open the **[Project Settings]** dialog box.

- In the tree view of the dialog box, click the **Job Settings** node to open the corresponding view.

- Select the **Use project settings when create a new job** check boxes of the **Implicit Context Load** and **Stats and Logs** areas.

- Click **Apply** to validate your changes and then **OK** to close the dialog box.

2.6.5 Stats & Logs

When you execute a Job, you can monitor the execution through the **tStatCatcher Statistics** option or through using a log component. This will enable you to store the collected log data in .csv files or in a database.

You can then set up the path to the log file and/or database once for good in the **[Project Settings]** dialog box so that the log data get always stored in this location.

- On the toolbar of the Studio main window, click [icon] or click **File** > **Edit Project Properties** from the menu bar to open the **[Project Settings]** dialog box.

- In the tree view of the dialog box, expand the **Job Settings** node and then click **Stats & Logs** to display the corresponding view.

Getting started with Talend Open Studio
Customizing project settings

If you know that the preferences for Stats & Logs will not change depending upon the context of execution, then simply set permanent preferences. If you want to apply the Stats & Logs settings individually, then it is better to set these parameters directly onto the Stats & Logs view. For more information about this view, see *How to automate the use of statistics & logs on page 120*.

- Select the **Use Statistics**, **Use Logs** and **Use Volumetrics** check boxes where relevant, to select the type of log information you want to set the path for.
- Select a format for the storage of the log data: select either the **On Files** or **On Database** check box. Or select the **On Console** check box to display the data in the console.

The relevant fields are enabled or disabled according to these settings. Fill out the **File Name** between quotes or the **DB name** where relevant according to the type of log information you selected.

You can now store the database connection information in the **Repository**. Set the **Repository Type** to **Repository** and browse to retrieve the relevant connection metadata. The fields get automatically completed.

Alternatively, if you save your connection information in a Context, you can also access them through Ctrl+Space.

2.6.6 Context settings

You can define default context parameters you want to use in your Jobs.

- On the toolbar of the Studio main window, click ![icon] or click **File** > **Edit Project Properties** from the menu bar to open the **[Project Settings]** dialog box.
- In the tree view of the dialog box, expand the **Job Settings** node and then select the **Implicit Context Load** check box to display the configuration parameters of the Implicit tContextLoad feature.

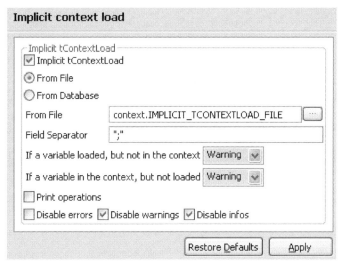

- Select the **From File** or **From Database** check boxes according to the type of file you want to store your contexts in.
- For files, fill in the file path in the **From File** field and the field separator in the **Field Separator** field.
- For databases, select the **Built-in** or **Repository** mode in the **Property Type** list and fill in the next fields.
- Fill in the **Table Name** and **Query Condition** fields.
- Select the type of system message you want to have (warning, error, or info) in case a variable is loaded but is not in the context or vice versa.
- Click **Apply** to validate your changes and then **OK** to close the dialog box.

2.6.7 Project Settings use

From the **[Project Settings]** dialog box, you can choose to which Job in the **Repository** tree view you want to apply the **Implicit Context Load** and **Stats and Logs** settings. To do so:

- On the toolbar of the Studio main window, click ![icon] or click **File** > **Edit Project Properties** from the menu bar to open the **[Project Settings]** dialog box.
- In the tree view of the dialog box, expand the **Job Settings** node and then click **Use Project Settings** to display the use of **Implicit Context Load** and **Stats and Logs** option in the Jobs.

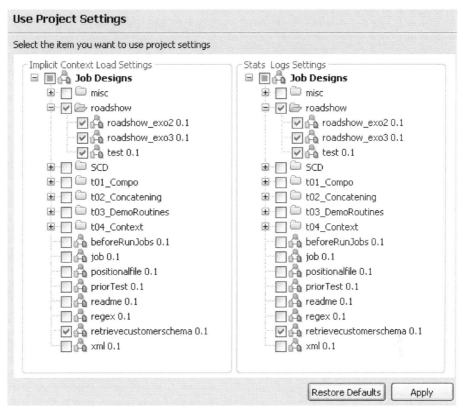

- In the **Implicit Context Load Settings** area, select the check boxes corresponding to the Jobs in which you want to use the implicit context load option.

- In the **Stats Logs Settings** area, select the check boxes corresponding to the Jobs in which you want to use the stats and logs option.

- Click **Apply** to validate your changes and then **OK** to close the dialog box.

2.6.8 Status settings

In the **[Project Settings]** dialog box, you can also define the Status.

- On the toolbar of the Studio main window, click or click **File** > **Edit Project Properties** from the menu bar to open the **[Project Settings]** dialog box.

- In the tree view of the dialog box, click the **Status** node to define the main properties of your **Repository** tree view elements.
  The main properties of a repository item gathers information data such as **Name**, **Purpose**, **Description**, **Author**, **Version** and **Status** of the selected item. Most properties are free text fields, but the **Status** field is a drop-down list.

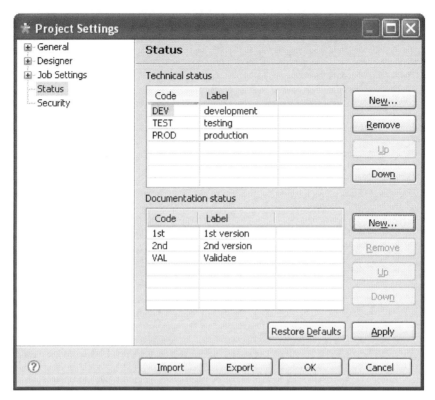

- Click the **New...** button to display a dialog box and populate the **Status** list with the most relevant values, according to your needs. Note that the **Code** can not be more than 3-character long and the **Label** is required.

Talend makes a difference between two status types: **Technical status** and **Documentation status**.

The **Technical status** list displays classification codes for elements which are to be running on stations, such as Jobs, metadata or routines.

The **Documentation status** list helps classifying the elements of the repository which can be used to document processes (Business Models or documentation).

- Once you completed the status setting, click **OK** to save

The **Status** list will offer the status levels you defined here when defining the main properties of your job designs and business models.

- In the [**Project Settings**] dialog box, click **Apply** to validate your changes and then **OK** to close the dialog box.

2.6.9 Security settings

You can hide or show your passwords on your documentations, metadata, contexts, and so on when they are stored in the **Repository** tree view.

- On the toolbar of the Studio main window, click 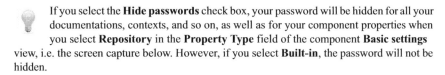 or click **File** > **Edit Project Properties** from the menu bar to open the **[Project Settings]** dialog box.
- In the tree view of the dialog box, click the **Security** node to open the corresponding view.
- Select the **Hide passwords** check box to hide your password.

    If you select the **Hide passwords** check box, your password will be hidden for all your documentations, contexts, and so on, as well as for your component properties when you select **Repository** in the **Property Type** field of the component **Basic settings** view, i.e. the screen capture below. However, if you select **Built-in**, the password will not be hidden.

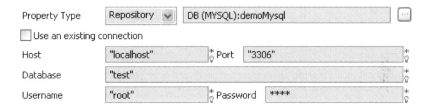

- In the **[Project Settings]** dialog box, click **Apply** to validate your changes and then **OK** to close the dialog box.

CHAPTER 3
Designing a Business Model

Talend Open Studio offers the best tool to formalize business descriptions into building blocks and their relationships. Talend Open Studio allows to design systems, connections, processes and requirements using standardized workflow notation through an intuitive graphical library of shapes and links.

This chapter aims at business managers, decision makers or developers who want to model their flow management needs at a macro level.

Before starting any business processes, you need to be familiar with Talend Open Studio Graphical User Interface (GUI). For more information, see *Talend Open Studio GUI on page 275*.

3.1 What is a Business Model

Talend's Business Models allow data integration project stakeholders to graphically represent their needs regardless of the technical implementation requirements. Business Models help the IT operation staff understand these expressed needs and translate them into technical processes (Jobs). They typically include both the systems and processes already operating in the enterprise, as well as the ones that will be needed in the future.

Designing Business Models is part of the enterprises' best practices that organizations should adopt at a very early stage of a data integration project in order to ensure its success. Because Business Models usually help detect and resolve quickly project bottlenecks and weak points, they help limit the budget overspendings and/or reduce the upfront investment. Then during and after the project implementation, Business Models can be reviewed and corrected to reflect any required change.

A Business Model is a non technical view of a business workflow need.

Generally, a typical Business Model will include the strategic systems or processes already up and running in your company as well as new needs. You can symbolize these systems, processes and needs using multiple shapes and create the connections among them. Likely, all of them can be easily described using repository attributes and formatting tools.

In the design workspace of Talend Open Studio, you can use multiple tools in order to:

- draw your business needs,
- create and assign numerous repository items to your model objects,
- define the business model properties of your model objects.

3.2 Opening or creating a Business Model

Open Talend Open Studio following the procedure as detailed in the paragraph *Launching Talend Open Studio on page 6.*,

In the **Repository** tree view, right-click the **Business Models** node.

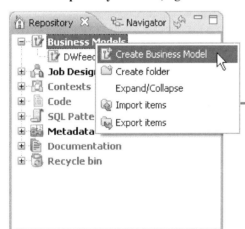

Select **Expand/Collapse** to display all existing Business Models (if any).

3.2.1 How to open a Business Model

Double-click the name of the Business Model to be opened.

The selected Business Model opens up on the design workspace.

3.2.2 How to create a Business Model

Right-click the **Business Models** node and select **Create Business Model**.

The creation wizard guides through the steps to create a new Business Model.

Select the **Location** folder where you want the new model to be stored.

And fill in a **Name** for it. The name you allocate to the file shows as a label on a tab at the top of the design workspace and the same name displays under the **Business Models** node in the **Repository** tree view.

The **Modeler** opens up on the empty design workspace.

You can create as many models as you want and open them all, they will display in a tab system on your design workspace.

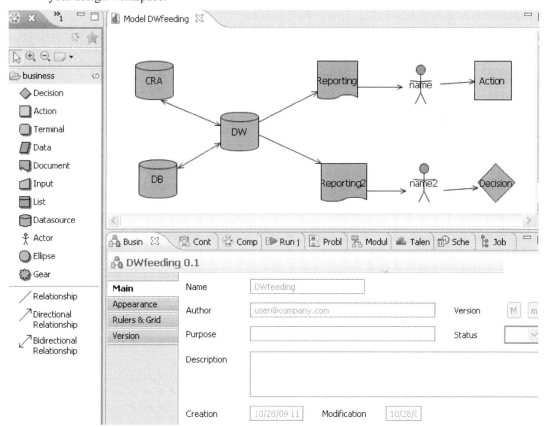

The **Modeler** is made of the following panels:

- Talend Open Studio's design workspace
- a **Palette** of shapes and lines specific to the business modeling
- the **Business Model** panel showing specific information about all or part of the model.

Designing a Business Model
Modeling a Business Model

3.3 Modeling a Business Model

If you have multiple tabs opened on your design workspace, click the relevant tab in order to show the appropriate model information.

In the **Business Model** view, you can see information relative to the active model.

Use the **Palette** to drop the relevant shapes on the design workspace and connect them together with branches and arrange or improve the model visual aspect by zooming in or out.

This **Palette** offers graphical representations for *objects* interacting within a Business Model.

The *objects* can be of different types, from strategic system to output document or decision step. Each one having a specific role in your Business Model according to the description, definition and assignment you give to it.

All objects are represented in the **Palette** as *shapes*, and can be included in the model.

Note that you must click the **business** folder to display the library of shapes on the **Palette**.

3.3.1 Shapes

Select the shape corresponding to the relevant *object* you want to include in your Business Model. Double-click it or click the shape in the **Palette** and drop it in the modeling area.

Alternatively, for a quick access to the shape library, keep your cursor still on the modeling area for a couple of seconds to display the quick access toolbar:

For instance, if your business process includes a decision step, select the diamond shape in the **Palette** to add this decision step to your model.

 When you move the pointer over the quick access toolbar, a tooltip helps you to identify the shapes.

Then a simple click will do to make it show on the modeling area.

The shape is placed in a dotted black frame. Pull the corner dots to resize it as necessary.

Also, a blue-edged input box allows you to add a label to the shape. Give an expressive name in order to be able to identify at a glance the role of this shape in the model.

Two arrows below the added shape allow you to create connections with other shapes. You can hence quickly define sequence order or dependencies between shapes.

Related topic: *Connecting shapes on page 47*.

The available shapes include:

Callout	Details
Decision	The diamond shape generally represents an **if** condition in the model. Allows to take context-sensitive actions.
Action	The square shape can be used to symbolize actions of any nature, such as transformation, translation or formatting.
Terminal	The rounded corner square can illustrate any type of output terminal
Data	A parallelogram shape symbolize data of any type.
Document	Inserts a Document object which can be any type of document and can be used as input or output for the data processed.
Input	Inserts an input object allowing the user to type in or manually provide data to be processed.
List	forms a list with the extracted data. The list can be defined to hold a certain nature of data
Database	Inserts a database object which can hold the input or output data to be processed.
Actor	This schematic character symbolizes players in the decision-support as well technical processes
Ellipse	Inserts an ellipse shape
Gear	This gearing piece can be used to illustrate pieces of code programmed manually that should be replaced by a **Talend** Job for example.

3.3.2 Connecting shapes

When designing your Business Model, you want to implement relations between a source shape and a target shape.

There are two possible ways to connect shapes in your design workspace:

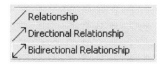

Either select the relevant **Relationship** tool in the **Palette**. Then, in the design workspace, pull a link from one shape to the other to draw a connection between them.

Or, you can implement both the relationship and the element to be related to or from, in few clicks.

- Simply mouse over a shape that you already dropped on your design workspace, in order to display the double connection arrows.

Designing a Business Model
Modeling a Business Model

- Select the relevant arrow to implement the correct directional connection if need be.
- Drag a link towards an empty area of the design workspace and release to display the connections popup menu.
- Select the appropriate connection from the list. You can choose among **Create Relationship To**, **Create Directional Relationship To** or **Create Bidirectional Relationship To**.
- Then, select the appropriate element to connect to, among the items listed.

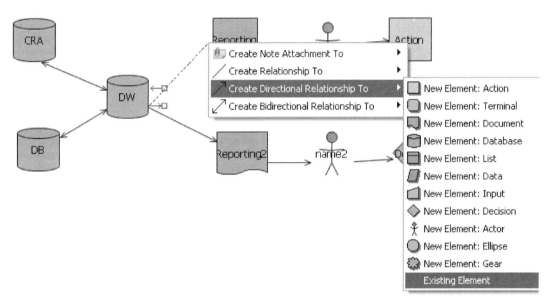

You can create a connection to an existing element of the model. Select **Existing Element** in the popup menu and choose the existing element you want to connect to in the displaying list box.

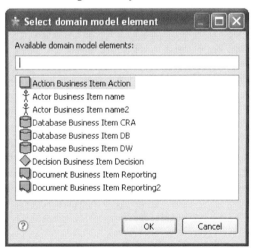

The connection is automatically created with the selected shape.

The nature of this connection can be defined using **Repository** elements, and can be formatted and labelled in the **Properties** panel, see *Business Models on page 50*.

When creating a connection, an input box allows you to add a label to the connection you've created. Choose a meaningful name to help you identify the type of relationship you created.

 You can also add notes and comments to your model to help you identify elements or connections at a later date.

Related topic: *How to comment and arrange a model* on page 49

3.3.3 How to comment and arrange a model

The tools of the **Palette** allow you to customize your model:

Callout	Details
Select	Select and move the shapes and lines around in the design workspace's modeling area.
Zoom	Zoom in to a part of the model. To watch more accurately part of the model. To zoom out, press *Shift* and click the modeling area.
Note/Text/Note attachment	Allows comments and notes to be added in order to store any useful information regarding the model or part of it.

How to add a note or free text

To add a note, select the **Note** icon in the **Palette**, docked to the right of the design workspace.

Alternatively right-click the model or the shape you want to link the note to, and select *Add Note*. Or select the Note tool in the quick access toolbar.

A sticky note displays on the modeling area. If the note is linked to a particular shape, a line is automatically drawn to the shape.

Type in the text in the input box or, if the latter doesn't show, type in directly on the sticky note.

If you want to link your notes and specific shapes of your model, click the down arrow next to the **Note** tool on the **Palette** and select **Note attachment**. Pull the black arrow towards an empty area of the design workspace, and release. The popup menu offers you to attach a new Note to the selected shape.

You can also select the *Add Text* feature to type in free text directly in the modeling area. You can access this feature in the **Note** drop-down menu of the **Palette** or via a shortcut located next to the *Add Note* feature on the quick access toolbar.

How to arrange the model view

You can also rearrange the look and feel of your model via the right-click menu.

Designing a Business Model
Modeling a Business Model

Place your cursor in the design area, right-click to display the menu and select *Arrange all*. The shapes automatically move around to give the best possible reading of the model.

Alternatively, you can select manually the whole model or part of it.

To do so, right-click any part of the modeling area, and click *Select*.

You can select:

• **All** shapes and connectors of the model,

• **All shapes** used in the design workspace,

• **All connectors** branching together the shapes.

From this menu you can also zoom in and out to part of the model and change the view of the model.

3.3.4 Business Models

The information in the **Business Models** view corresponds to the current selection, if any. This can be the whole model if you selected all shapes of it or more specifically one of the shapes it is made of. If nothing is selected, the **Business Models** tab gives general information about the model.

The **Business Models** view contains different types of information grouped in the **Main**, **Appearance**, **Rules & Grid**, and **Assignment** tabs.

The **Main** tab displays basic information about the selected item in the design workspace, being a Business Model or a Job. For more information about the **Main** tab, see *Configuration tabs on page 282*.

Appearance tab

From the **Appearance** tab you can apply filling or border colors, change the appearance of shapes and lines in order to customize your Business Model or make it easier to read.

The **Business Model** view includes the following formats:

- fill the shape with selected color.
- color the shape border
- insert text above the shape
- insert gradient colors to the shape
- insert shadow to the shape

You can also move and manage shapes of your model using the edition tools. Right-click the relevant shape to access these editing tools.

Rulers and Grid tab

To display the **Rulers & Grid** tab, click on the **Palette**, then click any empty area of the design workspace to deselect any current selection.

Click the **Rulers & Grid** tab to access the ruler and grid setting view.

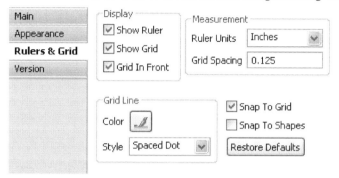

In the Display area, select the **Show Ruler** check box to show the **Ruler**, the **Show Grid** check box to show the **Grid**, or both heck boxes. **Grid in front** sends the grid to the front of the model.

In the Measurement area, select the ruling unit among **Centimeters**, **Inches** or **Pixels**.

In the **Grid Line** area, click the Color button to set the color of the grid lines and select their style from the **Style** list.

Select the **Snap To Grid** check box to bring the shapes into line with the grid or the **Snap To Shapes** check box to bring the shapes into line with the shapes already dropped in the Business Model.

You can also click the **Restore Defaults** button to restore the default settings.

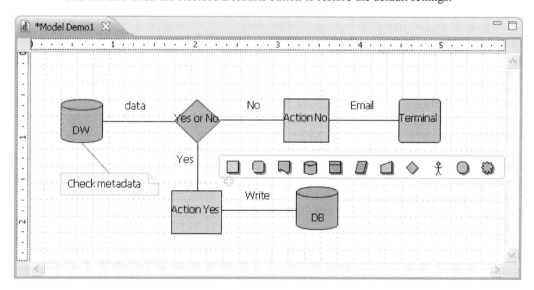

Assignment tab

The **Assignment** tab displays in a tabular form details of the **Repository** attributes you allocated to a shape or a connection.

Designing a Business Model
Assigning repository elements to a Business Model

To display any assignment information in the table, select a shape or a connection in the active model, then click the **Assignment** tab in the **Business Model** view.

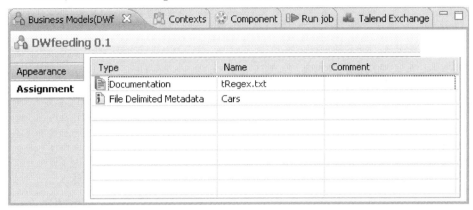

You can also display the assignement list placing the mouse over the shape you assigned information to.

You can modify some information or attach a comment. Also, if you update data from the **Repository** tree view, assignment information gets automatically updated.

For further information about how to assign elements to a Business Model, see *Assigning repository elements to a Business Model on page 52*.

3.4 Assigning repository elements to a Business Model

The **Assignment** tab in the **Business Models** view lists the elements from the **Repository** tree view which have been assigned to a shape in the Business Model.

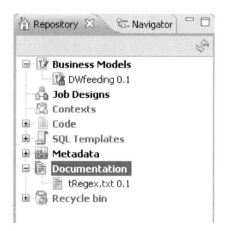

You can define or describe a particular object in your Business Model by simply associating it with various types of information, i.e. by adding metadata items.

You can set the nature of the metadata to be assigned or processed, thus facilitating the job design phase.

To assign a metadata item, simply drop it from the **Repository** tree view to the relevant shape in the design workspace.

The **Assignment** table, located underneath the design workspace, gets automatically updated accordingly with the assigned information of the selected object.

The types of items that you can assign are:

Element	Details
Job designs	If any job designs developed for other projects in the same repository are available, you can reuse them as metadata in the active Business Model
Metadata	You can assign any descriptive data stored in the repository to any of the objects used in the model. It can be connection information to a database for example.
Business Models	You can use in the active model all other Business Models stored in the repository of the same project.
Documentation	You can assign any type of documentation in any format. It can be a technical documentation, some guidelines in text format or a simple description of your databases.
Routines (Code)	If you have developed some routines in a previous project, to automate tasks for example, you can assign them to your Business Model. Routines are stored in the **Code** folder of the **Repository** tree view.

For more information about the **repository** elements, see *Designing a data integration Job on page 57*

3.5 Editing a Business Model

Follow the relevant procedure according to your needs:

3.5.1 How to rename a Business Model

Right-click the relevant Business Model label on the **Repository** tree view then select **Edit properties** to display the corresponding **Main** properties information in the **[Edit properties]** dialog box.

Edit the model name in the **Name** field, then click Finish to close the dialog box. The model label changes automatically in the **Repository** tree view and will be reflected on the model tab of the design workspace, the next time you open the Business Model.

 If the Business Model is open, the information in the **[Edit properties]** dialog box will be read-only so you won't be able to edit them.

3.5.2 How to copy and paste a Business Model

In **Repository** > **Business model,** right-click the Business Model name to be copied and select **Copy** in the popup menu, or press **Ctrl+c**.

Then right-click where you want to paste your Business Model, and select **Paste**.

3.5.3 How to move a Business Model

To move a Business Model from a location to another in your business models project folder, select a Business Model in the **Repository** > **Business Models** tree.

Then simply drop it to the new location.

3.5.4 How to delete a Business Model

Right-click the name of the model to be deleted and select **Delete** in the popup menu.

Alternatively, simply select the relevant Business Model, then drop it into the **Recycle bin** of the **Repository** tree view.

3.6 Saving a Business Model

To save a Business Model, click **File** > **Save** or press **Ctrl+s**. The model is saved under the name you gave during the creation process.

An asterisk displays in front of the business model name on the tab to indicate that changes have been made to the model but not yet saved.

To save a Business Model and increment its version in the same time, click **File**>**Save as....**The **[Save as]** dialog box displays.

- Next to the **Version** field, click the **M** button to increment the major version and the **m** button to increment the minor version.

- Click **Finish** to validate the modification

Designing a Business Model
Saving a Business Model

 By default, when you open a Business Model, you open its last version.
Any previous version of the Business Model is read-only and thus can not be modified

You can access a list of the different versions of a Business Model and perform certain operations. To do that:

- In the **Repository** tree view, select the Business Model you want to consult the versions of.
- Click the **Business Models>Version** in succession to display the version list of the selected Job.
- Right-click the Business Model version you want to consult.
- Do one of the followings:

Select	To...
Edit properties	edit Business Model properties. **Note:** The Business Model should not be open on the design workspace, otherwise it will be in read-only mode.
Read Business Model	consult the Business Model in read-only mode.

 You can open and modify the last version of a Business Model from the **Version** view if you select **Edit Business Model** from the drop-down list.

Designing a Business Model
Saving a Business Model

CHAPTER 4
Designing a data integration Job

Talend Open Studio is the tool with the capabilities that treat all of the different sources and targets required in data integration processes and all other associated operations.

Talend Open Studio helps you to design data integration Jobs that allow you to put in place up and run dataflow management processes.

This chapter addresses the needs of programmers or IT managers who are ready to implement the technical aspects of a business model (regardless of whether it was designed in Talend Open Studio's Business Modeler).

Before starting any data integration processes, you need to be familiar with the Talend Open Studio Graphical User Interface (GUI). For more information, see *Talend Open Studio GUI on page 275*.

4.1 What is a job design

A job design is the runnable layer of a business model. It is the graphical design, of one or more components connected together, that allows you to set up and run dataflow management processes. A job design translates business needs into code, routines and programs, in other words it technically implements your data flow.

The Jobs you design can address all of the different sources and targets that you need for data integration processes and any other related process.

When you design a Job in Talend Open Studio, you can:

- put in place data integration actions using a library of technical components.
- change the default setting of components or create new components or family of components to match your exact needs.
- set connections and relationships between components in order to define the sequence and the nature of actions.
- access code at any time to edit or document the components in the designed Job.
- create and add items to the repository for reuse and sharing purposes (in other projects or Jobs or with other users).

In order to be able to execute the Jobs you design in Talend Open Studio, you need to install a JVM Sun 1.5 or later (IBM JVM is not supported). You can download it from http://java.sun.com/javase/downloads/index.jsp.

4.2 Getting started with a basic job design

Until a Job is created, the design workspace is unavailable and the Palette does not display.

A job design is made of one or several Subjobs, which are themselves defined by one or, most likely, several components linked together. The properties of each component require to be configured individually, in order to function properly.

For more information, see *How to connect components together on page 64* and *How to define component properties on page 65*.

4.2.1 How to create a Job

Talend Open Studio enables you to create a data integration Job by dropping different technical components from the **Palette** onto the design workspace and then connecting these components together.

You can also create different folders to better classify these Jobs.

To create a data integration Job, complete the following:

- Open Talend Open Studio following the procedure as detailed in chapter *Launching Talend Open Studio on page 6*.

Designing a data integration Job
Getting started with a basic job design

- In the **Repository** tree view, right-click the **Job Designs** node and select **Create job** from the contextual menu.

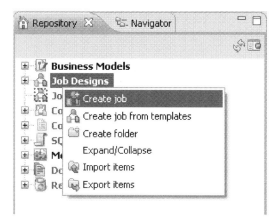

The **[New job]** wizard opens to help you define the main properties of the new Job.

- Enter the job properties as the following:

Field	Description
Name	the name of the new Job. A message comes up if you enter prohibited characters.
Purpose	job purpose or any useful information regarding the Job use.

Talend Open Studio 59

Designing a data integration Job
Getting started with a basic job design

Field	Description
Description	job description.
Author	a read-only field that shows by default the current user login.
Locker	a read-only field that shows by default the login of the user who owns the lock on the current Job. This field is empty when you are creating a Job and has data only when you are editing the properties of an existing Job.
Version	a read-only field. You can manually increment the version using the **M** and **m** buttons. For more information, see *Managing Job versions on page 149*.
Status	a list to select from the status of the Job you are creating.
Path	a list to select from the folder in which the Job will be created.

An empty design workspace opens up showing the name of the Job as a tab label.

- Drop the components you want to use in your job design from the **Palette** onto the design workspace and connect them together. For more information, see *How to drop components to the workspace on page 61* and *How to connect components together on page 64*.

- Define the properties of each of the components used in the Job. For more information, see *How to define component properties on page 65*.

- Save your Job and then press **F6** to execute it. For more information, see *How to run a Job on page 71*.
  The Job you created is now listed under the **Job Designs** node in the **Repository** tree view.

 You can open one or more of the created Jobs by simply double-clicking the job label in the **Repository** tree view.

To create different folders for your Jobs, complete the following:

- In the **Repository** tree view, right-click **Job Designs** and select **Create folder** from the contextual menu.
  The **[New folder]** dialog box displays.

- In the **Label** field, enter a name for the folder and then click **Finish** to confirm your changes and close the dialog box.
  The created folder is listed under the **Job Designs** node in the **Repository** tree view.

 If you have already created Jobs that you want to move into this new folder, simply drop them into the folder.

Designing a data integration Job
Getting started with a basic job design

For a scenario showing how to create a real-life data integration Job, see *Theory into practice: Job example on page 287*.

4.2.2 How to drop components to the workspace

How to drop components from the Palette

To actually start building a Job, click a Component, on the **Palette**. Then click again on the design workspace to drop it there and add it to your job design.

 If the **Palette** does not show in the Studio, see *How to show, hide the Palette and change its position on page 77*.

 You can drop a note to your Job the same way you drop components. For more information, see *How to add notes to a Job design on page 116*.

Each newly added component displays generally in a blue square that symbolizes it as an individual Subjob.

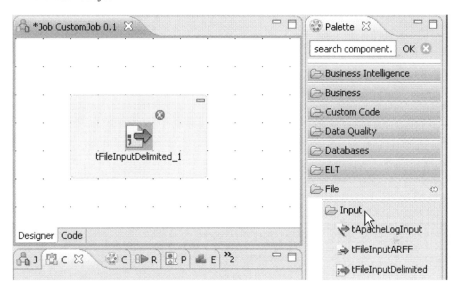

Connect components together in a logical order using the connections offered, in order to build a full Job or Subjob. For more information about component connection types, see *Connection types on page 81*.

The Job or Subjob gets highlighted in one single blue rectangle. For more information about Job and Subjob background color, see *How to manage the subjob display on page 118*.

Multiple information or warnings may show next to the component. Browse over the component icon to display the information tooltip. This will display until you fully completed your job design and defined all basic (and sometimes advanced) component properties of the **Component** view.

 You will be required to use the relevant code, i.e. Perl code in Perl jobs and java code in Java jobs.

Related topics:

Designing a data integration Job
Getting started with a basic job design

- *How to connect components together on page 64.*
- *Warnings and error icons on components on page 115.*
- *How to define component properties on page 65.*

How to drop components from the Metadata node

For recurrent use of files and DB connections in various Jobs, we recommend you to store the connection and schema metadata in the **Repository** tree view under the **Metadata** node. Different folders under the **Metadata** node will group the established connections including those to databases, files and systems.

Different wizards will help you centralize connection and schema metadata in the **Repository** tree view. For more information about the **Metadata Manager** wizards, see *How to centralize the Metadata items on page 88*.

Once the relevant metadata is stored under the **Metadata** node, you will be able to drop the corresponding components directly onto the design workspace.

- In the **Repository** tree view, expand **Metadata** and the folder holding the connection you want to use in your Job.
- Drop the relevant connection/schema onto the design workspace.

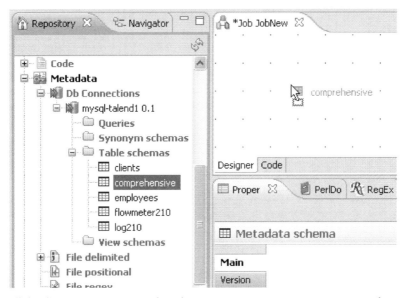

A dialog box prompts you to select the component you want to use among those offered.

Designing a data integration Job
Getting started with a basic job design

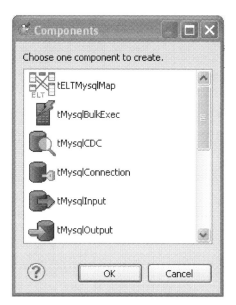

- Select the component and then click **OK**. The selected component displays on the design workspace.

Or, according to the type of component (Input or Output) that you want to use, perform one of the following operations:

- **Output**: Press **Ctrl** on your keyboard while you are dropping the component onto the design workspace to directly include it in the active Job.

- **Input**: Press **Alt** on your keyboard while you drop the component onto the design workspace to directly include it in the active Job.

If you double-click the component, the **Component** view shows the selected connection details as well as the selected schema information.

> If you select the connection without selecting a schema, then the properties will be filled with the first encountered schema.

4.2.3 How to search components in the Palette

If you do not want to browse the components families in the **Palette** to find the components you want to use in your Job, you can search the desired component directly in the search field at the top of the **Palette**.

To search for a component, do the following:

- Click to clear the search field of any text.

- Enter the name of the component you want to look for and click **OK**.

Designing a data integration Job
Getting started with a basic job design

The **Palette** displays only the family/families that hold(s) the component.

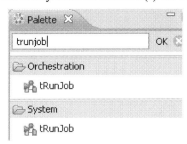

To go back to the default **Palette** settings, click .

4.2.4 How to connect components together

A Job or a Subjob is defined by a group of components interconnected in a logical way. The Job itself can be built with several Subjobs carrying out various processings.

The component forming a Subjob, as well as the Subjobs are connected to each other using various types of connections.

Also, a Job (made of one or more subjobs) can be preceded by a pre-job and followed by a post-job components, in order to ensure that some specific tasks (often not related to the actual data processing) are performed first or last in the process. For more information, see *How to use the tPrejob and tPostjob components on page 112*.

To connect two components, right-click the source component on your design workspace, select your type of connection from the contextual menu, and click the target component.

When dragging the link from your source component towards the target component, a graphical plug indicates if the destination component is valid or not. The black crossed circle disappears only when you reach a valid target component.

Only the connections authorized for the selected component are listed on the right-click contextual menu.

The types of connections proposed are different for each component according to its nature and role within the Job, i.e. if the connection is meant to transfer data (from a defined schema) or if no data is handled.

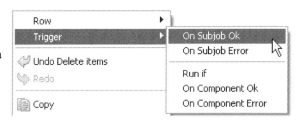

The types of connections available also depend if data comes from one or multiple input files and gets transferred towards one or multiple outputs.

For more information about the various types of connections and their specific settings, see *Using connections on page 81*.

Designing a data integration Job
Getting started with a basic job design

4.2.5 How to define component properties

The properties information for each component forming a Job or a sub-job allows to set the actual technical implementation of the active Job.

Each component is defined by basic and advanced properties shown respectively on the **Basic Settings** tab and the **Advanced Settings** tab of the **Component** view of the selected component in the design workspace. The **Component** view gathers also other collateral information related to the component in use, including **View** and **Documentation** tabs.

For detailed configuration for each component displaying in the **Palette**, check out the Talend Open Studio Components Reference Guide.

Basic Settings tab

The **Basic Settings** tab is part of the **Component** view, which is located on the lower part of the designing editor of Talend Open Studio.

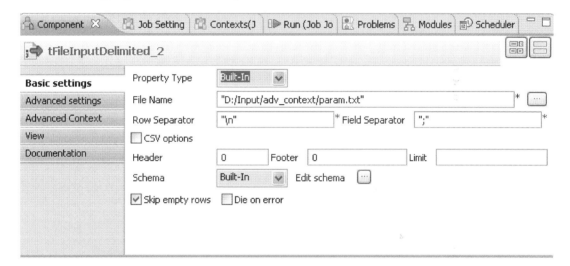

Each component has specific basic settings according to its function requirements within the Job. For a detailed description of each component properties and use, see the Talend Open Studio Components Reference Guide.

 Some components require code to be input or functions to be set. Where relevant, make sure you use the correct code, i.e. Perl code in perl properties and Java code in Java properties.

For **File** and **Database** components you can centralize properties in metadata files located in the **Metadata** directory of the **Repository** tree view. This means that on the **Basic Settings** tab you can set properties on the spot, using the **Built-In Property** type or use the properties you stored in the **Metadata Manager** using the **Repository Property** type. The latter option helps you save time.

Select **Repository** as **Property type** and choose the metadata file holding the relevant information. Related topic: *How to centralize the Metadata items on page 88.*

Or you can drop the **Metadata** item from the **Repository** tree view directly to the component already dropped on the design workspace, for its properties to be filled in automatically.

Talend Open Studio 65

For all components that handle a data flow (most components), you can define a **Talend** schema in order to describe and possibly select the data to be processed. Like the **Properties** data, this schema is either **Built-in** or stored remotely in the repository in a metadata file that you created. A detailed description of the Schema setting is provided in the next sections.

How to set a built-in schema

A schema created as **Built-in** is meant for a single use in a Job, hence cannot be reused in another Job.

Select **Built-in** in the **Property Type** list of the **Basic settings** view, and click the **Edit Schema** button to create your built-in schema by adding columns and describing their content, according to the input file definition.

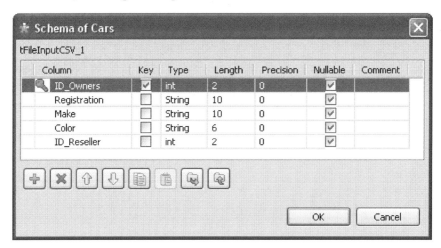

In all output properties, you also have to define the schema of the output. To retrieve the schema defined in the input schema, click the **Sync columns** tab in the **Basic settings** view.

 In Java, some extra information is required. For more information about Date pattern for example, check out:
http://java.sun.com/j2se/1.5.0/docs/api/index.html.

How to set a repository schema

If you often use certain database connections or specific files when building your data integration Jobs, you can avoid defining the same properties over and over again by creating metadata files and storing them in the **Metadata** node in the **Repository** tree view

To recall a metadata file into your current Job, select **Repository** in the **Schema** list and then select the relevant metadata file. Or, drop the metadata item from the **Repository** tree view directly to the component already dropped on the design workspace. Then click **Edit Schema** to check that the data is appropriate.

Designing a data integration Job
Getting started with a basic job design

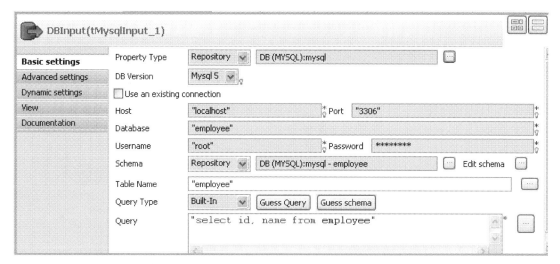

You can edit a repository schema used in a Job from the **Basic settings** view. However, note that the schema hence becomes **built-in** in the current Job.

 You cannot change the schema stored in the repository from this window. To edit the schema stored remotely, right-click it under the **Metadata** node and select the corresponding edit option (**Edit connection** or **Edit file**) from the contextual menu.

Related topics: *How to centralize the Metadata items on page 88*

How to set a field dynamically (Ctrl+Space bar)

On any field of your Job/component **Properties** view, you can use the **Ctrl+Space** bar to access the global and context variable list and set the relevant field value dynamically.

- Place the cursor on any field of the **Component** view.
- Press **Ctrl+Space bar** to access the proposal list.
- Select on the list the relevant parameters you need. Appended to the variable list, an information panel provides details about the selected parameter.

This can be any parameter including: error messages, number of lines processed, or else... The list varies according to the component in selection or the context you're working in.

Related topic: *How to centralize contexts and variables on page 89*

Talend Open Studio 67

Advanced settings tab

Some components, especially **File** and **Database** components, provides numerous advanced use possibilities.

[Screenshot of tFileInputDelimited_1 Advanced settings panel showing options: Advanced separator (for numbers), Extract lines at random, Encoding Type ISO-8859-15, Trim all column, Check each row structure against schema, Check column to trim (with Column/Trim table listing key and value), Split row before field, tStatCatcher Statistics, Enable parallel execution.]

The content of the Advanced settings tab changes according to the selected component.

Generally you will find on this tab the parameters that are not required for a basic or usual use of the component but may be required for a use out of the standard scope.

How to measure data flows

You can also find in the **Advanced settings** view the option **tStatCatcher Statistics** that allows you, if selected, to display logs and statistics about the current Job without using dedicated components. For more information regarding the stats & log features, see *How to automate the use of statistics & logs on page 120*.

Dynamic settings tab

All components **Basic Settings** and **Advanced Settings** tabs display various check boxes and drop-down lists for component parameters. Usually, available values for these types of parameters is either true or false and can only be edited when designing your Job.

The **Dynamic settings** tab, on the **Component** view, allows you to customize these parameter into code or variable.

This feature allows you, for example, to define these parameters as variables and thus let them become context-dependent, whereas they are not meant to be by default.

Another benefit of this feature is that you can now change the context setting at execution time. This makes full sense when you intend to export your job script in order to deploy it onto a job execution server for example.

Designing a data integration Job
Getting started with a basic job design

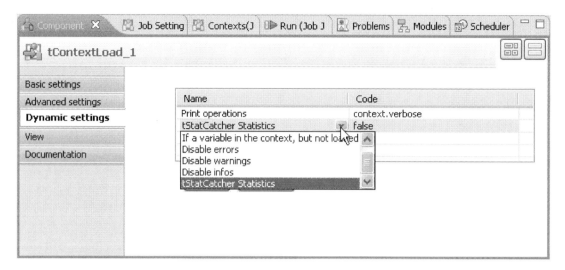

To customize these types of parameters, as context variables for example, follow the following steps:

- Select the relevant component basic settings or advanced settings view that contains the parameter you want to define as a variable.
- Click the **Dynamic settings** tab.
- Click the **plus** button to display a new parameter line in the table.
- Click the **Name** of the parameter displaying to show the list of available parameters. For example: *Print operations*
- Then click in the facing **Code** column cell and set the code to be used. For example: *context.verbose* if you create the corresponding context variable, called *verbose*.

 As code, you can input a context variable or a piece of code (in Java or Perl) according to your generation language.

The corresponding lists or check boxes thus become unavailable and are highlighted in yellow in the **Basic** or **Advanced Settings** tab.

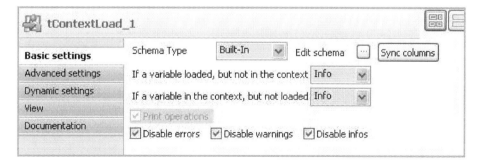

 If you want to set a parameter as context variable, make sure you create the corresponding variable in the **Context** view.
For more information regarding the context variable definition, see *How to use variables in the Contexts view on page 90*.

You could also use a global variable or pieces of java or perl code, to store the values to be used for each parameter.

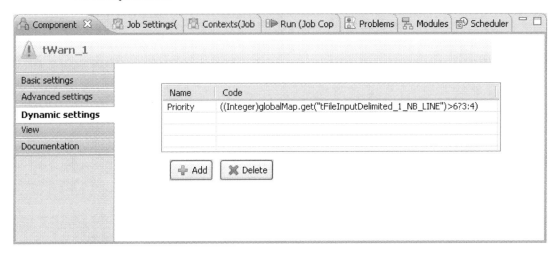

For example, use some global variable available through the **Ctrl+Space** bar keys, and adapt it to your context.

View tab

The **View** tab of the **Component** view allows you to change the default display format of components on the design workspace.

Field	Description
Label format	Free text label showing on the design workspace. Variables can be set to retrieve and display values from other fields. The field tooltip usually shows the corresponding variable where the field value is stored.
Hint format	Hidden tooltip, showing only when you mouse over the component.
Connection format	Indicates the type of connection accepted by the component.

You can graphically highlight both **Label** and **Hint** text with HTML formatting tags:

- Bold: <b> YourLabelOrHint </b>
- Italic: <i> YourLabelOrHint </i>
- Return carriage: YourLabelOrHint
 ContdOnNextLine
- Color: <Font color= '#RGBcolor'> YourLabelOrHint </Font>

To change your preferences of this View panel, click **Window>Preferences>Talend>Designer**.

Documentation tab

Feel free to add any useful comment or chunk of text or documentation to your component.

Designing a data integration Job
Getting started with a basic job design

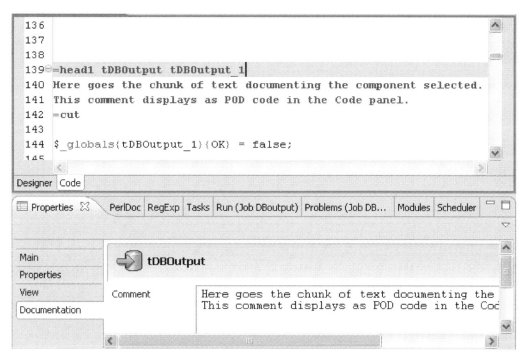

The content of this **Comment** field will be formatted using Pod markup and will be integrated in the generated code. You can view your comment in the **Code** panel.

You can show the Documentation in your hint tooltip using the associated variable (_COMMENT_)

For advanced use of Documentations, you can use the **Documentation** view in order to store and reuse any type of documentation.

4.2.6 How to run a Job

You can execute a Job in several ways. This mainly depends on the purpose of your job execution and on your user level.

If you are an advanced Perl/Java user and want to execute your Job step by step to check and possibly modify it on the run, see *How to run a Job in Java Debug mode on page 72*.

If you do not have advanced Perl/Java knowledge and want to execute and monitor your Job in normal mode, see *How to run a Job in normal mode on page 71*.

How to run a Job in normal mode

 Make sure you saved your **Job** before running it in order for all properties to be taken into account.

To run your Job in a normal mode, complete the following:

- Click the **Run** view to access it.
- Click the **Basic Run** tab to access the normal execution mode.

Designing a data integration Job
Getting started with a basic job design

- In the **Context** area to the right of the view, select in the list the proper context for the Job to be executed in. You can also check the variable values.

If you have not defined any particular execution context, the context parameter table is empty and the context is the default one. Related topic: *How to centralize contexts and variables on page 89*.

- Click **Run** to start the execution.
- On the same view, the console displays the progress of the execution. The log includes any error message as well as start and end messages. It also shows the job output in case of a **tLogRow** component is used in the job design.

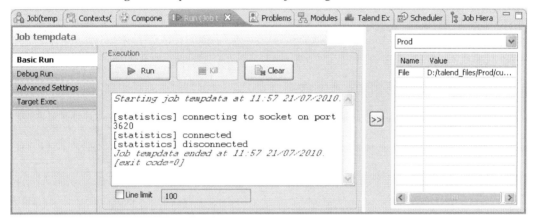

Before running again a Job, you might want to remove the execution statistics and traces from the designing workspace. To do so, click the **Clear** button.

If for any reason, you want to stop the Job in progress, simply click the **Kill** button. You will need to click the **Run** button again, to start again the Job.

Talend Open Studio offers various informative features displayed during execution, such as statistics and traces, facilitating the job monitoring and debugging work. For more information, see the following sections.

How to run a Job in Java Debug mode

To follow step by step the execution of a Job to identify possible bugs, you can run it in Debug mode.

To access the Debug mode:

- Click the **Run** view to access it.
- Click the **Debug Run** tab to access the debug execution modes.

 In order to be able to run a Job in Debug mode, you need the EPIC module to be installed.

Before running your Job in Debug mode, add breakpoints to the major steps of your job flow.

Designing a data integration Job
Getting started with a basic job design

This will allow you to get the Job to automatically stop at each breakpoint. This way, components and their respective variables can be verified individually and debugged if required.

To add breakpoints to a component, right-click it on the design workspace, and select **Add breakpoint** on the contextual menu.

A pause icon displays next to the component where the break is added.

To switch to debug mode, click the **Java Debug** button on the **Debug Run** tab of the **Run** panel. Talend Open Studio's main window gets reorganized for debugging.

You can then run the Job step by step and check each breakpoint component for the expected behavior and variable values.

To switch back to Talend Open Studio designer mode, click **Window**, then **Perspective** and select Talend Open Studio.

How to run a Job in Traces Debug mode

The traces feature allows you to monitor data processing when running a Job in Talend Open Studio.

It provides a row by row view of the component behavior and displays the dynamic result next to the **Row** link on the design workspace.

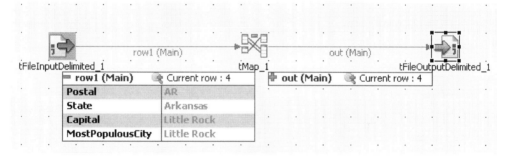

This feature allows you to monitor all the components of a Job, without switching to the debug mode, hence without requiring advanced Perl/Java knowledge.

The **Traces** function displays the content of processed rows in a table.

 Exception is made for external components which cannot offer this feature if their design does not include it.

You can activate or deactivate **Traces** or decide what processed columns to display in the traces table that displays on the design workspace when launching the current Job.

To activate the **Traces** mode in a Job:

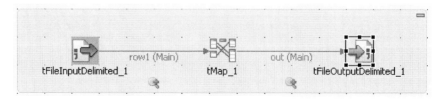

Talend Open Studio 73

Designing a data integration Job
Getting started with a basic job design

- Click the **Run** view.
- Click the **Debug Run** tab to access the debug and traces execution modes.
- Click the down arrow of the **Java Debug** button and select the **Traces Debug** option. An icon displays under every flow of your Job to indicate that process monitoring is activated.
- Click the **Traces Debug** to execute the Job in Traces mode.

To deactivate the **Traces** on one of the flows in your Job:

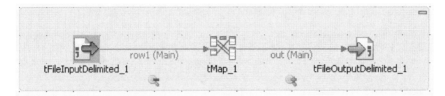

- Right-click the **Traces** icon under the relevant flow, then select **Disable Traces** from the list. A red minus sign replaces the green plus sign on the icon to indicate that the **Traces** mode has been deactivated for this flow.

To choose which columns of the processed data to display in the traces table, do as follows:

- Right-click the **Traces** icon for the relevant flow, then select **Setup Traces** from the list. The **[Setup Traces]** dialog box displays.

- In the dialog box, clear the check boxes corresponding to the columns you do not want to display in the Traces table.
- Click **OK** to close the dialog box.

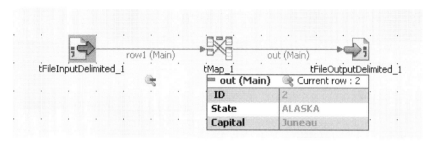

Monitoring data processing starts when you execute the Job and stops at the end of the execution.

Click the **Clear** button in the **Debug Run** tab to remove the displayed monitoring information.

How to set advanced execution settings

Several advanced execution settings are available to make the execution of the Jobs handier:

- Statistics, this feature displays processing performance rate. For more information, see *How to display Statistics on page 75*.

- Exec time, this feature displays the execution time in the console at the end of the execution. For more information, see *How to display the execution time and other options on page 76*.

- Save Job before execution, this feature allows to automatically save the job before its execution.

- Clear before run, this feature clears all the results of a previous execution before re-executing the Job.

- JVM Setting, this feature allows you to define the parameters of your JVM according to your needs, for example the parameters used to display special characters.

How to display Statistics

The **Statistics** feature displays each component performance rate, under the flow links on the design workspace.

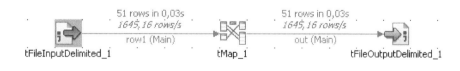

It shows the number of rows processed and the processing time in row per second, allowing you to spot straight away any bottleneck in the data processing flow.

For trigger links like **OnComponentOK**, **OnComponentError**, **OnSubjobOK**, **OnSubjobError** and **If**, the **Statistics** option displays the state of this trigger during the execution time of your Job: Ok or Error and True or False.

 Exception is made for external components which cannot offer this feature if their design does not include it.

Designing a data integration Job
Getting started with a basic job design

In the **Run** view, click the **Advanced Settings** tab and select the **Statistics** check box to activate the Stats feature and clear the box to disable it.

The calculation only starts when the job execution is launched, and stops at the end of it.

Click the **Clear** button from the **Basic** or **Debug Run** views to remove the calculated stats displayed. Select the **Clear before Run** check box to reset the Stats feature before each execution.

 The statistics thread slows down job execution as the Job must send these stats data to the design workspace in order to be displayed.

You can also save your Job before the execution starts. Select the relevant option check box.

How to display the execution time and other options

To display the job total execution time after job execution, select in the **Advanced Settings** tab of the **Run** view the **Exec time** check box before running the Job.

This way you can test your Job before going to production.

You can also clear the design workspace before each job execution by selecting the check box **Clear before Run**.

You can also save your Job before the execution starts. Select the relevant option check box.

How to display special characters in the console

Talend Open Studio can display special characters in the console. Take the Chinese, the Japanese or the Korean characters for example, proceed as follows before executing the Job:

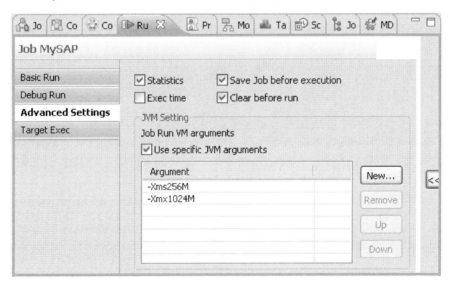

- Select the **Advanced Settings** tab.
- In the **JVM settings** area of the tab view, select the **Use specific JVM arguments** checkbox to activate the **Argument** table.
- Next to the **Argument** table, click the **New...** button to pop up the **[Set the VM argument]** dialog box.

76   Talend Open Studio

- In the dialog box, type in `-Dfile.encoding=UTF-8`.
- Click **OK** to close the dialog box.

This argument can be applied for all of your Job executions in Talend Open Studio. For further information about how to apply this JVM argument for all of the Job executions, see *Debug and job execution preferences on page 23*.

4.2.7 How to customize your workspace

When using Talend Open Studio to design a data integration Job, you can customize the **Palette** layout and setting according to your needs. You can as well change the position of any of the panels that exist in the Studio to meet your requirements.

How to change the Palette layout and settings

The **Palette** contains all basic technical components necessary to create the most complex Jobs in the design workspace. These components are grouped in families and sub-families.

For specific component configuration, check out the Talend Open Studio Components Reference Guide.

Talend Open Studio enables you to change the layout and position of your **Palette** according to your requirements. the below sections explain all management options you can carry out on the **Palette**.

How to show, hide the Palette and change its position

By default, the **Palette** might be hidden on the right hand side of your design workspace.

If you want the **Palette** to show permanently, click the left arrow, at the upper right corner of the design workspace, to make it visible at all times.

You can also move around the **Palette** outside the design workspace within Talend Open Studio's main window. To enable the standalone **Palette** view, click the **Window** menu > **Show View...** > **General** > **Palette**.

If you want to set the Palette apart in a panel, right-click the **Palette** head bar and select **Detached** from the contextual menu. The **Palette** opens in a separate view that you can move around wherever you like within Talend Open Studio's main window.

How to display/hide components families

You can display/hide components families according to your needs in case of visibility problems, for example. To do so, right-click the **Palette** and select **Display folder** to display components families and **Hide folder** to display components without their families.

Designing a data integration Job
Getting started with a basic job design

 This display/hide option can be very useful when you are in the **Favorite** view of the **Palette**. In this view, you usually have a limited number of components that if you display without their families, you will have them in an alphabetical list and thus facilitate their usage. for more information about the **Palette** favorite, see *How to set the Palette favorite on page 78*.

How to maintain a component family open

If you often use one or many component families, you can add a pin on their names to stop them from collapsing when you select components from other families.

To add a pin, click the pin icon on the top right-hand corner of the family name.

How to filter the Palette

You can select the components to be shown or hidden on your **Palette**. You can also add to the **Palette** the components that you developed yourself.

For more information about filtering the **Palette**, see *Palette Settings on page 31*.

For more information about adding components to the **Palette**, either from **Talend Exchange** or from your own development, see *How to download external community components on page 106* and/or *External or User components on page 22*.

How to set the Palette favorite

The **Palette** offers you search and favorite possibilities that by turn facilitate its usage.

You can add/remove components to/from the **Palette** favorite view of Talend Open Studio in order to have a quick access to all the components that you mostly use.

To do so:

- From the **Palette**, right-click the component you want to add to **Palette** favorite and select **Add To Favorite**.

Designing a data integration Job
Getting started with a basic job design

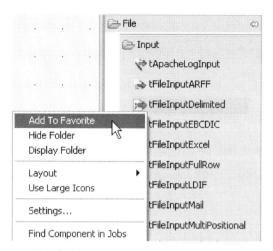

- Do the same for all the components you want to add to the **Palette** favorite then click the **Favorite** button in the upper right corner of the **Palette** to display the **Palette** favorite.

Only the components added to the favorite are displayed.

To delete a component from the **Palette** favorite:

- Right-click the component you want to remove from the favorite and select **Remove From Favorite**.

To restore the **Palette** standard view, click the **Standard** button in the upper right corner of the **Palette**.

How to change components layout in the Palette

You can change the layout of the component list in the **Palette** to display them in columns or in lists, as icons only or as icons with short description.

You can also enlarge the component icons for better readability of the component list.

Talend Open Studio 79

Designing a data integration Job
Getting started with a basic job design

To do so, right-click any component family in the **Palette** and select the desired option in the contextual menu or click **Settings** to open the **[Palette Settings]** window and fine-tune the layout.

How to add external components to the Palette

Talend Open Studio enables you to add external components to the **Palette** of your Studio and use them in your job designs.

For more information about the creation and development of user components, refer to our wiki *Component creation tutorial section*.

For more information about how to download user components in your Studio, see *External or User components on page 22*.

How to change panels positions

All panels in the open Studio can be moved around according to your needs.

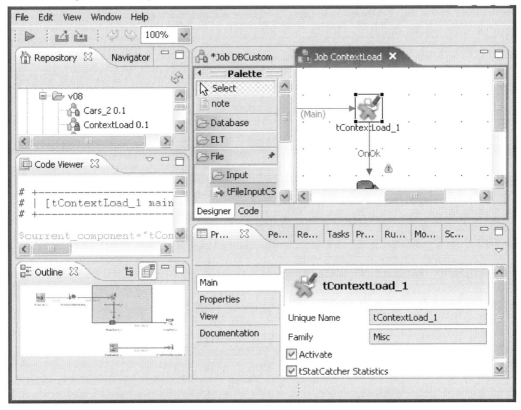

All you need to do is to click the head border of a panel or to click a tab, hold down the mouse button and drag the panel to the target destination. Release to change the panel position.

Click the minimize/maximize icons (□/□) to minimize the corresponding panel or maximize it. For more information on how to display or hide a panel/view, see *How to display job configuration tabs/views on page 81*.

Designing a data integration Job
Using connections

Click the close icon ( ) to close a tab/view. To reopen a view, click **Window** > **Show View** > **Talend**, then click the name of the panel you want to add to your current view or see *Shortcuts and aliases on page 284*.

If the **Palette** does not show or if you want to set it apart in a panel, go to **Window** > **Show view...** > **General** > **Palette**. The **Palette** opens in a separate view that you can move around wherever you like within Talend Open Studio's main window.

How to display job configuration tabs/views

The configuration tabs are located in the lower half of the design workspace. Each tab opens a view that displays detailed information about the selected element in the design workspace.

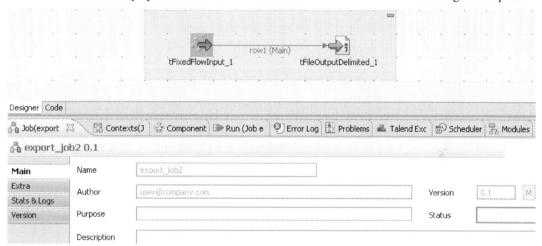

The **Component**, **Run Jobs**, **Problems** and **Error Log** views gather all information relative to the graphical elements selected in the design workspace or the actual execution of the open Job.

The **Modules** and **Scheduler** tabs are located in the same tab system as the **Component**, **Logs** and **Run Job** tabs. Both views are independent from the active or inactive Jobs open on the design workspace.

Some of the configuration tabs are hidden by default such as the **Error Log, Job Hierarchy**, **Modules** and **Scheduler** tabs. You can show hidden tabs in this tab system and directly open the corresponding view if you select **Window** > **Show view** and then, in the open dialog box, expand the corresponding node and select the element you want to display.

For detail description about these tabs, see *Configuration tabs on page 282*.

4.3 Using connections

In Talend Open Studio, a Job or a Subjob is composed of a group of components logically linked to one another via connections. This section will describe the types of connections and their related settings.

4.3.1 Connection types

There are various types of connections which define either the data to be processed, the data output, or the job logical sequence.

Designing a data integration Job
Using connections

Right-click a component on the design workspace to display a contextual menu that lists all available links for the selected component.

The sections below describe all available connection types.

Row connection

A **Row** connection handles the actual data. The **Row** connections can be **main**, **lookup**, **reject** or **output** according to the nature of the flow processed.

Main

This type of row connection is the most commonly used connection. It passes on data flows from one component to the other, iterating on each row and reading input data according to the component properties setting (schema).

Data transferred through main rows are characterized by a schema definition which describes the data structure in the input file.

You cannot connect two Input components together using a **main Row** connection. Only *one* incoming **Row** connection is possible per component. You will not be able to link twice the same target component using a main Row connection. The second row linking a component will be called **Lookup**.

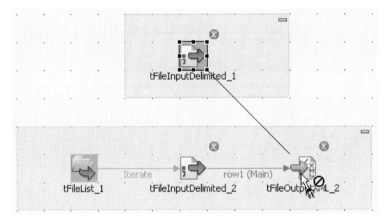

- Right-click the input component and select **Row** > **Main** on the connection list.
- Alternatively click the component to highlight it, then right-click it and drag the cursor towards the destination component. This will automatically create a **Row** > **Main** type of connection.

To be able to use multiple **Row** connections, see *Multiple Input/Output on page 84*.

Lookup

This row link connects a sub-flow component to a main flow component (which should be allowed to receive more than one incoming flow). This connection is used only in the case of multiple input flows.

Talend Open Studio

Designing a data integration Job
Using connections

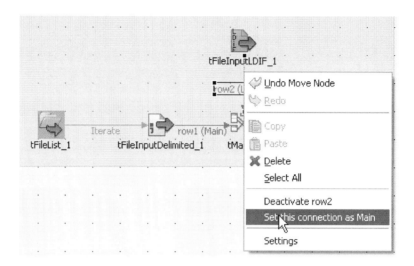

A **Lookup** row can be changed into a main row at any time (and reversely, a main row can be changed to a lookup row). To do so, right-click the row to be changed, and on the pop-up menu, click **Set this connection as Main**.

Related topic: *Multiple Input/Output on page 84*.

Filter

This row link connects specifically a **tFilterRow** component to an output component. This row link gathers the data matching the filtering criteria. This particular component offers also a **Reject** link to fetch the non-matching data flow.

Rejects

This row link connects a processing component to an output component. This row link gathers the data that does NOT match the filter or are not valid for the expected output. This link allows you to track the data that could not be processed for any reason (wrong type, undefined null value, etc.). On some components, this link is enabled when the **Die on error** option is deactivated. For more information, refer to the relevant component properties available in the Talend Open Studio Reference Guide.

ErrorReject

This row link connects a **tMap** component to an output component. This link is enabled when you clear the **Die on error** check box in the **tMap editor** and it gathers data that could not be processed (wrong type, undefined null value, unparseable dates, etc.).

Related topic: *Handling errors on page 174*.

Output

This row link connects a **tMap** component to one or several output components. As the job output can be multiple, you get prompted to give a name for each output row created.

 The system also remembers deleted output link names (and properties if they were defined). This way, you do not have to fill in again property data in case you want to reuse them.

Designing a data integration Job
Using connections

Related topic: *Multiple Input/Output on page 84*.

Uniques/Duplicates

These row links connect a **tUniqRow** to output components.

The **Uniques** link gathers the rows that are found first in the incoming flow. This flow of unique data is directed to the relevant output component or else to another processing subjob.

The **Duplicates** link gathers the possible duplicates of the first encountered rows. This reject flow is directed to the relevant output component, for analysis for example.

Multiple Input/Output

Some components help handle data through multiple inputs and/or multiple outputs. These are often processing-type components such as the **tMap**.

If this requires a join or some transformation in one flow, you want to use the **tMap** component, which is dedicated to this use.

For further information regarding data mapping, see *Mapping data flows on page 155*.

For properties regarding the **tMap** component as well as use case scenarios, see *tMap* in the Talend Open Studio Components Reference Guide.

Iterate connection

The **Iterate** connection can be used to loop on files contained in a directory, on rows contained in a file or on DB entries.

A component can be the target of only one **Iterate** link. The **Iterate** link is mainly to be connected to the start component of a flow (in a subjob).

Some components such as the **tFileList** component are meant to be connected through an iterate link with the next component. For how to set an **Iterate** connection, see *Iterate connection settings on page 87*.

 The name of the **Iterate** link is read-only unlike other types of connections.

Trigger connections

Trigger connections define the processing sequence, i.e. no data is handled through these connections.

The connection in use will create a dependency between Jobs or sub-jobs which therefore will be triggered one after the other according to the trigger nature.

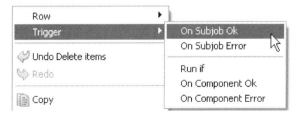

Trigger connections fall into two categories:

- subjob triggers: **On Subjob Ok**, **On Subjob Error** and **Run if**,
- component triggers: **On Component Ok**, **On Component Error** and **Run if**.

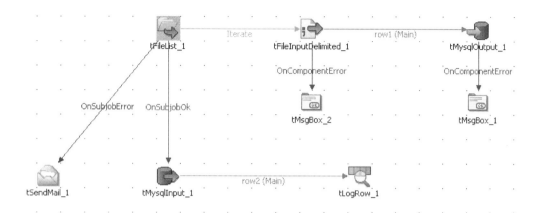

OnSubjobOK (previously **Then Run**): This link is used to trigger the next subjob on the condition that the main subjob completed without error. This connection is to be used only from the start component of the Job.

These connections are used to orchestrate the subjobs forming the Job or to easily troubleshoot and handle unexpected errors.

OnSubjobError: This link is used to trigger the next subjob in case the first (main) subjob do not complete correctly. This "on error" subjob helps flagging the bottleneck or handle the error if possible.

Related topic: *How to define the Start component on page 114*.

OnComponentOK and **OnComponentError** are component triggers. They can be used with any source component on the subjob.

OnComponentOK will only trigger the target component once the execution of the source component is complete without error. Its main use could be to trigger a notification subjob for example.

OnComponentError will trigger the sub-job or component as soon as an error is encountered in the primary Job.

Run if triggers a subjob or component in case the condition defined is met. For how to set a trigger condition, see *Run if connection settings on page 88*.

Link connection

The **Link** connection can only be used with ELT components. These links transfer table schema information to the ELT mapper component in order to be used in specific DB query statements.

Related topics: *ELT components* in the Talend Open Studio Components Reference Guide.

The **Link** connection therefore does not handle actual data but only the metadata regarding the table to be operated on.

When right-clicking the ELT component to be connected, select **Link** > **New Output**.

Designing a data integration Job
Using connections

 Be aware that the name you provide to the link MUST reflects the actual table name.

In fact, the link name will be used in the SQL statement generated through the ETL Mapper, therefore the same name should never be used twice.

4.3.2 How to define connection settings

You can display the properties of a connection by selecting it and clicking the **Component** view tab, or by right-clicking the connection and selecting **Settings** from the contextual menu. This section summarizes connection property settings.

Row connection settings

The **Basic settings** vertical tab of the **Component** view of the connection displays the schema of the data flow handled by the connection. You can change the schema by clicking the **Edit schema** button. Once you change the schema of the data flow, the schema type of the two components across the connection will become **Built-In**. For more information, see *How to set a built-in schema on page 66*.

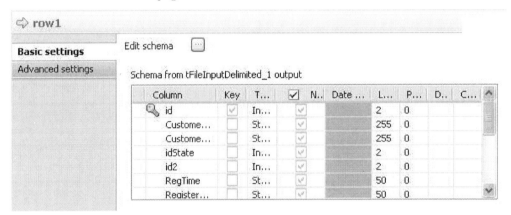

The **Advanced settings** vertical tab lets you monitor the data flow over the connection in a Job without using a separate **tFlowMeter** component. The measured information will be interpreted and displayed in a supervising tool such as Talend Activity Monitoring Console. For information about Talend Activity Monitoring Console, see Talend Activity Monitoring Console **User Guide**.

Designing a data integration Job
Using connections

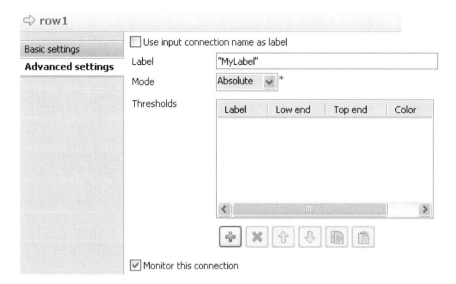

To monitor the data over the connection, perform the following settings in the **Advanced settings** vertical tab:

- Select the **Monitor this connection** check box.

- Select **Use input connection name as label** to use the name of the input flow to label your data to be logged, or enter a label in the **Label** field.

- From the **Mode** list, select **Absolute** to log the actual number of rows passes over the connection, or **Relative** to log the ratio (%) of the number of rows passed over this connection against a reference connection. If you select **Relative**, you need to select a reference connection from the **Connections List** list.

- Click the plus button to add a line in the **Thresholds** table and define a range of the number of rows to be logged.

Related topics: *Scenario: Catching flow metrics from a Job on page 1317* in the Talend Open Studio Components **Reference Guide** and *Connection Monitoring* in the Talend Activity Monitoring Console **User Guide**.

Iterate connection settings

You can set an **Iterate** link to run parallel iterations:

- Simply select the **Iterate** link of your Subjob to display the related **Basic settings** view of the **Components** tab.

- Select the **Enable parallel execution** check box and set the number of executions to be carried out in parallel.

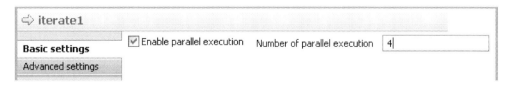

Talend Open Studio 87

When executing your Job, the number of parallel iterations will be distributed onto the available processors.

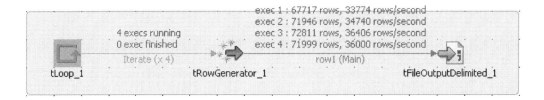

- Select the **Statistics** check box of the **Run** view to show the real time parallel executions on the design workspace.

Trigger connection settings

Run if connection settings

In the **Basic settings** view of a **Run if** connection, you can set the condition to the Subjob in Perl or in Java according to the generation language you selected. Pressing **Ctrl+Space** allows you to access all global and context variables.

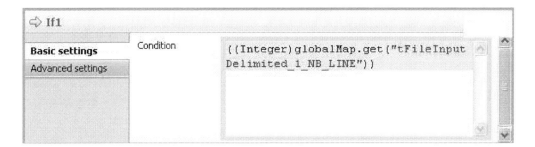

4.4 Using the Metadata Manager

Talend Open Studio is a metadata-driven solution, and can therefore help you ensure the whole Job consistency and quality through a centralized Metadata Manager in the repository.

Talend Open Studio provides a Metadata Manager that consolidates all project information in a centralized repository shared by all users in the integration processes. This shared repository facilitates collaboration between team members by allowing them to store and share their business models, integration jobs and metadata.

4.4.1 How to centralize the Metadata items

The **Metadata** node in the **Repository** tree view gathers various wizards to help you set up connections to the files, databases, and/or systems you may connect to.

This way you can store centrally the connection details you need to connect to your usual utilities and you can easily reuse them over and over again in all your job designs without filling them manually every time when configuring the job components.

From the metadata wizards, you can collect and centralize connection details to various utilities including:

- DB Connection: connection details and table data description (schema) of any type of database and JDBC connections
- File Delimited/Positional/Regex/XML/Excel/Ldif: file access details and description of data from the types of file listed.
- LDAP: access details and data description of an LDAP directory.
- Salesforce: access details and data description of a Salesforce table.
- WSDL: access details and data description of a webservice.
- Generic schema: access details and data description of any sort of sources.

For more information about these Metadata creation procedures, see *Managing Metadata on page 181*.

4.4.2 How to centralize contexts and variables

Depending on the circumstances the Job is being used in, you might want to manage it differently for various execution types (Prod and Test in the example given below). For instance, there might be various testing stages you want to perform and validate before a Job is ready to go live for production use.

Talend Open Studio offers you the possibility to create multiple context data sets. Furthermore you can either create context data sets on a one-shot basis, from the context tab of a Job or you can centralize the context data sets in the **Contexts** node of the **Repository** tree view in order to reuse them in different Jobs.

A context is characterized by parameters. These parameters are mostly context-sensitive variables which will be added to the list of variables for reuse in the component-specific properties on the **Component** view through the **Ctrl+Space bar** keystrokes.

How to use variables in a Job

Variables represent values which change throughout the execution of a program. A global variable is a system variable which can be accessed by any module or function. It retains its value after the function or program using it has completed execution. A context variable is a variable which is defined by the user for a particular context.

You can use an existing global variable or context variable in any component properties field. Press **Ctrl+Space bar** to display the full list of global and context variables used in various predefined Perl or Java functions.

```
Description: Error Message

Global variable, property of component tMap [tMap_1].
Type: String
Availability: After

Variable Name: ((String)globalMap.get("tMap_1_ERROR_MESSAGE"))
```

```
tFileInputDelimited_2.ERROR_MESSAGE
tFileInputDelimited_2.NB_LINE
tMap_1.ERROR_MESSAGE
tFileOutputDelimited_1.ERROR_MESSAGE
tFileOutputDelimited_1.NB_LINE
tFileOutputDelimited_2.ERROR_MESSAGE
tFileOutputDelimited_2.NB_LINE
tFileInputDelimited_3.ERROR_MESSAGE
tFileInputDelimited_3.NB_LINE
tFlowMeter_1.ERROR_MESSAGE
tFlowMeter_2.ERROR_MESSAGE
```

The list grows along with new user-defined variables (context variables).

Related topics:

- *How to define variables from the Component view on page 95*
- *How to use variables in the Contexts view on page 90*

How to use variables in the Contexts view

Various ways are at your disposal to create and define variables. You can manage your variables through the **Contexts** view or directly on the **Component** view.

For more information regarding the variable definition directly on the **Component** view, see *How to define variables from the Component view on page 95*.

The **Contexts** view is positioned on the lower part of the design workspace and is made of three tabs: **Variables**, **Values as tree** and **Values as table**.

 If you cannot find the **Contexts** view on the tab system of Talend Open Studio, go to **Window** > **Show view** > **Talend**, and select **Contexts**.

Variables tab

The **Variables** tab is part of the **Contexts** tab and shows all of the variables that have been defined for each component in the current Job.

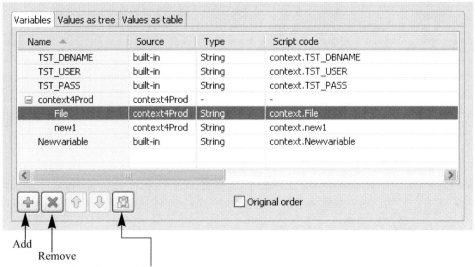

From this panel, you can manage your built-in variables:

- Add a parameter line to the table by clicking on **Plus** (+)
- Edit the **Name** of the new variable and type in the *<Newvariable>* name.
- Delete built-in variables. (Reminder: repository variables are read-only.)
- Import variables from a repository context source, using the **Repository variables** button.

- Display the context variables in their original order. They are sorted automatically by the studio upon creation in the tab view or when imported from the **Repository**. To do this, select the **Original order** check box.

- Reorganize the context variables by selecting the variable of interest and then using the ⬆ and ⬇ buttons. To do so, you need select the **Original order** check box to activate the two arrow buttons.

To define the actual value of a newly created variable, click the **Value as tree** tab.

You can add as many entries as you need on the **Variables** tab. By default the variable created is of built-in type.

Fields	Description
Name	Name of the variable. You can edit this field, on the condition that the variable is of Built-in type. Repository variables are read-only.
Source	**Built-in**: The variable is created in this Job and will be used in this Job only. **<Repository entry name>**: The variable has been defined in a context stored in the repository. The source is thus the actual context group you created in the repository.
Type	Select the type of data being handled. This is required in Java.
Script code	Code corresponding to the variable value. It depends on the Generation language you selected (Java or Perl) such as in Perl: `$_context{YourParameterName`. In Java, it will be: `context.YourParameterName`. This **Script code** is automatically generated when you define the variable in the **Component** view.
Comment	Add any useful comment

You cannot create contexts from the **Variables** view, but only from the **Values as table** or **as tree** views.

For further information regarding variable definition on the component view, see *How to define variables from the Component view on page 95*.

For more information about the repository variables, see *How to store contexts in the repository on page 96*.

Values as tree tab

This tab shows the variables as well as their values in a tree view.

Designing a data integration Job
Using the Metadata Manager

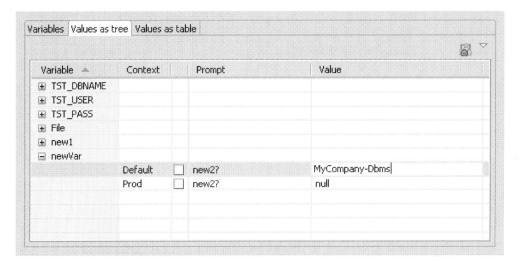

From this view, you can:

- Define the value of a built-in variable directly in the **Value** field. Note that repository variables values are read-only and can only be edited in the relevant repository context.
- Define a question to prompt the user for variable value confirmation at execution time.
- Create or Edit a context name through the top right dedicated button.
- Rearrange the variable/context groupby display.

Fields	Description
Variable	Name of the variables.
Context	Name of the contexts.
Prompt	Select this check box, if you want the variable to be editable in the confirmation dialog box at execution time.
	If you asked for a prompt to popup, fill in this field to define the message to show on the dialog box.
Value	Value for the corresponding variable. Define the value of your built-in variables. Note that repository variables are read-only.

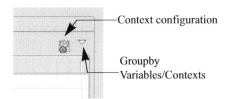

You can manage your contexts from this tab, through the dedicated button placed on the top right hand side of the **Contexts** view. See *How to configure contexts on page 93* for further information regarding the context management.

On the **Values as tree** tab, you can display the values based on the *contexts* or on the *variables* for more clarity.

To change the way the values are displayed on the tree, click the small down arrow button, then click the **group by** option you want.

For more information regarding variable definition, see *How to define variables from the Component view on page 95* and *How to store contexts in the repository on page 96*.

Values as table tab

This **Values as table** tab shows the context and variable settings in the form of a table.

Fields	Description
Name	Name of the variable.
<YourContextName>	Corresponding value for the variable.

You can manage your contexts from this tab, through the **Configure contexts** button placed on the top right hand side of the **Contexts** panel. See *How to configure contexts on page 93* for further information regarding the context management.

For more information regarding variable definition, see *How to define variables from the Component view on page 95* and *How to store contexts in the repository on page 96*.

How to configure contexts

You can only manage your contexts from the **Values as table** or **Values as tree** tabs. A dedicated button shows up on the top right hand side of the **Contexts** view.

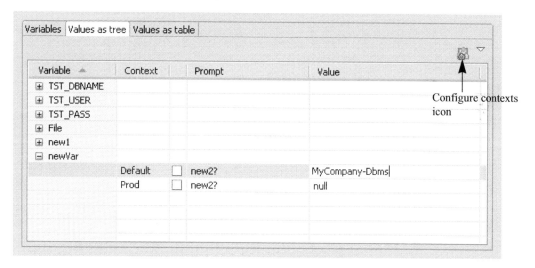

Click the **Configure Contexts...** icon to open the management dialog box.

 The default context cannot be removed, therefore the **Remove** button is unavailable. To make it editable, select another context on the list.

Creating a context

Based on the default context you set, you can create as many contexts as you need.

- To create a new context, click **New** on the **[Configure Contexts]** dialog box.
- Type in a name for the new context.

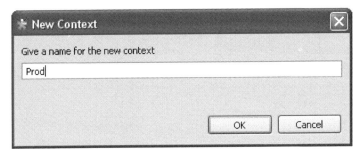

Click **OK** to validate the creation.

When you create a new context, the entire default context legacy is copied over to the new context. You hence only need to edit the relevant fields on the **Value as tree** tab to customize the context according to your use.

The drop-down list **Default Context** shows all the contexts you created.

You can switch default context by simply selecting the new default context on the **Default Context** list on the **Variables** tab of the **Contexts** view.

Note that the Default (or last) context can never be removed. There should always be a context to run the Job, be this context called Default or any other name.

Designing a data integration Job
Using the Metadata Manager

Renaming or editing a context

To change the name of an existing context, click **Edit** on the **[Configure contexts]** dialog box and enter the new context name in the dialog box showing up.

Click **OK** to validate the change.

To carry out changes on the actual values of the context variables, go to the **Values as tree** or **Values as table** tabs. For more information about these tabs, see *How to use variables in the Contexts view on page 90*.

How to define variables from the Component view

Various ways are at your disposal to create and define context variables. You can mostly manage your variables from the **Contexts** view, but you can also create them directly on the **Component** view.

For more information related to the variable definition through the **Contexts** view, see *How to use variables in the Contexts view on page 90*.

For more information regarding the variable definition in the repository, see *How to store contexts in the repository on page 96*.

Context variables creation

The quickest way to create context variables on the spot is to use the **F5** key:

- On the relevant **Component** view, place your cursor on the field that you want to parameterize.
- Press **F5** to display the context parameter dialog box:

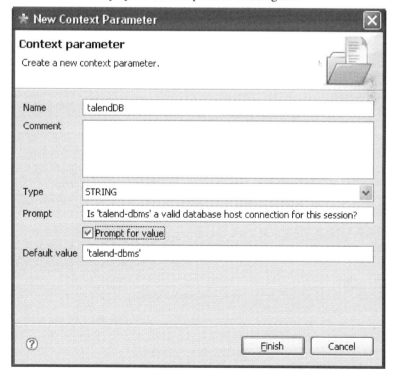

- Give a **Name** to this new variable, fill in the **Comment** area and choose the **Type**.
- Enter a **Prompt** to be displayed to confirm the use of this variable in the current Job execution (generally used for test purpose only). And select the **Prompt for value** check box to display the field as editable value.
- If you filled in a value already in the corresponding properties field, this value is displayed in the **Default value** field. Else, type in the default value you want to use for one context.
- Click **Finish** to validate.
- Go to the **Contexts** view tab. Notice that the context variables tab lists the newly created variables.

The newly created variables are listed in the **Contexts** view.

 The variable name should follow some typing rules and should not contain any forbidden characters, such as space char.

The variable created this way is automatically stored in all existing contexts, but you can subsequently change the value independently in each context.

For more information on how to create or edit a context, see *How to configure contexts on page 93*.

StoreSQLQuery

StoreSQLQuery is a user-defined variable and is mainly dedicated to debugging.

StoreSQLQuery is different from other context variables in the fact that its main purpose is to be used as parameter of the specific global variable called **Query**. It allows you to dynamically feed the global query variable.

The global variable **Query**, is available on the proposals list (**Ctrl+Space bar**) for some DB input components.

For further details on **StoreSQLQuery** settings, see the Talend Open Studio Components Reference Guide, and in particular **tDBInput** *Scenario 2: Using StoreSQLQuery variable*.

How to store contexts in the repository

You can store centrally all contexts if you need to reuse them across various Jobs.

How to create a context group

Right-click the **Contexts** node in the **Repository** tree view and select **Create new context group** in the list.

Designing a data integration Job
Using the Metadata Manager

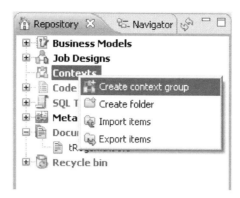

A 2-step wizard helps you to define the various contexts and context parameters, that you'll be able to select on the **Contexts** view of the design workspace.

- On the Step 1, type in a name for the context group to be created.
- Add any general information such as a description.
- Click **Next**.

The Step 2 allows you to define the various contexts and variables that you need.

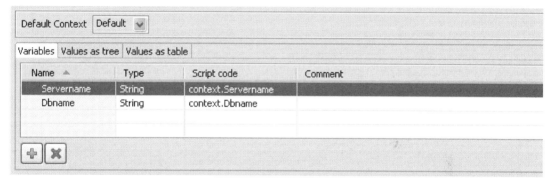

First define the default context's variable set that will be used as basis for the other contexts.

- On the **Variables** tab, click the **Plus (+)** button to add as many new variable lines as needed and define the name of the variables. In this example, we define the variables that could be used in the **Name** field of the **Component** view.
- Select the **Type** of variable on the list.
- The **Script code** varies according to the type of variable you selected (and the generation language). It will be used in the generated code. The screen shot above shows the Java code produced.

On the **Tree** or **Table** views, define the various contexts and the values of the variables.

Designing a data integration Job
Using the Metadata Manager

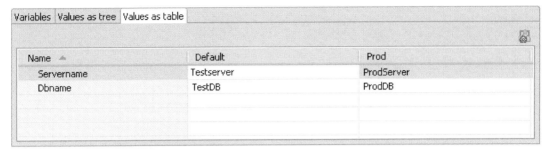

- Define the values for the default (first) context variables.
- Then create a new context that will be based on the variables values that you just set. For more information about how to create a new context, see *How to configure contexts on page 93*.

On the **Values as tree** tab, you can also add a prompt if you want the variable to be editable in a confirmation dialog box at execution time.

- To add a prompt message, select the facing check box.
- And type in the message you want to display at execution time.

Once you created and adapted as many context sets as you want, click **Finish** to validate. The group of contexts thus displays under the **Contexts** node in the **Repository** tree view.

How to create a context from a Metadata

When creating a Metadata (through the File or DB metadata wizards), you have the possibility to Export the metadata connection information as a Context.

For more information about this feature, see *Exporting Metadata as context on page 252*.

How to apply context variables to a Job from the repository

Once a context group is created and stored in the **Repository**, there are two ways of applying it to a Job:

- Drop a context group. This way, the group is applied as a whole.
- Use the context icon button . This way, the variables of a context group can be applied separately.

Designing a data integration Job
Using the Metadata Manager

How to drop a context group onto a Job

To drop a context group onto a Job, proceed as follows:

- Double-click the Job to which a context group is to be added.

- Once the Job is opened, drop the context group of your choice either onto the Job workspace or onto the **Contexts** view beneath the workspace.

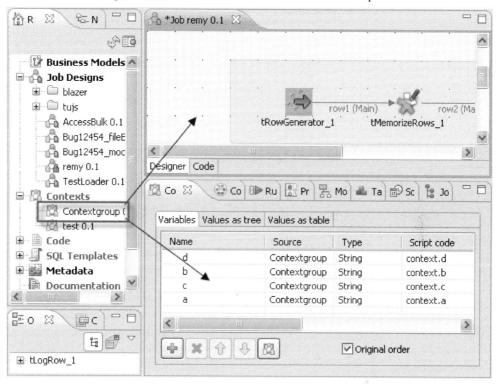

How to use the context icon button

To use the context icon button [icon] to apply context variables to a Job, proceed as follows:

- Double-click the Job to which a context variable is to be added.

- Once the Job is opened in the workspace, click the **Contexts** view beneath the workspace to open it.

- At the bottom of the **Contexts** view, click the [icon] button to open the wizard to select the context variables to be applied.

Talend Open Studio   99

Designing a data integration Job
Using the Metadata Manager

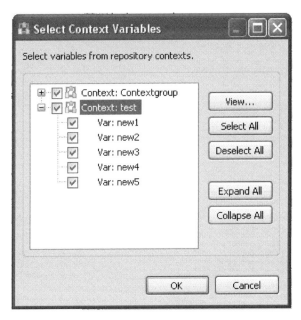

- In the wizard, select the context variables you need to apply or clear those you do not need to.

 The context variables that have been applied are automatically selected and cannot be cleared.

- Click **OK** to apply the selected context variables to the Job.

How to run a Job in a selected context

You can select the context you want the job design to be executed in.

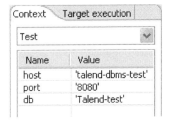

Click the **Run Job** tab, and in the **Context** area, select the relevant context among the various ones you created.

If you didn't create any context, only the **Default** context shows on the list.

All the context variables you created for the selected context display, along with their respective value, in a table underneath. If you clear the **Prompt** check box next to some variables, you will get a dialog box allowing you to change the variable value for this job execution only.

To make a change permanent in a variable value, you need to change it on the Context view if your variable is of type built-in or in the Context group of the repository.

Related topics:

- *How to use variables in the Contexts view on page 90*
- *How to store contexts in the repository on page 96*

4.4.3 How to use the SQL Templates

Talend Open Studio allows you to benefit from using some system SQL templates since many query structures are standardized with common approaches.

Talend Open Studio lists system SQL templates under the **SQL Templates** node in the **Repository** tree view. There, you can find several standardized SQL templates including Generic, MySQL, Oracle, and Teradata.

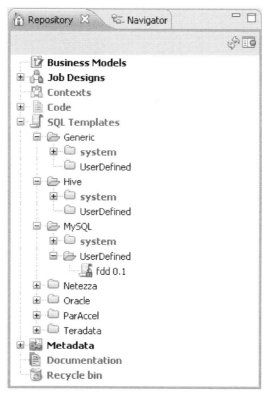

In each of the above categories, you can create your own user-defined SQL templates using the SQL templates wizard and thus centralize them in the repository for reuse.

For more information about the use of SQL templates in Talend Open Studio, see *Using SQL templates on page 263*.

For more information about how to create a user-defined SQL template and use it in a job context, see *Scenario: Iterating on DB tables and deleting their content using a user-defined SQL template* in the Talend Open Studio Components Reference Guide.

4.5 Handling Jobs: advanced subjects

The sections below give detail information about various advanced configuration situations of a data integration Job including handling multiple input and output flows, using SQl queries, using external components in the Job, scheduling a task to run your Job.

4.5.1 How to map data flows

The most common way to handle multiple input and output flows in your Job including transformations and data re-routing is to use the **tMap** component.

For more information about the principles of using this component, see *Mapping data flows on page 155*.

For examples of Jobs using this component, see *tMap* in the Talend Open Studio Components Reference Guide.

4.5.2 How to create queries using the SQLBuilder

SQLBuilder helps you build your SQL queries and monitor the changes between DB tables and metadata tables. This editor is available in all DBInput and DBSQLRow components (specific or generic).

You can build a query using the SQLbuilder whether your database table schema is stored in the **Repository** tree view or built-in directly in the Job.

Fill in the DB connection details and select the appropriate repository entry if you defined it.

Remove the default query statement in the **Query** field of the **Basic settings** view of the **Component** panel. Then click the three-dot button to open the **[SQL Builder]** editor.

Designing a data integration Job
Handling Jobs: advanced subjects

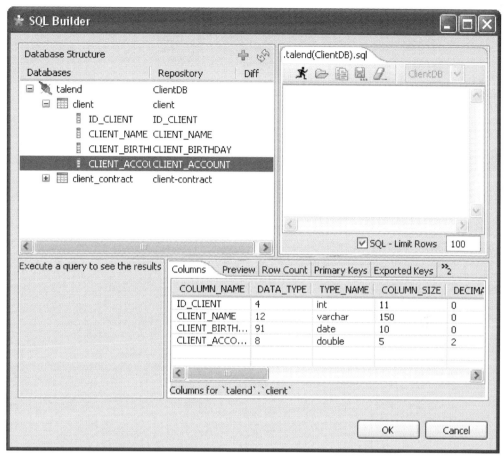

The **[SQL Builder]** editor is made of the following panels:

- Database structure,
- Query editor made of editor and designer tabs,
- Query execution view,
- Schema view.

The Database structure shows the tables for which a schema was defined either in the repository database entry or in your built-in connection.

The schema view, in the bottom right corner of the editor, shows the column description.

How to compare database structures

On the **Database Structure** panel, you can see all tables stored in the DB connection metadata entry in the **Repository** tree view, or in case of built-in schema, the tables of the database itself.

 The connection to the database, in case of built-in schema or in case of a refreshing operation of a repository schema might take quite some time.

Click the refresh icon to display the differences between the DB metadata tables and the actual DB tables.

Talend Open Studio

Designing a data integration Job
Handling Jobs: advanced subjects

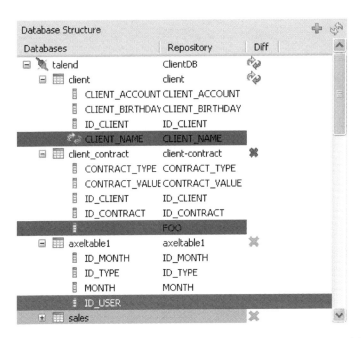

The **Diff** icons point out that the table contains differences or gaps. Expand the table node to show the exact column containing the differences.

The red highlight shows that the content of the column contains differences or that the column is missing from the actual database table.

The blue highlight shows that the column is missing from the table stored in **Repository > Metadata**.

How to build a query

The **[SQL Builder]** editor is a multiple-tab editor that allows you to write or graphically design as many queries as you want.

To create a new query, right-click the table or on the table column and select **Generate Select Statement** on the pop-up list.

Click the empty tab showing by default and type in your SQL query or press **Ctrl+Space** to access the autocompletion list. The tooltip bubble shows the whole path to the table or table section you want to search in.

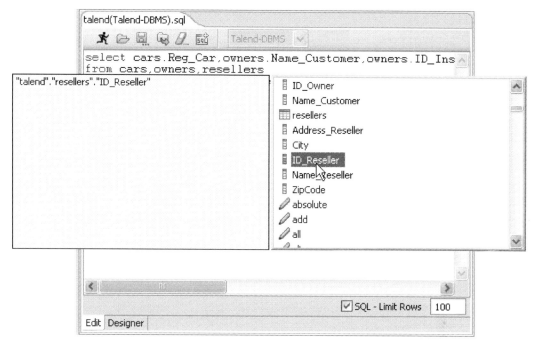

Alternatively the graphical query **Designer** allows you to handle tables easily and have real-time generation of the corresponding query in the **Edit** tab.

Click the **Designer** tab to switch from the manual **Edit** mode to the graphical mode.

 You may get a message while switching from one view to the other as some SQL statements cannot be interpreted graphically.

If you selected a table, all columns are selected by default. Clear the check box facing the relevant columns to exclude them from the selection.

Add more tables in a simple right-click. On the **Designer** view, right-click and select **Add tables** in the pop-up list then select the relevant table to be added.

If joins between these tables already exist, these joins are automatically set up graphically in the editor.

You can also very easily create a join between tables. Right-click the first table columns to be linked and select **Equal** on the pop-up list, to join it with the relevant field of the second table.

Designing a data integration Job
Handling Jobs: advanced subjects

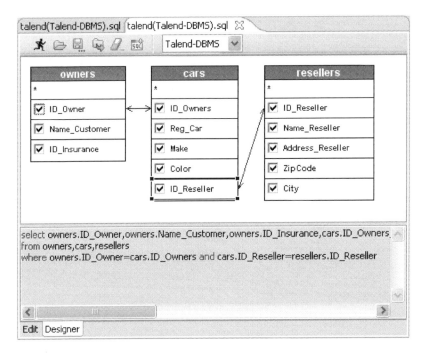

The SQL statement corresponding to your graphical handlings is also displayed on the viewer part of the editor or click the **Edit** tab to switch back to the manual **Edit** mode.

 In the **Designer** view, you cannot include graphically filter criteria. You need to add these in the **Edit** view.

Once your query is complete, execute it by clicking the icon on the toolbar.

The toolbar of the query editor allows you to access quickly usual commands such as: execute, open, save and clear.

On the **Results** view in the lower left corner, are displayed the results of the active query.

How to store a query in the repository

To be able to retrieve and reuse queries, we recommend you to store them in the repository.

In the **[SQL Builder]** editor, click the icon on the toolbar to bind the query with the DB connection and schema in case these are also stored in the repository.

The query can then be accessed from the **Database structure** view, on the left-hand side of the editor.

4.5.3 How to download external community components

Talend Open Studio enables you to access a list of all community components in **Talend Exchange** that are compatible with your current version of Talend Open Studio and are not yet installed in your **Palette**. You can then download these components to use them later in the job designs you carry out in the Studio.

Designing a data integration Job
Handling Jobs: advanced subjects

 The community components available for download in **Talend Exchange** view are not validated by **Talend**. This explains the component-load errors you may have sometimes when trying to download certain components from the view.

How to install community components from Talend Exchange

To copy community components from **Talend Exchange** onto the **Palette** of your current Talend Open Studio:

- Click the **Talend Exchange** tab in the lower part of Talend Open Studio to open the **Compatible components** list.
  This list is empty till you click the refresh button in the upper right corner of the view.

- Click the refresh button in the upper right corner of the view.
  Components from **Talend Exchange** that are compatible with your current version of Talend Open Studio display.

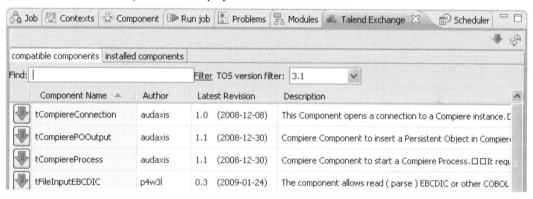

- Click the install button next to the component name you want to load to the **Palette**.
  A progress indicator displays to show the percentage of the download process that has been completed. When the component is successfully installed, a confirmation dialog box displays to confirm the download operation and indicate where in the **Palette** the component has been loaded.

   To download a group of selected components simultaneously, select the components to download and click the install button in the upper right corner of the view.

- Click **OK** in the confirmation dialog box to close it and restart Talend Open Studio.
  All downloaded components display in their relative families in the **Palette**.

You can also download components compatible with older versions of Talend Open Studio. To do so:

- On the **Talend Exchange** view, select the desired version from the **Talend Studio version filter** list. The **Compatible components** list is refreshed automatically.

How to manage installed components

From the **Talend Exchange** view, you can reload or delete components you already installed in the **Palette**.

To install the updated version of a component you already downloaded from the **Compatible components** list, do as follows:

Designing a data integration Job
Handling Jobs: advanced subjects

- In the upper left corner of the view, click the **Installed components** tab to open a list of all the components you downloaded from **Talend Exchange**.

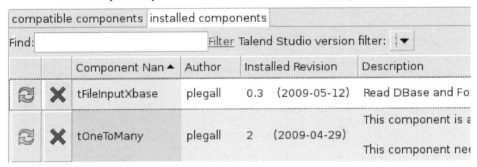

- Click the refresh button next to the component name for which you want to install the newer version.

> If the already downloaded community component is modified in **Talend Exchange**, the refresh button next to its name will become blue in color. Otherwise, it is grey.

To delete a component that you previously downloaded from the **Compatible components** list, do as follows:

- In the **Installed components** list, click the remove button next to the component name you want to delete from your system. You will always be able to re-install it later if you feel like.

4.5.4 How to install external modules

The use of some components in Talend Open Studio requires specific modules to be installed.

The **Modules** view lists all modules necessary to use the components embedded in the Studio. Few of these modules do not exist by default and thus you must install them in order to be able to run smoothly the Jobs that use such components.

> If the **Modules** tab does not show on the tab area of your design workspace, go to **Window** > **Show View...** > **Talend** and then select **Modules** from the list.

To access the **Modules** view, click the **Modules** tab in the design workspace.

Designing a data integration Job
Handling Jobs: advanced subjects

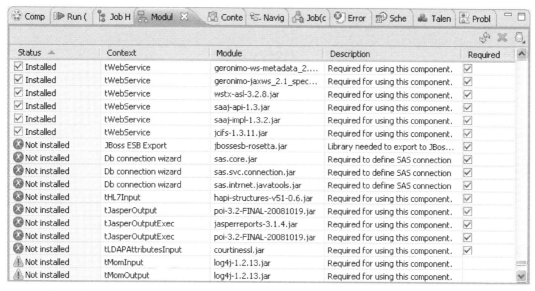

The table below describes the information presented in the **Modules** view.

Column	Description
Status	points out if a module is installed or not installed on your system. The ⚠ icon indicates that the module is not necessarily required for the corresponding component listed in the **Context** column. The ⊗ icon indicates that the module is absolutely required for the corresponding component.
Context	lists the name of **Talend** component using the module. If this column is empty, the module is then required for the general use of Talend Open Studio. 💡 This column lists any external libraries added to the routines you create and save in the Studio library folder. For more information, see *How to edit user routine libraries on page 259*.
Module	lists the module exact name.
Description	explains why the module/library is required.
Required	the selected check box indicates that the module is required.

To install any missing module, complete the following:

- In the **Modules** view, click the 🔍 icon in the upper right corner of the view.
  The **[Open]** dialog box of your operating system displays.

- Browse to the module you want to install, select it and then click **Open** on the dialog box.
  The dialog box closes and the selected module is installed in the library folder of the current Studio.
  You can now use the component dependent on this module in any of your job designs.

Designing a data integration Job
Handling Jobs: advanced subjects

4.5.5 How to launch a Job periodically

The **Scheduler** view in Talend Open Studio helps you to schedule a task that will launch periodically a Job via a task scheduling (crontab) program.

Through the **Scheduler** view, you can generate a crontab file that holds cron-compatible entries (the data required to launch the Job). These entries will allow you to launch periodically a Job via the crontab program.

This job launching feature is based on the *crontab* command, found in Unix and Unix-like operating systems. It can be also installed on any Windows system.

To access the **Scheduler** view, click the **Scheduler** tab in the design workspace.

 If the **Scheduler** tab does not display on the tab system of your design workspace, go to **Window** > **Show View...** > **Talend**, and then select **Scheduler** from the list.

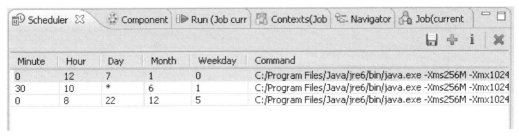

This view is empty if you have not scheduled any task to run a Job. Otherwise, it lists the parameters of all the scheduled tasks.

The below procedure explains how to schedule a task in the **Scheduler** view to run a specific Job periodically and then generate the crontab file that will hold all the data required to launch the selected Job. It also points out how to use the generated file with the *crontab* command in Unix or a task scheduling program in Windows.

- Click the ✚ icon in the upper right corner of the **Scheduler** view.
  The **[Open Scheduler]** dialog box displays.

Designing a data integration Job
Handling Jobs: advanced subjects

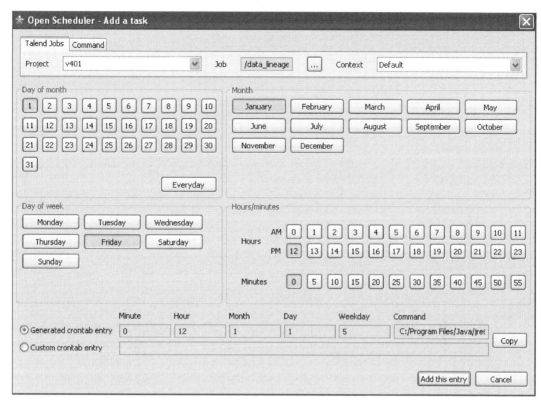

- From the **Project** list, select the project that holds the Job you want to launch periodically.

- Click the three-dot button next to the **Job** field and select the Job you want to launch periodically.

- From the **Context** list, if more than one exists, select the desired context in which to run the Job.

- Set the time and date details necessary to schedule the task.
  The command that will be used to launch the selected Job is generated automatically and attached to the defined task.

- Click **Add this entry** to validate your task and close the dialog box.
  The parameters of the scheduled task are listed in the **Scheduler** view.

- Click the [icon] icon in the upper right corner of the **Scheduler** view to generate a crontab file that will hold all the data required to start the selected Job.
  The **[Save as]** dialog box displays.

- Browse to set the path to the crontab file you are generating.

- In the **File name** field, enter a name for the crontab file and then click **Save** to close the dialog box.
  The crontab file corresponding to the selected task is generated and stored locally in the defined path.

- In Unix, paste the content of the crontab file into the crontab configuration of your Unix system.

Talend Open Studio   111

- In Windows, install a task scheduling program that will use the generated crontab file to launch the selected Job.

You can use the ✖ icon to delete any of the listed tasks and the icon to edit the parameters of any of the listed tasks.

4.5.6 How to use the tPrejob and tPostjob components

The prejob and postjob parts display as components on the design workspace, and are thus available in the **Palette** of components. To use these **tPrejob** and **tPostjob** components, simply drop them to the design workspace as you would do with any other components. An orange square shows the pre and post-job parts which are different types of subjobs.

However note that their use slightly differs from typical components, in the way that these two components do not actually process data nor flows but are meant to help you make your job design clearer.

> As **tPrejob** and **tPostjob** are not meant to take part in any data processing, they can not be part of multi thread execution. The tasks included in the **tPrejob** and **tPostjob** are done once for all following subjobs, whether the subjobs are executed in sequence or in parallel.

Connect to these **tPrejob** and **tPostjob** components, all the components that perform organizing tasks that are not directly related to the data processing or the main subjob to help orchestrating the processing that will follow.

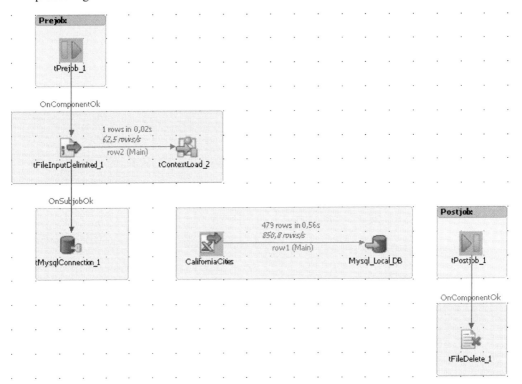

Tasks that require a **tPrejob** component to be used include for example:

- loading context information required for the subjob execution,

- opening a database connection,
- making sure that a file exists.

Many more tasks that are collateral to your Job and might be damaging the overall readability of your Job may as well need a prejob component.

Tasks that require a **tPostjob** component to be used include, for example:

- clearing a folder or deleting a file,
- any tasks to be carried out even though the preceding subjob(s) failed.

4.6 Handling Jobs: miscellaneous subjects

The sections below give detail information about various subjects related to the management of a data integration Job including defining the start component, handling errors, using the **tPrejob** and **tPostjob** components and searching for jobs that use specific components.

4.6.1 How to share a database connection

If you have various Jobs using the same database connection, you can now factorize the connection by using the **Use or Register a shared connection** option.

This option box has been added to all Connection components in order to reduce the number of connection opening and closing.

Assuming that you have two related Jobs (a parent job and a child job) that both need to connect to your remote MySQL database, then perform the operations below:

- Drag and drop a **tMySQLConnection** (assuming that you work with a MySQL database)
- Connect it to the first component of your parent Job

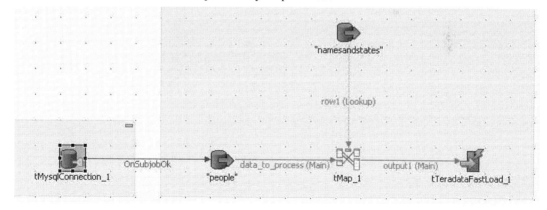

Designing a data integration Job
Handling Jobs: miscellaneous subjects

- On the Connection Component view, tick the box **Use or Register a shared connection**.
- Give a name to the connection you want to share, in the **Shared DB Connection Name** field.

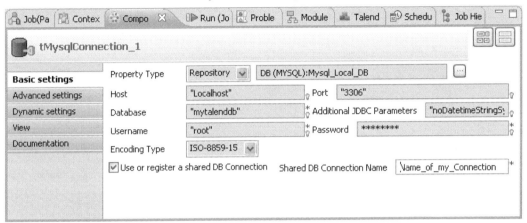

- You are now able to re-use the connection in your Child Job (and any other Job that requires a connection to the same database).
- Simply follow the same steps again and make sure you use the same name in the **Shared DB Connection Name** field.

For more information about how to use the Connection components, see *Talend Open Studio Components* Reference Guide.

4.6.2 How to define the Start component

The **Start** component is the trigger of a Job. There can be several Start components per job design if there are several flows running in parallel. But for one flow and its *connected* subflows, only one component can be the Start component.

Drop a component to the design workspace, all possible start components take a distinctive bright green background color. Notice that most of the components, can be **Start** components.

Only components which do not make sense to trigger a flow, will not be proposed as Start components, such as the **tMap** component for example.

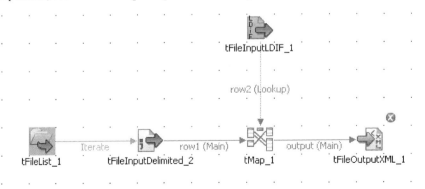

To distinguish which component is to be the **Start** component of your Job, identify the main flow and the secondary flows of your Job

114 Talend Open Studio

- The main flow should be the one connecting a component to the next component using a Row type link. The Start component is then automatically set on the first component of the main flow (icon with green background).

- The secondary flows are also connected using a Row-type link which is then called Lookup row on the design workspace to distinguish it from the main flow. This Lookup flow is used to enrich the main flow with more data.

Be aware that you can change the Start component hence the main flow by changing a main Row into a Lookup Row, simply through a right-click the row to be changed.

Related topics:

- *How to connect components together on page 64*
- *Activating/Deactivating a Job or a sub-job on page 126*

4.6.3 How to handle error icons on components or Jobs

When the properties of a component are not properly defined and contain one or several errors that can prevent the job code to compile properly, error icons will automatically show next to the component icon on the design workspace and the job name in the **Repository** tree view.

Warnings and error icons on components

When a component is not properly defined or if the link to the next component does not exist yet, a red checked circle or a warning sign is docked at the component icon.

Mouse over the component, to display the tooltip messages or warnings along with the label. This context-sensitive help informs you about any missing data or component status.

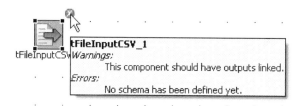

Error icons on Jobs

When the component settings contain one or several errors that can prevent the job code to compile properly, an icon will automatically show next to the job name in the **Repository** tree view.

The error icon displays as well on the tab next to the job name when you open the Job on the design workspace.

The compilation or code generation does only take place when carrying out one of the following operations:

- opening a Job,

- clicking on the **Code Viewer** tab,
- executing a Job (clicking on **Run Job**),
- saving the Job.

Hence, the red error icon will only show then.

When you execute the Job, a warning dialog box opens to list the source and description of any error in the current Job.

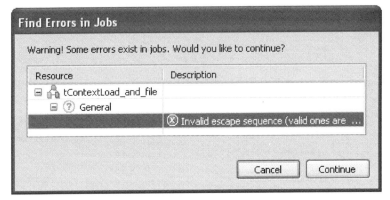

Click **Cancel** to stop your job execution or click **Continue** to continue it.

For information on errors on components, see *Warnings and error icons on components on page 115*.

4.6.4 How to add notes to a Job design

In the **Palette**, click the **Misc** family and then drop the **Note** element to the design workspace to add a text comment to a particular component or to the whole Job.

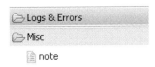

You can change the note format. To do so, select the note you want to format and click the **Basic setting** tab of the **Component** view.

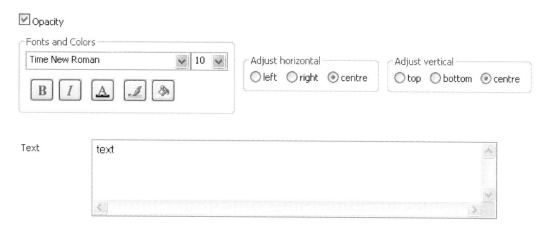

Select the **Opacity** check box to display the background color. By default, this box is selected when you drop a note on the design workspace. If you clear this box, the background becomes transparent.

You can select options from the **Fonts and Colors** list to change the font style, size, color, and so on as well as the background and border color of your note.

You can select the **Adjust horizontal** and **Adjust vertical** boxes to define the vertical and horizontal alignment of the text of your note.

The content of the **Text** field is the text displayed on your note.

4.6.5 How to display the code or the outline of your Job

This panel is located below the **Repository** tree view. It displays detailed information about the open Job or Business Model in the design workspace.

The Information panel is composed of two tabs, **Outline** and **Code Viewer**, which provide information regarding the displayed diagram (either Job or Business Model).

Outline

The **Outline** tab offers a quick view of the business model or the open Job on the design workspace and also a tree view of all used elements in the Job or Business Model. As the design workspace, like any other window area can be resized upon your needs, the **Outline** view is convenient to check out where about on your design workspace, you are located.

Designing a data integration Job
Handling Jobs: miscellaneous subjects

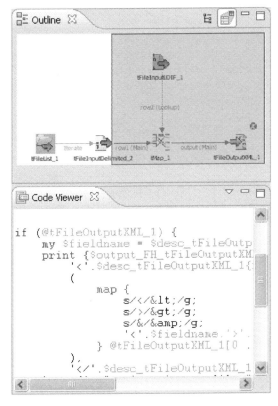

This graphical representation of the diagram highlights in a blue rectangle the diagram part showing in the design workspace.

Click the blue-highlighted view and hold down the mouse button. Then, move the rectangle over the Job.

The view in the design workspace moves accordingly.

The **Outline** view can also be displaying a folder tree view of components in use in the current diagram. Expand the node of a component, to show the list of variables available for this component.

To switch from the graphical outline view to the tree view, click either icon docked at the top right of the panel.

Code viewer

The **Code viewer** tab provides lines of code generated for the selected component, behind the active job design view, as well the run menu including Start, Body and End elements.

 This view only concerns the job design code, as no code is generated from Business Models.

Using a graphical colored code view, the tab shows the code of the component selected in the design workspace. This is a partial view of the primary Code tab docked at the bottom of the design workspace, which shows the code generated for the whole Job.

4.6.6 How to manage the subjob display

A subjob is graphically defined by a blue square gathering all connected components that belong to this subjob. Each individual component can be considered as a subjob when they are not yet connected to one another.

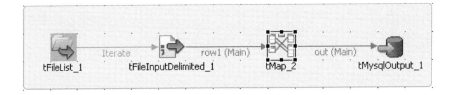

This blue highlight helps you easily distinguish one subjob from another.

A Job can be made of one single subjob. An orange square shows the prejob and postjob parts which are different types of subjobs.
For more information about prejob and postjob, see *How to use the tPrejob and tPostjob components* on page 112.

How to format subjobs

You can modify the subjob color and its title color. To do so, select your subjob and click the **Component** view.

In the **Basic setting** view, select the **Show subjob title** check box if you want to add a title to your subjob, then fill in a title.

To modify the title color and the subjob color:

- In the **Basic settings** view, click the **Title color/Subjob color** button to display the **[Colors]** dialog box.

- Set your colors as desired. By default, the title color is blue and the subjob color is transparent blue.

How to collapse the subjobs

If your Job is made of numerous subjobs, you can collapse them to improve the readability of the whole Job. The minus (-) and plus (+) signs on the top right-hand corner of the subjob allow you to collapse and restore the complete subjob.

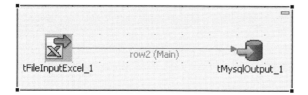

click the minus sign (-) to collapse the subjob. When reduced, only the first component of the subjob is displayed.

Click the plus sign (+) to restore your subjob.

How to remove the subjob background color

If you do not want your subjobs to be highlighted, you can remove the background color on all or specific subjobs.

To remove the background color of all your subjobs, click the **Toggle Subjobs** icon on the toolbar of Talend Open Studio.

Designing a data integration Job
Handling Jobs: miscellaneous subjects

To remove the background color of a specific subjob, right-click the subjob and select the **Hide subjob** option on the pop-up menu.

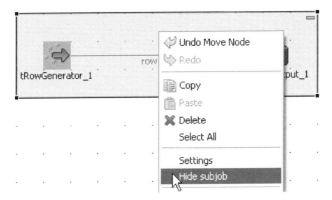

4.6.7 How to define options on the Job view

On the **Job** view located on the bottom part of the design workspace, you can define Job's optional functions. This view is made of two tabs: **Stats & Logs** tab and **Extra** tab.

The **Stats & Logs** tab allows you to automate the use of **Stats & Logs** features and the Context loading feature. For more information, see *How to automate the use of statistics & logs on page 120*.

The **Extra** tab lists various options you can set to automate some features such as the context parameters use, in the **Implicit Context Loading** area. For more information, see *How to use the features in the Extra tab on page 121*.

How to automate the use of statistics & logs

If you have a great need of log, statistics and other measurement of your data flows, you are facing the issue of having too many log-related components loading your job designs. You can automate the use of **tFlowMeterCatcher**, **tStatCatcher**, **tLogCatcher** component functionalities without using the components in your Job via the **Stats & Logs** tab.

For more information regarding the Log component, see the Talend Open Studio Components Reference Guide.

The **Stats & Logs** panel is located on the **Job** tab underneath the design workspace and prevents your jobs designs to be overloaded by components.

 This setting supersedes the log-related components with a general log configuration.

To set the **Stats & Logs** properties:

- Click the **Job** tab.
- Select the **Stats & Logs** panel to display the configuration view.

120 Talend Open Studio

Designing a data integration Job
Handling Jobs: miscellaneous subjects

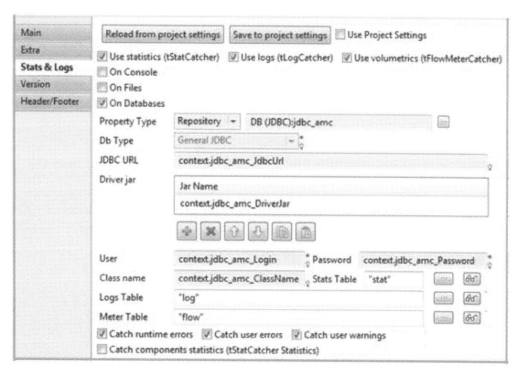

 When you use a database connection, for example, to JDBC, you need create the stats table, the logs table or meter table manually.

- Set the relevant details depending on the output you prefer (console, file or database).
- Select the relevant **Catch** check box according to your needs.

 You can automatically save the settings into your Preference. Or else, you can access the preferences via **Window > Preferences > Talend > Stats & Logs**.

When you use **Stats & Logs** functions in your Job, you can apply them to all its subjobs.

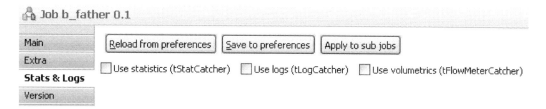

To do so, click the **Apply to subjobs** button in the **Stats & Logs** panel of the **Job** view and the selected stats & logs functions of the main Job will be selected for all of its subjobs.

How to use the features in the Extra tab

The **Extra** tab offers some optional function parameters.

- Select the **Multithread execution** check box to allow two job executions to start at the same time.

Talend Open Studio   121

Designing a data integration Job
Handling Jobs: miscellaneous subjects

- Set the **Implicit tContextLoad** option parameters to avoid using the **tContextLoad** component on your Job and automate the use of context parameters.
  Choose between **File** or **Database** as source of your context parameters and set manually the file or database access.
  Set notifications (error/warning/info) for unexpected behaviors linked to context parameter setting.

- When you fill in **Implicit tContextLoad** manually, you can store these parameters in your project by clicking the **Save to project settings** button, and thus reuse these parameters for other components in different Jobs.

- Select the **Use Project Settings** check box to recuperate the context parameters you have already defined in the **Project Settings** view.
  The **Implicit tContextLoad** option becomes available and all fields are filled in automatically.
  For more information about context parameters, see *Context settings on page 37*.

- Click **Reload from project settings** to update the context parameters list with the latest context parameters from the project settings.

4.6.8 How to find components in Jobs

 You should open one Job at least in the Studio to display the **Palette** to the right of the design workspace and thus start the search.

From the **Palette**, you can search for all the Jobs that use the selected component. To do so:

- In the **Palette**, right-click the component you want to look for and select **Find Component in Jobs**.

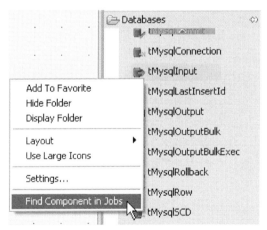

A progress indicator displays to show the percentage of the search operation that has been completed then the **[Find a Job]** dialog box displays listing all the Jobs that use the selected component.

Designing a data integration Job
Handling Jobs: miscellaneous subjects

- From the list of Jobs, click the desired Job and then click **OK** to open it on the design workspace.

CHAPTER 5
Managing data integration Jobs

This chapter describes the management procedures you can carry out on the Jobs you design in Talend Open Studio or you can carry out on any of the items included in a project, for example routines or metadata.

These management procedures include importing and ing Jobs and items between different projects or machines, scheduling job execution and running and deploying jobs on distant servers and copying Jobs onto different SVN branches.

Before starting any data integration processes, you need to be familiar with Talend Open Studio Graphical User Interface (GUI). For more information, see *Talend Open Studio GUI on page 275*.

5.1 Activating/Deactivating a Job or a sub-job

You can enable or disable the whole Job or a sub-job directly connected to the selected component. By default, a component is activated.

In the **Main** properties of the selected component, select or clear the **Activate** check box.

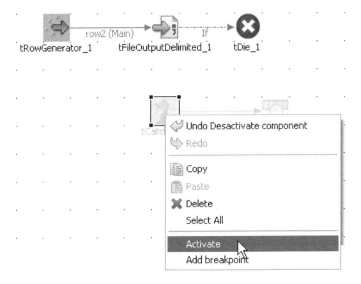

Alternatively, right-click the component and select the relevant **Activate/Deactivate** command according to the current component status.

If you disable a component, no code will be generated, you will not be able to add or modify links from the disabled component to active or new components.

Related topic: *How to define the Start component on page 114*.

5.1.1 How to disable a Start component

In the case the component you deactivated is a **Start** component, components of all types and links of all nature connected directly and indirectly to it will get disabled too.

5.1.2 How to disable a non-Start component

When you clear the **Activate** check box of a regular (non Start) component, are deactivated only the selected component itself along with all direct links.

If a direct link to the disabled component is a main Row connection to a sub-job. All components of this sub-job will also get disabled.

5.2 Importing/exporting items or Jobs

Talend Open Studio enables you to import/export your Jobs or items in your Jobs from/to various projects or various versions of the Studio. It enables you as well to export Jobs and thus deploy and execute the Jobs created in the Studio on any server.

5.2.1 How to import items

You can import items from previous versions of Talend Open Studio or from a different project of your current version.

The items you can possibly import are multiple:

- Business Models
- Jobs Designs
- Routines
- Documentation
- Metadata

Follow the steps below to import them to the repository:

- In the **Repository** tree view, right-click any entry such as **Job Designs** or **Business Models**.
- On the pop-up menu, select the **Import Items** option.

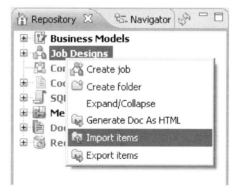

- A dialog box prompts you to select the root directory or the archive file to extract the items from.
- If you exported the items from your local repository into an archive file (including source files and scripts), select the archive filepath, browse to the file then click **OK**.
- If the items to import are still stored on your local repository, select **Root Directory** and browse to the relevant project directory on your system.
- Browse down to the relevant **Project** folder within the workspace directory. It should correspond to the project name you picked up.

Managing data integration Jobs
Importing/exporting items or Jobs

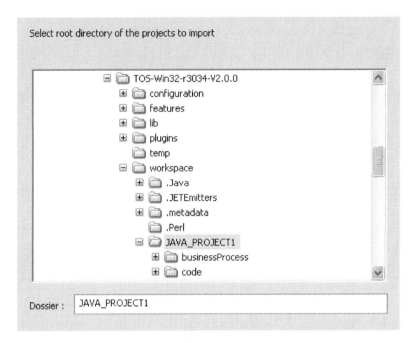

- If you only want to import very specific items such as some **Job Designs**, you can select the specific folder, such as Process where all the job designs for the project are stored. If you only have **Business Models** to import, select the specific folder: **BusinessProcess**.

- But if your project gather various types of items (Business Models, Jobs Designs, Metadata, Routines...), we recommend you to select the **Project** folder to import all items in one go.

- Then click **OK** to continue.

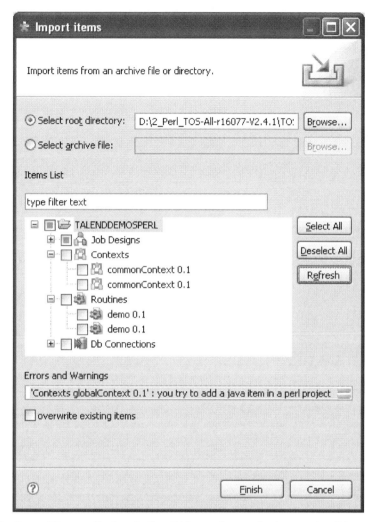

- In the **Items List** are displayed all valid items that can be imported. All items are selected by default, but you can individually clear the check boxes of unwanted items.

- Click **Finish** to validate the import.

- The imported items display on the repository in the relevant folder respective to their nature.

 If there are several versions of the same items, they will all be imported into the Project you are running, unless you already have identical items.

5.2.2 How to export Jobs in Java

The export Job feature allows you to deploy and execute a job on any server, independent of Talend Open Studio.

The export Job feature adds all of the files required to execute the job to an archive, including the .bat and .sh along with any context-parameter files or other related files.

Managing data integration Jobs
Importing/exporting items or Jobs

 The **[Export Jobs]** dialog boxes vary in appearance, depending on whether you work on a Java or Perl version of the product.

To export jobs, complete the following:

- In the **Repository** tree view, right-click the Job(s) you want to export.
- Select **Export Job** to open the **[Export Jobs]** dialog box.

 You can show/hide a tree view of all created Jobs in Talend Open Studio directly from the **[Export Jobs]** dialog box by clicking the `»` and the `«` buttons respectively. The Jobs you earlier selected in the Studio tree view display with selected check boxes. This accessibility helps to modify the selected items to be exported directly from the dialog box without having to close it and go back to the **Repository** tree view in Talend Open Studio to do that.

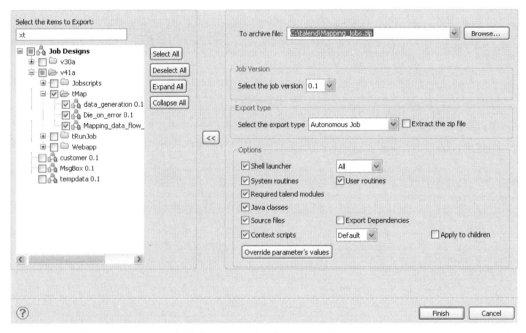

- On the **To archive file** field, browse to the directory where you want to save your exported Job.

- On the **Job Version** area, select the version number of the Job you want to export if you have created more than one version of the Job.

- Select the **Export Type** in the list between **Autonomous Job, Axis Webservice (WAR), Axis Webservice (Zip), JBoss ESB** and **Petals ESB**.

- Select the **Extract the zip file** check box to automatically extract the archive file in the target directory.

- In the **Options** area, select the file type(s) you want to add to the archive file. The check boxes corresponding to the file types necessary for the execution of the Job are selected by default. You can clear these check boxes depending on what you want to export.

- To export the .bat and/or .sh files necessary to launch the exported Job, select **Shell launcher** check box. In the corresponding list, you can select:
  - **All** to export the .bat and .sh files,
  - **Unix** to export the .sh file,
  - **Windows** to export the .bat file.

- To export the user or system routines used in the specified Job, select the **System routines** or **User routines** check boxes.

- To export **Talend** modules, select the **Required Talend modules** check box.

- To export the .java file holding Java classes generated by the Job when designing it, select the **Java classes** check box.

- To export the sources used by the Job during its execution including the .item and .properties files, Java and Talend sources, select the **Source files** check box.

   If you select the **Source files** check box, you can reuse the exported Job in a Talend Open Studio installed on another machine. These source files are only used in Talend Open Studio.

- Select the **Export Dependencies** check box if you want to export the dependencies of your Job, i.e. contexts, routines, connections, etc.

- Select the **Context script** check box to export ALL context parameters files and not just those you select in the corresponding list.

- To export only one context, select the context that fits your needs from the **Context script** list, including the .bat or .sh files holding the appropriate context parameters. Then you can, if you wish, edit the .bat and .sh files to manually modify the context type.

- Select the **Apply to children** check box if you want to apply the context selected from the list to all child Jobs.

- Click the **Override parameters' values** button.
  In the window which opens you can update, add or remove context parameters and values of the Job context you selected in the list, if necessary.

- Click **Finish** to validate your changes, complete the export operation and close the dialog box.

A zipped file for the Jobs is created in the defined place.

How to export Jobs as Autonomous Job

In the case of a Plain Old Java Object export, if you want to reuse the Job in Talend Open Studio installed on another machine, make sure you selected the **Source files** check box. These source files (.item and .properties) are only needed within Talend Open Studio.

Select a context in the list when offered. Then once you click the **Override parameters' values** button below the **Context script** checkbox, the opened window will list all of the parameters of the selected context. In this window, you can configure the selected context as needs.

All contexts parameter files are exported along in addition to the one selected in the list.

 After being exported, the context selection information is stored in the .bat/.sh file and the context settings are stored in the context **.properties** file.

How to export Jobs as Webservice

In the **[Export Jobs]** dialog box, you can change the type of export in order to export the job selection as Webservice archive.

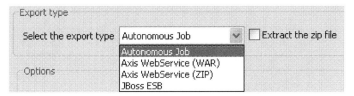

Select the type of archive you want to use in your Web application.

Archive type	Description
WAR	The options are read-only. Indeed, the WAR archive generated includes all configuration files necessary for the execution or deployment from the Web application.
ZIP	All options are available. In the case the files of your Web application config are all set, you have the possibility to only set the Context parameters if relevant and export only the Classes into the archive.

Once the archive is produced, place the WAR or the relevant Class from the ZIP (or unzipped files) into the relevant location, of your Web application server.

The URL to be used to deploy the job, typically reads as follow:
`http://localhost:8080/Webappname/services/JobName?method=runJob&args=null`

where the parameters stand as follow:

URL parameters	Description
http://localhost:8080/	Type in the Webapp host and port
/Webappname/	Type in the actual name of your web application
/services/	Type in "services" as the standard call term for web services
/JobName	Type in the exact name of the Job you want to execute
?method=runJob&args=null	The method is RunJob to execute the Job.

The call return from the Web application is 0 when there is no error and different from 0 in case of error. For a real-life example of creating and exporting a Job as a Websrvice and calling the exported Job from a browser, see *An example of exporting a Job as a Web service on page 132*.

The **tBufferOutput** component was especially designed for this type of deployment. For more information regarding this component, see *tBufferOutput* of the Talend Open Studio Components Reference Guide.

An example of exporting a Job as a Web service

This scenario describes first a simple Job that creates a .txt file and writes in it the current date along with first and last names. Second, it shows how to export this Job as a Webservice. And finally, it calls the Job exported as a Webservice from a browser. The exported Job as a Webservice will simply return the "return code" given by the operating system.

Creating the Job:

- Drop the following components from the **Palette** onto the design workspace: **tFixedFlowInput** and **tFileOutputDelimited**.

- Connect **tFixedFlowInput** to **tFileOutputDelimited** using a **Row Main** link.

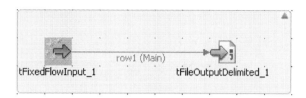

- In the design workspace, select **tFixedFlowInput**.

- Click the **Component** tab to define the basic settings for **tFixedFlowInput**.

- Set the **Schema** to **Built-In** and click the three-dot **[...]** button next to **Edit Schema** to describe the data structure you want to create from internal variables. In this scenario, the schema is made of three columns, *now*, *firstname*, and *lastname*.

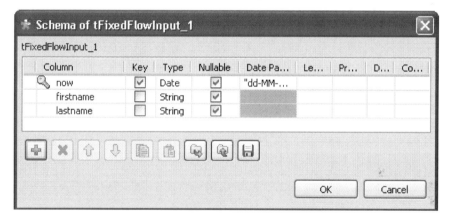

- Click the plus button to add the three parameter lines and define your variables.

- Click **OK** to close the dialog box and accept propagating the changes when prompted by the system. The three defined columns display in the **Values** table of the **Basic settings** view of **tFixedFlowInput**.

- Click in the **Value** cell of each of the three defined columns and press **Ctrl+Space** to access the global variable list.

- From the global variable list, select *TalendDate.getCurrentDate()*, *talendDatagenerator.getFirstName*, and *talendDataGenerator.getLastName* for the *now*, *firstname*, and *lastname* columns respectively.

- In the **Number of rows** field, enter the number of lines to be generated.

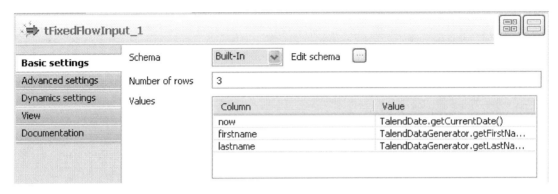

- In the design workspace, select **tFileOutputDelimited**.
- Click the **Component** tab for **tFileOutputDelimited** and browse to the output file to set its path in the **File name** field. Define other properties as needed.

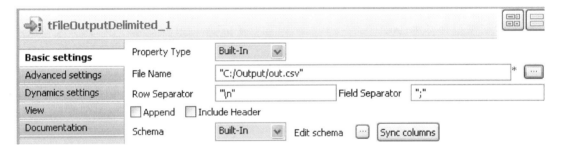

If you press **F6** to execute the Job, three rows holding the current date and first and last names will be written to the set output file.

Exporting the Job as a Webservice:

- In the **Repository** tree view, right-click the above created Job and select **Export Job**. The **[Export Jobs]** dialog box displays.

Managing data integration Jobs
Importing/exporting items or Jobs

- Click the **Browse...** button to select a directory to archive your Job in.
- In the **Job Version** area, select the version of the Job you want to export as a web service.
- In the **Export type** area, select the export type you want to use in your Web application (WAR in this example) and click **Finish**. The **[Export Jobs]** dialog box disappears.
- Copy the War folder and paste it in the Tomcat webapp directory.

Calling the Job from a browser:

Type the following URL into your browser:
http://localhost:8080//export_job/services/export_job2?method=runJob where "export_job" is the name of the webapp directory deployed in Tomcat and "export_job2" is the name of the Job.

Click **Enter** to execute the Job from your browser.

Managing data integration Jobs
Importing/exporting items or Jobs

```
Ce fichier XML ne semble pas avoir d'information de style lui

- <soapenv:Envelope>
  - <soapenv:Body>
    - <runJobReturn xsi:type="ns1:runJobReturn">
      - <ns1:item xsi:type="ns1:ArrayOf_xsd_string">
          <ns1:item xsi:type="xsd:string">0</ns1:item>
        </ns1:item>
      </runJobReturn>
    </soapenv:Body>
  </soapenv:Envelope>
```

The return code from the Web application is 0 when there is no error and 1 if an error occurs.

For a real-life example of creating and exporting a Job as a Webservices using the **tBufferOutput** component, see *Scenario 2: Buffering output data on the webapp server* of the Talend Open Studio Components **Reference Guide**.

How to export Jobs as JBoss ESB

Talend Open Studio provides the possibility to expose **Talend** Jobs as services into JBoss ESB (Enterprise Service Bus) in order to execute these Jobs on the messaging engine (the bus).

 In order to be able to export a Job to be deployed on a JBoss ESB server, make sure that the jar specific to JBoss ESB is installed in the Java library and that it displays in the Modules view of Talend Open Studio. For more information about the Modules view, see How to install external modules on page 108.

In the **[Export Jobs]** dialog box, you can change the type of export in order to export the selected Job as an ESB archive. You can then deploy this exported Job on a JBoss ESB server.

To export a Job on ESB:

- In the **Job Version** area, select the version of the Job you want to execute on a JBoss ESB server.
- From the **Select export type** list in the **Export type** area, select **JBoss ESB**.
- In the **Option** area, select the file type you want to add to the archive. When the **Context script** list displays more than one context, select the one you need.
- Select the **Apply to children** check box if you want to apply the context selected from the list to all child Jobs.
- To export the sources used by the Job during its execution including the files .item, .properties and java sources of Jobs and routines, select the **Source files** check box.

     If you select the **Source files** check box, you can reuse the exported Job in a Talend Open Studio installed on another machine. These source files are only used in Talend Open Studio.

- Select the **Export Dependencies** check box if you want to export dependencies with your Job, i.e. contexts, routines, connections, etc.

- In the **ESB Export type** list, select between *JBoss MQ* or *JBoss Messaging*.

- In the **Service Name** field, type in the name of the service on which you will deploy your Job.

- In the **Category** field, type in the category of the service on which the Job will be deployed.

- In the **Message Queue Name** field, type in the name of the queue that is used to deploy the Job.

- Click the **Browse...** button next to the **To archive file** field and browse to set the path to the archive file in which you want to export the Job.

- Click **Finish**.
  The dialog box closes. A progress indicator displays to show the progress percentage of the export operation. The Job is exported in the selected archive.

When you copy the ESB archive in the deployment directory and launch the server, the Job is automatically deployed and will be ready to be executed on the ESB server.

How to export Jobs as Petals ESB

Talend Open Studio provides the possibility to expose **Talend** Jobs as services into petals ESB (Enterprise Service Bus) in order to execute these Jobs on the messaging engine (the bus). .

Integrating Talend with petals ESB

Talend provides a smooth approach to expose services on petals ESB and thus facilitates:

- application integration on the bus: This will enable the integration of systems and applications across the enterprise.

- service interactions: The ESB provides connectivity between services. i.e. allows services with varying interfaces to communicate.

The Java Business Integration (JBI) is the approach used to implement a service-oriented architecture (SOA) and export **Talend** Jobs on petals ESB.

Petals ESB is complemented with Binding Components (BC) and **Talend** Service Engine (SE) in order to provide: first the access methods necessary for different types of services including FileTransfer, WebService, MOM, and second the engine to deploy the service. For more information about interaction between Petals and **Talend** Jobs, check http://doc.petalslink.com/display/petalsesb/A+Simple+Talend+Job.

Then, with the integration of **Talend** and petals ESB, you can execute the Jobs designed in Talend Open Studio on petals ESB. For more information, see *How to export Jobs as Petals ESB on page 137*. Several mechanisms are provided to pass information and data to a Job and to retrieve information and data from a Job.

Using Talend Open Studio and petals ESB, you can execute a Job which has no specific interaction with Petals. You can:

- expose a context as a parameter into the service's WSDL,

- pass attachment files to a Job,

Managing data integration Jobs
Importing/exporting items or Jobs

- pass native parameters and options to a Job,
- get the Job's execution result.

How to export Jobs to petals ESB

From the **[Export Jobs]** dialog box, you can export a selected Job as a petals ESB archive. You can then execute the exported Job on the bus (the messaging engine).

To export a Job as a petals ESB archive, complete the following:

- In the **Repository** tree view, right-click the Job you want to export and then select **Export Job** from the contextual menu.
  The **[Export Jobs]** dialog box displays.

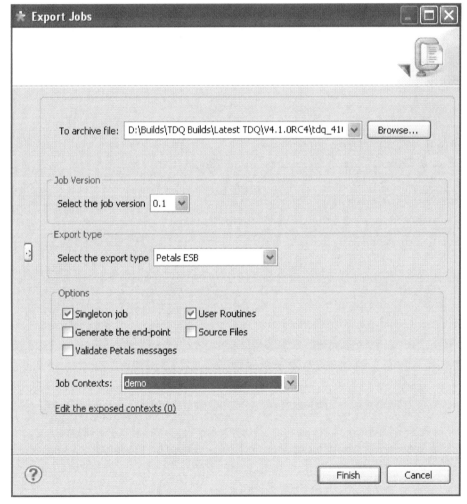

- In the **To archive file** field, browse to set the path to the archive file in which you want to export the Job.
- From the **Select the job version** list, select the job version you want to export.

- From the **Select export type** list in the **Export type** area, select **Petals ESB**. The three following options in the **Options** area are selected by default: **Singleton job**, **User Routines** and **Source file**. You can select any of the other options as needed.

The table below explains the export options:

Option	Description
Singleton job	Exports the Job as singleton: A singleton Job can have only one instance running at a time on a given **Talend** Service Engine in petals ESB.
Generate the end-point	Generates the end-point at deployment time. If this option is not selected, the end-point name is the job name with the suffix `Endpoint`.
Validate Petals messages	Validates all the messages / requests against the WSDL. Selecting this option reduces system performance (disk access).
User routines	Embeds the user routines in the service-unit.
Source files	Embeds the source files in the generated service-unit.
Jobs contexts	A list from which to select the context that will be used by default by the Job.

- In the **[Export Jobs]** dialog box, click the **Edit the exposed contexts** link to open the **[Context Export]** dialog box.

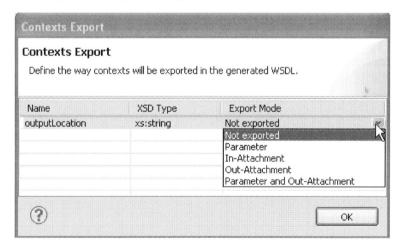

This dialog box will display a list of all the context variables that are used in the exported Job. Here you can specify how each context variable should be exported in the generated WSDL file.

- Click in the **Export Mode field** and select from the list the context export mode for each of the listed context variables.
The table below explains the export mode options:

Managing data integration Jobs
Importing/exporting items or Jobs

Export Mode	Description
Not exported	The context is not exported (not visible as a parameter). But the context can still be overridden using the native parameters (options) of the job.
Parameter	The context is exported as a parameter in the WSDL.
In-Attachment	The context will pass the path of a temporary file which content is attached in the input message.
Out-Attachment	The context will be read after the job execution. -This context must point to a file, -The file content will be read by the service engine and attached to the response, -The context name will be used as the attachment name, -The file will be deleted by the service engine right after its content was loaded.
Parameter and Out-Attachment	A mix between the **Parameter** and the **Out-Attachment** modes. -The context is exposed as a parameter, -It will also be read after the job execution, -The file will be deleted anyway, The advantage of this export mode is to define the output file destination dynamically.

- Click **OK** to validate your choice and close the **[Context Export]** dialog box.

- In the **[Export Jobs]** dialog box, click **Finish**.
  The dialog box closes. A progress indicator displays to show the progress percentage of the export operation. The Job is exported in the selected archive.

The **Talend** Job is now exposed as a service into petals ESB and can be executed inside the bus.

5.2.3 How to export Jobs in Perl

The export Jobs feature allows you to deploy and execute a job on any server, independent to Talend Open Studio.

Exporting a Job adds all the files required to execute the job to an archive, including the .bat and .sh along with any context-parameter files or other related files.

 The **[Export Jobs]** dialog boxes vary in appearance, depending on whether you work on a Java or Perl version of the product.

To export Jobs, complete the following:

- Right-click the relevant job in the **Repository** tree view.

- Select **Export Job** to open the **[Export Jobs]** dialog box.

Managing data integration Jobs
Importing/exporting items or Jobs

> You can show/hide a tree view of all created Jobs in Talend Open Studio directly from the **[Export Jobs]** dialog box by clicking the » and the « buttons respectively. The Jobs you earlier selected in the Studio tree view display with selected check boxes. This accessibility helps to modify the selected items to be exported directly from the dialog box without having to close it and go back to the **DQ Repository** tree view in Talend Open Studio to do that.

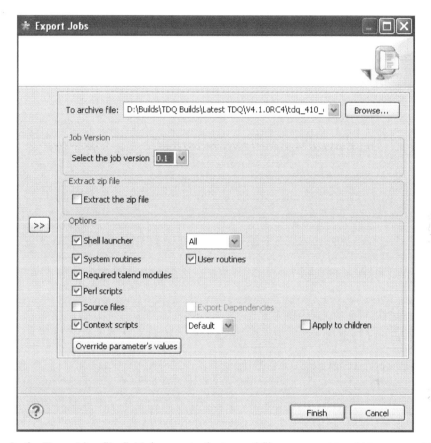

- In the **To archive file field**, browse to the type of files you want to add to your archive.

- From **Select the job version list**, select the version number of the Job you want to export.

- Select **Extract the zip file** check box to export the archive file and its version extracted from your Job.

- In the **Options** zone, select the file type(s) you want to add to the archive file. The check boxes corresponding to the file types necessary for the execution of the Job are selected by default. You can clear these check boxes depending on what you want to export.

- To export the .bat and .sh files necessary to launch the exported Job, select **Shell launcher** check box.

- To export the user or system routines used in the specified Job, select the **System routines** and **User routines** check boxes.

- To export **Talend** modules, select the **Required Talend modules** check box.

Talend Open Studio 141

Managing data integration Jobs
Importing/exporting items or Jobs

- To export the .jar file holding Perl classes necessary for job execution in Perl, select the **Perl scripts** check box.
- To export the sources used by the Job during its execution including the files .item, .properties and perl sources of Jobs and routines, select the **Source files** check box.

   If you select the **Source files** check box, you can reuse the exported Job in a Talend Open Studio installed on another machine. These source files are only used in Talend Open Studio.

- Select the **Export Dependencies** check box if you want to export the dependencies with your Job, i.e. contexts, routines, connections, etc.
- Select the **Context script** check box to export all context parameters files and not just those you select in the list.
- From the **Context script** list, select the context that fits your needs, including the .bat or .sh files holding the appropriate context parameters. Then you can, if you wish, edit the .bat and .sh files to manually modify the context type.
- Select the **Apply to children** check box if you want to apply the context selected from the list to all children jobs.

   If you want to change the context selection, simply edit the `.bat/.sh` file and change the following setting: `--context=Prod` to the relevant context.
  If you want to change the context settings, then edit the relevant context properties file.

- Click **Finish** to validate your changes, complete the export operation and close the dialog box.

A zipped file for the Jobs is created in the defined place.

 You cannot import jobs into a different version of Talend Open Studio than the one the jobs were created in. To be able to reuse previous jobs in a later version of Talend Open Studio, use the Import Project function. See How to import a project on page 17.

5.2.4 How to export items

You can export multiple items from the repository onto a directory or an archive file. Hence you have the possibility to export metadata information such as DB connection or Documentation along with your Job or your Business Model, for example.

- In the **Repository** tree view, select the items you want to export.
- To select several items at a time, press the **Ctrl** key and select the relevant items.

Managing data integration Jobs
Importing/exporting items or Jobs

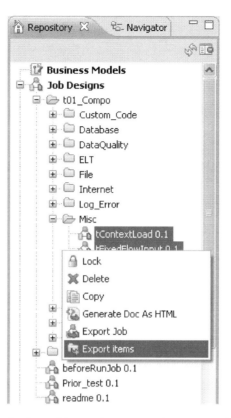

 If you want to export a database table metadata entry, make sure you select the whole DB connection, and not only the relevant table as this will prevent the export process to complete correctly.

- Right-click while maintaining the **Ctrl** key down and select **Export items** on the pop-up menu:

Managing data integration Jobs
Importing/exporting items or Jobs

You can select additional items on the tree for exportation if required.

- Click **Browse** to browse to where you want to store the exported items. Alternatively, define the archive file where to compress the files for all selected items.

If you have several versions of the same item, they will all be exported.

Select the **Export Dependencies** check box if you want to set and export routine dependencies along with Jobs you are exporting. By default, all of the user routines are selected. For further information about routines, see *What are routines*.

- Click **Finish** to close the dialog box and export the items.

5.2.5 How to change context parameters in Jobs

As explained in sections *How to export Jobs in Java on page 129* and *How to export Jobs in Perl on page 140*, you can edit the context parameters:

If you want to change the context selection, simply edit the .bat/.sh file and change the following setting: `--context=Prod` to the relevant context.

If you want to change individual parameters in the context selection, edit the .bat/.sh file and add the following setting according to your need:

Operations	Setting
to change *value1* for parameter *key1*	`--context_param key1=value1`
to change *value1* and *value2* for respective parameters *key1* and *key2*	`--context_param key1=value1` `--context_param key2=value2`
to change a value containing space characters such as in a file path	`--context_param key1="path to file"`

5.3 Managing repository items

Talend Open Studio enables you to edit the items centralized in the repository and to update the Jobs that use these items accordingly.

5.3.1 How to handle updates in repository items

You can update the metadata, context or joblets parameters that are centralized in the **Repository** tree view any time in order to update the database connection or the context group details, for example.

When you modify any of the parameters of an entry in the **Repository** tree view, all Jobs using this repository entry will be impacted by the modification. This is why, the system will prompt you to propagate these modifications to all the Jobs that use the repository entry.

The below sections explain how to modify the parameters of a repository entry and how to propagate the modifications to all or some of the Jobs that use the entry in question.

How to modify a repository item

To update the parameters of a repository item, complete the following:

- Expand the **Metadata**, **Contexts** or **Joblets Designs** node in the **Repository** tree view and browse to the relevant entry that you need to update.
- Right-click this entry and select the corresponding edit option in the contextual menu.

A respective wizard displays where you can edit each of the definition steps for the entry parameters.

When updating the entry parameters, you need to propagate the changes throughout numerous Jobs or all your Jobs that use this entry.

A prompt message pops up automatically at the end of your update/modification process when you click the **Finish** button in the wizard.

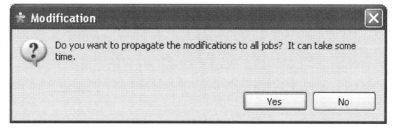

- Click **Yes** to close the message and implement the changes throughout all Jobs impacted by these changes. For more information about the first way of propagating all your changes, see *How to update impacted Jobs automatically on page 146*.

- Click **No** if you want to close the message without propagating the changes. This will allow you to propagate your changes on the impacted Jobs manually on one by one basis. For more information on another way of propagating changes, see *How to update impacted Jobs manually on page 147*.

How to update impacted Jobs automatically

After you update the parameters of any item already centralized in the **Repository** tree view and used in different Jobs, a message will prompt you to propagate the modifications you did to all Jobs that use these parameters.

Click **Yes** if you want the system to scan your **Repository** tree view for the Jobs that get impacted by the changes you just made. This aims to automatically propagate the update throughout all your Jobs (open or not) in one click.

The **[Update Detection]** dialog box displays to list all Jobs impacted by the parameters that are modified.

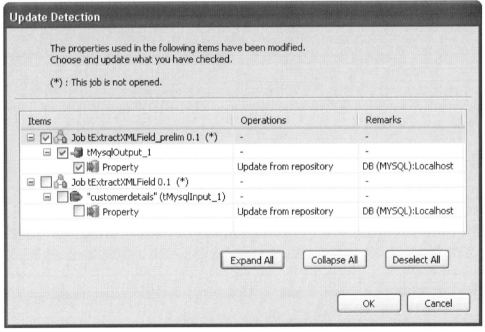

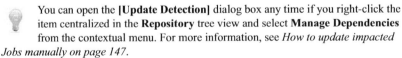

You can open the **[Update Detection]** dialog box any time if you right-click the item centralized in the **Repository** tree view and select **Manage Dependencies** from the contextual menu. For more information, see *How to update impacted Jobs manually on page 147*.

- If needed, clear the check boxes that correspond to the Jobs you do not wish to update. You can update them any time later through the **Detect Dependencies** menu. For more information, see *How to update impacted Jobs manually on page 147*.

- Click **OK** to close the dialog box and update all selected Jobs.

How to update impacted Jobs manually

Before propagating changes in the parameters of an item centralized in the tree view throughout the Jobs using this entry, you might want to view all Jobs that are impacted by the changes. To do that, complete the following:

- In the **Repository** tree view, expand the node holding the entry you want to check what Jobs use it.

- Right-click the entry and select **Detect Dependencies**.
  A progress bar indicates the process of checking for all Jobs that use the modified metadata or context parameter. Then a dialog box displays to list all Jobs that use the modified item.

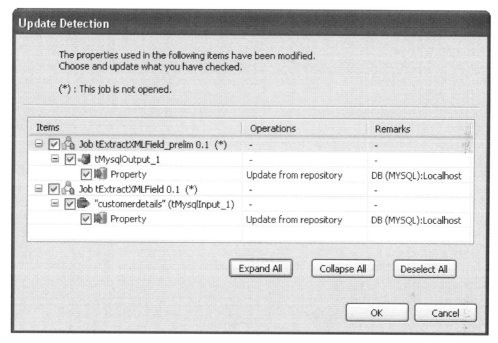

- Select the check boxes corresponding to the Jobs you want to update with the modified metadata or context parameter and clear those corresponding to the Jobs you do not want to update.

- Click **OK** to validate and close the dialog box.

 The Jobs that you choose not to update will be switched back to **Built-in**, as the link to the Repository cannot be maintained. It will thus keep their setting as it was before the change.

5.4 Searching a Job in the repository

If you want to open a specific Job in the **Repository** tree view of the current Talend Open Studio and you can not find it for one reason or another, you can simply click on the quick access toolbar.
To find a Job in the **Repository** tree view, complete the following:

Managing data integration Jobs
Searching a Job in the repository

- On **Talend Open Studio** toolbar, click to open the **[Find a Job]** dialog box that lists automatically all the Jobs you created in the current Studio.

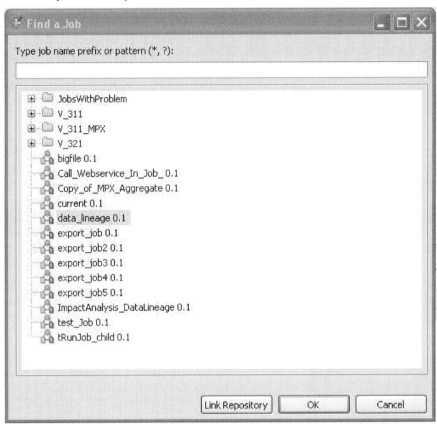

- Enter the job name or part of the job name in the upper field.
  When you start typing your text in the field, the job list is updated automatically to display only the Job(s) which name(s) match(es) the letters you typed in.

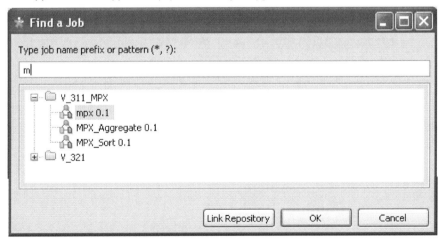

- Select the desired Job from the list and click **Link Repository** to automatically browse to the selected Job in the **Repository** tree view.

- If needed, click **Cancel** to close the dialog box and then right-click the selected Job in the **Repository** tree view to perform any of the available operations in the contextual menu.
- Otherwise, click **Ok** to close the dialog box and open the selected Job on the design workspace.

5.5 Managing Job versions

When you create a Job in Talend Open Studio, by default its version is 0.1 where 0 stands for the major version and 1 for the minor version.

You can create many versions of the same Job. To do that:

- Close your Job if it is open on the design workspace, otherwise, its properties will be read-only and thus you can not modify them.
- In the **Repository** tree view, right-click your Job and select **Edit properties** in the drop-down list to open the **[Edit properties]** dialog box.
- Next to the **Version** field, click the **M** button to increment the major version and the **m** button to increment the minor version.
- Click **Finish** to validate the modification.

By default, when you open a Job, you open its last version.
Any previous version of the Job is read-only and thus can not be modified.

To change the version of your Job, you can also:

- Close your Job if it is open on the design workspace, otherwise, its properties will be read-only and thus you can not modify them.
- In the **Repository** tree view, right-click your Job and select **Open another version** in the drop-down list.
- In the dialog box, select the **Create new version and open it** check box and click the **M** button to increment the major version and the **m** button to increment the minor version.
- Click **Finish** to validate the modification and open this new version of your Job.

You can also save a Job and increment its version in the same time, by clicking **File>Save as...**.

This option does not overwrite your current Job, it saves your Job as another new Job and/or with another version.

You can access a list of the different versions of a Job and perform certain operations. To do that:

- In the **Repository** tree view, select the Job you want to consult the versions of.
- Click the **Job** > **Version** in succession to display the version list of the selected Job.
- Right-click the job version you want to consult.
- Do one of the followings:

Select	To...
Edit Job	open the last version of the job. This option is only available when you select the last version of the Job.

Managing data integration Jobs
Documenting a Job

Select	To...
Read job	consult the Job in read-only mode.
Open Job Hierarchy	consult the hierarchy of the Job.
Edit properties	edit job properties. **Note:** The Job should not be open on the design workspace, otherwise it will be in read-only mode. 💡 This option is only available when you select the last version of the Job.
Run job	execute the Job.

You can also manage the version of several Jobs and/or metadata at the same time, as well as Jobs and their dependencies and/or child Jobs from the Project Settings. For more information, see *Version management on page 33*.

5.6 Documenting a Job

Talend Open Studio enables you to generate documentation that gives general information about your projects, Jobs or joblets. You can automate the generation of such documentation and edit any of the generated documents.

5.6.1 How to generate HTML documentation

Talend Open Studio allows you to generate detailed documentation in HTML of the Job(s) you select in the **Repository** tree view of your Studio. This auto-documentation offers the following:

- The properties of the project where the selected Jobs have been created,
- The properties and settings of the selected Jobs along with preview pictures of each of the Jobs,
- The list of all the components used in each of the selected Jobs and component parameters.

To generate an HTML document for a Job, complete the following:

- In the **Repository** tree view, right-click a **Job** entry or select several **Job Designs** to produce multiple documentations.
- Select **Generate Doc as HTML** on the contextual menu.

Managing data integration Jobs
Handling job execution

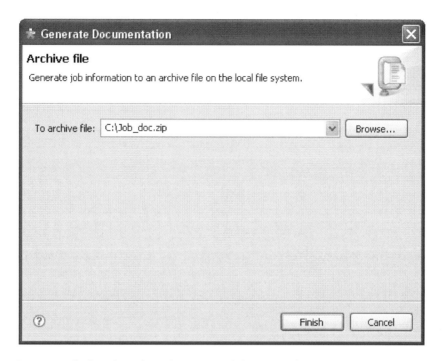

- Browse to the location where the generated documentation archive should be stored.
- In the same field, type in a name for the archive gathering all generated documents.
- Click **Finish** to validate the generation operation.

The archive file is generated in the defined path. It contains all required files along with the Html output file. You can open the HTML file in your favorite browser.

5.6.2 How to update the documentation on the spot

You can choose to manually update your documentation on the spot.

To update a single document, right-click the relevant documentation entry and select **Update documentation**.

5.7 Handling job execution

5.7.1 How to deploy a Job on SpagoBI server

From Talend Open Studio interface, you can deploy your jobs easily on a SpagoBI server in order to execute them from your SpagoBI administrator.

How to create a SpagoBI server entry

Beforehand, you need to set up your single or multiple SpagoBI server details in Talend Open Studio.

- On the menu bar, click **Window** > **Preferences** to open the **[Preferences]** dialog box.

Managing data integration Jobs
Handling job execution

- Expand the **Talend** > **Import/Export** nodes in succession and select **SpagoBI Server** to display the relevant view.

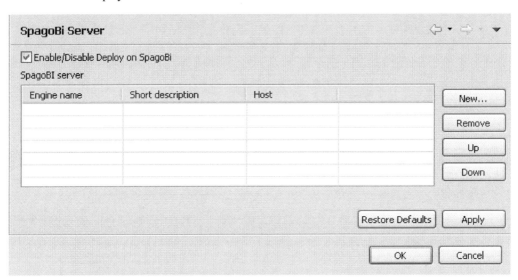

- Select the **Enable/Disable Deploy on SpagoBI** check box to activate the deployment operation.

- Click **New** to open the **[Create new SpagoBi server]** dialog box and add a new server to the list.

- In the **Engine Name** field, enter the internal name used in Talend Open Studio. This name is not used in the generated code.

- In the **Short description** field, enter a free text to describe the server entry you are recording.

- Fill in the host and port information corresponding to your server in the corresponding fields. Host can be the IP address or the DNS Name of your server.

- Type in the **Login** and **Password** as required to log on the SpagoBI server.

- In **Application Context**, type in the context name as you created it in Talend Open Studio

- Click **OK** to validate the details of the new server entry and close the dialog box.

152   Talend Open Studio

Managing data integration Jobs
Handling job execution

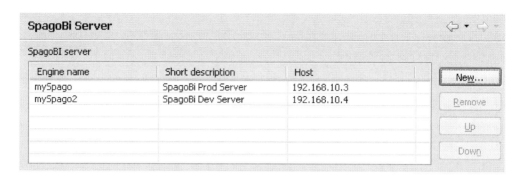

The newly created entry is added to the table of available servers. You can add as many SpagoBI entries as you need.

- Click **Apply** and then **OK** to close the **[Preferences]** dialog box.

How to edit or remove a SpagoBI server entry

Select the relevant entry in the table, click the **Remove** button next to the table to first delete the outdated entry.

Then if required, simply create a new entry including the updated details.

How to deploy your jobs on a SpagoBI server

Follow the steps below to deploy your Job(s) onto a SpagoBI server.

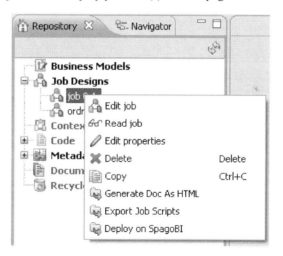

- In the **Repository** tree view, expand **Job Designs** and right-click the Job to deploy.
- In the drop-down list, select **Deploy on SpagoBI**.
- As for any job export, select a **Name** for the job archive that will be created and fill it in the **To archive file** field.
- Select the relevant **SpagoBI server** on the drop-down list.
- The **Label**, **Name** and **Description** fields come from the job main properties.

Talend Open Studio   153

Managing data integration Jobs
Handling job execution

- Select the relevant context in the list.
- Click **OK** once you've completed the setting operation.

The jobs are now deployed onto the relevant SpagoBI server. Open your SpagoBI administrator to execute your jobs.

CHAPTER 6
Mapping data flows

The most common way to handle multiple input and output flows including transformations and data re-routing is to use the **tMap** component.

This chapter gives details about the usage principles of this component, for further information or scenario and use cases, see *tMap* in the Talend Open Studio Components Reference Guide.

Before starting any data integration processes, you need to be familiar with Talend Open Studio Graphical User Interface (GUI). For more information, see *Talend Open Studio GUI on page 275*.

6.1 tMap operation overview

tMap allows the following types of operations:

- data multiplexing and demultiplexing,
- data transformation on any type of fields,
- fields concatenation and interchange,
- field filtering using constraints,
- data rejecting.

As all these operations of transformation and/or routing are carried out by **tMap**, this component cannot be a start or end component in the job design.

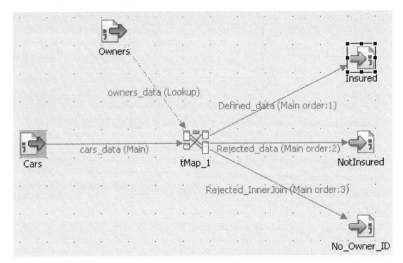

tMap uses incoming connections to pre-fill input schemas with data in the **Map Editor**. Therefore, you cannot create new input schemas directly in the **Map Editor**. Instead, you need to implement as many **Row** connections incoming to **tMap** component as required, in order to create as many input schemas as needed.

The same way, create as many output row connections as required. However, you can fill in the output with content directly in the **Map Editor** through a convenient graphical editor.

Note that there can be only one **Main** incoming rows. All other incoming rows are of **Lookup** type. Related topic: *Row connection on page 82*.

Lookup rows are incoming connections from secondary (or reference) flows of data. These reference data might depend directly or indirectly on the primary flow. This dependency relationship is translated with a graphical mapping and the creation of an expression key.

The **Map Editor** requires the connections to be implemented in your Job in order to be able to define the input and output flows in the **Map Editor**. You also need to create the actual mapping in your Job in order to display the **Map Editor** in the **Preview** area of the **Basic settings** view of the **tMap** component.

Mapping data flows
tMap interface

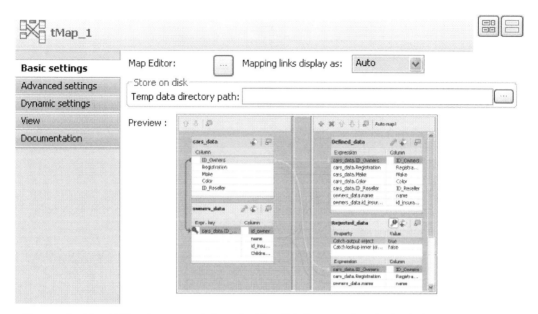

To open the **Map Editor** in a new window, double-click the **tMap** icon in the design workspace or click the three-dot button next to the **Map Editor** in the **Basic settings** view of the **tMap** component.

The following sections give the information necessary to use the **tMap** component in any of your Job designs.

6.2 tMap interface

tMap is an advanced component which requires more detailed explanation than other **Talend** components. The **Map Editor** is an "all-in-one" tool allowing you to define all parameters needed to map, transform and route your data flows via a convenient graphical interface.

You can minimize and restore the **Map Editor** and all tables in the **Map Editor** using the window icons.

Mapping data flows
tMap interface

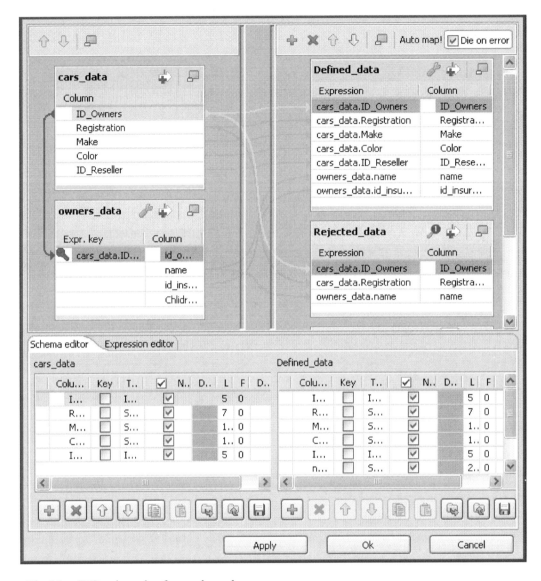

The **Map Editor** is made of several panels:

- The **Input panel** is the top left panel on the editor. It offers a graphical representation of all (main and lookup) incoming data flows. The data are gathered in various columns of input tables. Note that the table name reflects the main or lookup row from the job design on the design workspace.

- The **Variable panel** is the central panel on the **Map Editor**. It allows the centralization of redundant information through the mapping to variable and allows you to carry out transformations.

- The **Output panel** is the top right panel on the editor. It allows mapping data and fields from Input tables and Variables to the appropriate Output rows.

- Both bottom panels are the Input and Output schemas description. The **Schema editor** tab offers a schema view of all columns of input and output tables in selection in their respective panel.

- **Expression editor** is the edition tool for all expression keys of Input/Output data, variable expressions or filtering conditions.

The name of input/output tables in the mapping editor reflects the name of the incoming and outgoing flows (row connections).

6.3 Setting the input flow in the Map Editor

The order of the **Input** tables is essential. The top table reflects the **Main** flow connection, and for this reason, is given priority for reading and processing through the **tMap** component.

For this priority reason, you are not allowed to move up or down the **Main** flow table. This ensures that no Join can be lost.

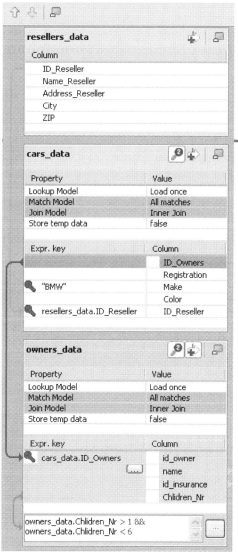

Although you can use the up and down arrows to interchange **Lookup** tables order, be aware that the **Joins** between two lookup tables may then be lost.

Related topic: *How to use Explicit Join on page 160.*

6.3.1 How to fill in Input tables with a schema

To fill in input tables, you need to define first the schemas of all input components connected to the **tMap** component on your design workspace.

Main and Lookup table content

The order of the **Input** tables is essential.

The **Main Row** connection determines the **Main** flow table content. This input flow is reflected in the first table of the **Map Editor's** Input panel.

The **Lookup** connections' content fills in all other (secondary or subordinate) tables which displays below the **Main** flow table. If you have not define the schema of an input component yet, the input table displays as empty in the Input area.

The key is also retrieved from the schema defined in the Input component. This **Key** corresponds to the key defined in the input schema where relevant. It has to be distinguished from the hash key that is internally used in the **Map Editor**, which displays in a different color.

Variables

You can use global or context variables or reuse the variable defined in the **Variables** area. Press **Ctrl+Space bar** to access the list of variables. This list gathers together global, context and mapping variables.

Mapping data flows
Setting the input flow in the Map Editor

The list of variables changes according to the context and grows along new variable creation. Only valid mappable variables in the context show on the list.

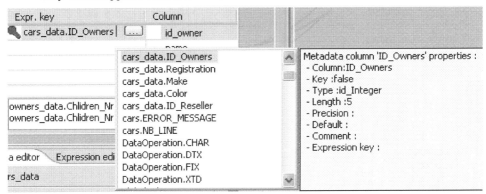

Docked at the **Variable** list, a metadata tip box display to provide information about the selected column.

Related topic: *Mapping variables on page 165*

6.3.2 How to use Explicit Join

In fact, **Joins** let you select data from a table depending upon the data from another table. In the **Map Editor** context, the data of a **Main** table and of a **Lookup** table can be bound together on **expression keys**. In this case, the order of table does fully make sense.

Simply drop column names from one table to a subordinate one, to create a **Join** relationship between the two tables. This way, you can retrieve and process data from multiple inputs.

The join displays graphically as a purple link and creates automatically a key that will be used as a hash key to speed up the match search.

You can create direct joins between the main table and lookup tables. But you can also create indirect joins from the main table to a lookup table, via another lookup table. This requires a direct join between one of the **Lookup** table to the **Main** one.

 You cannot create a **Join** from a subordinate table towards a superior table in the **Input** area.

The **Expression key** field which is filled in with the dragged and dropped data is editable in the input schema, whereas the column name can only be changed from the **Schema editor** panel.

You can either insert the dragged data into a new entry or replace the existing entries or else concatenate all selected data into one cell.

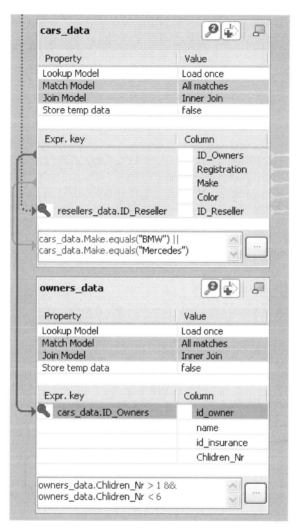

For further information about possible types of drag & drops, see *Mapping the Output setting on page 171*.

 If you have a big number of input tables, you can use the minimize/maximize icon to reduce or restore the table size in the **Input** area. The Join binding two tables remains visible even though the table is minimized.

Creating a join automatically assigns a hash key onto the joined field name. The key symbol displays in violet on the input table itself and is removed when the join between the two tables is removed.

Related topics:

- *Describing the schema editor on page 175*
- *How to use Inner join on page 162*

Along with the explicit Join you can select whether you want to filter down to a unique match or if you allow several matches to be taken into account. In this last case, you can choose to only consider the first or the last match or all of them.

Unique Match

This is the default selection when you implement an explicit Join. This means that only the last match from the Lookup flow will be taken into account and passed on to the output.

The other matches will be then ignored.

First Match

This selection implies that several matches can be expected in the lookup. The First Match selection means that in the lookup only the first encountered match will be taken into account and passed onto the main output flow.

The other matches will then be ignored.

All Matches

This selection implies that several matches can be expected in the lookup flow. In this case, all matches are taken into account and passed on to the main output flow.

6.3.3 How to use Inner join

The **Inner join** is a particular type of Join that distinguishes itself by the way the rejection is performed.

This option avoids that null values are passed on to the main output flow. It allows also to pass on the rejected data to a specific table called **Inner Join Reject** table.

If the data searched cannot be retrieved through the explicit join or the filter (inner) join, in other words, the Inner Join cannot be established for any reason, then the requested data will be rejected to the Output table defined as **Inner Join Reject** table if any.

Simply drop column names from one table to a subordinate one, to create a **Join** relationship between the two tables. The join displays graphically as a purple link and creates automatically a key that will be used as a hash key to speed up the match search.

Click the **tMap settings** button located at the top a lookup table, and select the **Inner Join** option in the **Join Model** list to define this table as **Inner Join** table.

Mapping data flows
Setting the input flow in the Map Editor

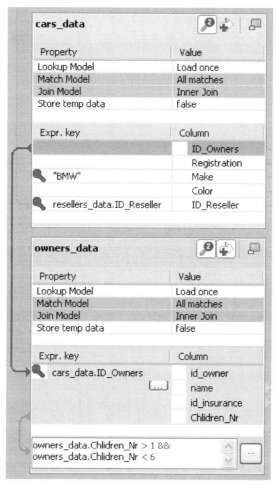

On the **Output** area, click the **tMap settings** button and select **true** in the **Catch lookup inner join reject** list to define the Inner Join Reject output.

 An **Inner Join** table should always be coupled to an **Inner Join Reject** table.

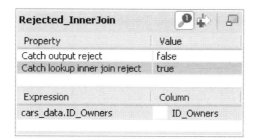

You can also use the filter button to decrease the number of rows to be searched and improve the performance (in java).

Related topics:

- *Inner Join Rejection on page 173*

Mapping data flows
Setting the input flow in the Map Editor

- *How to filter an input flow on page 164*

6.3.4 How to use the All Rows option

By default, in each input table of the input area of the tMap editor, the **All rows** match model option is selected. This **All rows** option means that all the rows are loaded from the **Lookup** flow and searched against the **Main** flow.

The output corresponds to the Cartesian product of both table (or more tables if need be).

 If you create an explicit or an inner join between two tables, the All rows option is no longer available. You then have to choose between Unique match, First match and All matches match model. For more information, see *How to use Explicit Join on page 160* and *How to use Inner join on page 162*.

6.3.5 How to filter an input flow

Click the **Filter** button next to the **tMap settings** button to add a **Filter** area.

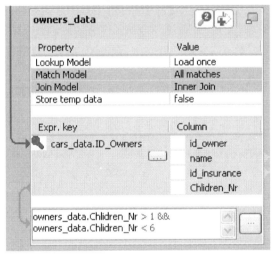

In the Filter area, type in the condition to be applied. This allows to reduce the number of rows parsed against the main flow, enhancing the performance on long and heterogeneous flows.

You can use the Autocompletion tool via the **Ctrl+Space bar** keystrokes in order to reuse schema columns in the condition statement.

 This feature is only available in Java therefore the filter condition needs to be written in Java.

6.3.6 How to remove input entries from table

To remove input entries, click the red cross sign on the Schema Editor of the selected table. Press Ctrl or Shift and click fields for multiple selection to be removed.

 If you remove Input entries from the **Map Editor** schema, this removal also occurs in your component schema definition.

6.4 Mapping variables

The **Var** table (variable table) regroups all mapping variables which are used numerous times in various places.

You can also use the **Expression** field of the **Var** table to carry out any transformation you want to, using Java Code or Perl code.

Variables help you save processing time and avoid you to retype many times the same data.

There are various possibilities to create variables:

- Type in freely your variables in Perl or Java. Enter the strings between quotes or concatenate functions using the relevant operator.
- Add new lines using the plus sign and remove lines using the red cross sign. And press **Ctrl+Space** to retrieve existing global and context variables.
- Drop one or more **Input** entries to the **Var** table.

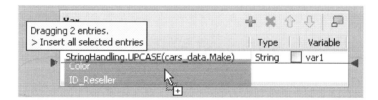

Select an entry on the Input area or press Shift key to select multiple entries of one Input table.

Press **Ctrl** to select either non-appended entries in the same input table or entries from various tables. When selecting entries in the second table, notice that the first selection displays in grey. Hold the **Ctrl** key down to drag all entries together. A tooltip shows you how many entries are in selection.

Then various types of drag-and-drops are possible depending on the action you want to carry out.

To...	you need to...
Insert all selected entries as separated variables.	Simply drag & drop to the Var table. Arrows show you where the new Var entry can be inserted. Each Input is inserted in a separate cell.
Concatenate all selected input entries together with an existing Var entry.	Drag & drop onto the Var entry which gets highlighted. All entries gets concatenated into one cell. Add the required operators using Perl/Java operations signs. The dot concatenates string variables.
Overwrite a Var entry with selected concatenated Input entries.	Drag & drop onto the relevant Var entry which gets highlighted then press **Ctrl** and release. All selected entries are concatenated and overwrite the highlighted Var.

Mapping data flows
Using the expression editor

To...	you need to...
Concatenate selected input entries with highlighted Var entries and create new Var lines if needed	Drag & drop onto an existing Var then press **Shift** when browsing over the chosen Var entries. First entries get concatenated with the highlighted Var entries. And if necessary new lines get created to hold remaining entries.

6.4.1 How to access global or context variables

Press **Ctrl+Space** to access the global and context variable list.

Appended to the variable list, a metadata list provides information about the selected column.

6.4.2 How to remove variables

To remove a selected **Var** entry, click the red cross sign. This removes the whole line as well as the link.

Press **Ctrl** or **Shift** and click fields for multiple selection then click the red cross sign.

6.5 Using the expression editor

All expressions (**Input**, **Var** or **Output**) and constraint statements can be viewed and edited from the expression editor. This editor provides visual comfort to write any function or transformation in a handy dedicated view.

6.5.1 How to access the expression editor

You can write the expressions necessary for the data transformation directly in the **Expression editor** view located in the lower half of the expression editor, or you can open the **[Expression Builder]** dialog box where you can write the data transformation expressions.

To open the **Expression editor** view, complete the following:

- Double-click the **tMap** component in your job design to open the **Map Editor**.
- In the lower half of the editor, click the **Expression editor** tab to open the corresponding view.

 To edit an expression, select it in the **Input** panel and then click the **Expression editor** tab and modify the expression as required.

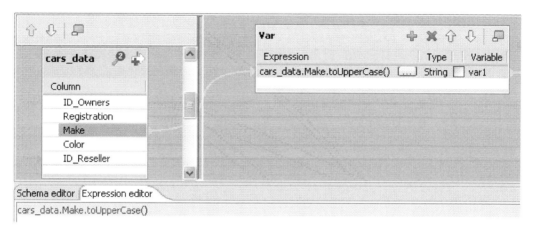

- Enter the Perl code or Java code according to your needs. The corresponding expression in the output panel is synchronized.

 Refer to the relevant Perl or Java documentation for more information regarding functions and operations.

To open the **[Expression Builder]** dialog box, complete the following:

- In the **Var** or **Output** panel of the **Map Editor**, click the three-dot button next to the expression you want to open.

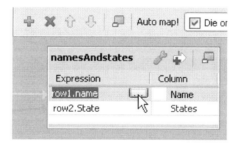

The **[Expression Builder]** dialog box opens on the selected expression.

Mapping data flows
Using the expression editor

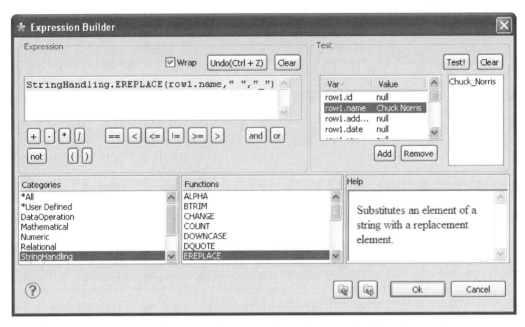

For a use case showing the usage of the expression editor, see the following section.

6.5.2 How to write code using the Expression Builder

Some jobs require pieces of code to be written in order to provide components with parameters. In the **Component** view of some components, an **Expression Builder** interface can help you build these pieces of code (in Java or Perl generation language).

The following example shows the use of the **Expression Builder** in a **tMap** component.

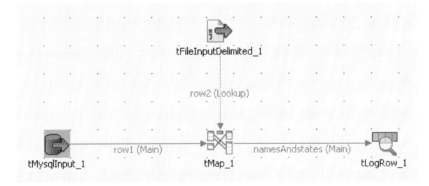

Two input flows are connected to the **tMap** component.

- From the DB input, comes a list of names made of a first name and a last name separated by a space char.

- From the File input, comes a list of US states, in lower case.

In the **tMap**, use the expression builder to: First, replace the blank char separating the first and last names with an underscore char, and second, change the states from lower case to upper case.

168   Talend Open Studio

- In the **tMap**, set the relevant inner join to set the reference mapping. For more information regarding **tMap**, see *tMap operation overview on page 156* and *tMap interface on page 157*.

- From the main (*row1*) input, drop the *Names* column to the output area, and the *State* column from the lookup (*row2*) input towards the same output area.

- Then click the first **Expression** field (*row1.Name*) to display the three-dot button.

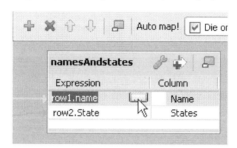

The **[Expression Builder]** dialog box opens up.

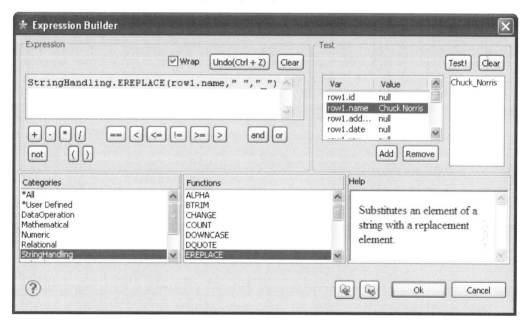

- In the **Category** area, select the relevant action you want to perform. In this example, select `StringHandling` and select the `EREPLACE` function.

- In the **Expression** area, paste *row1.Name* in place of the text expression, in order to get: `StringHandling.EREPLACE(row1.Name," ","_")`. This expression will replace the separating space char with an underscore char in the char string given.

- Now check that the output is correct, by typing in the relevant **Value** field of the **Test** area, a dummy value, e.g: *Chuck Norris*.

- Then click **Test!** and check that the correct change is carried out, e.g: *Chuck_Norris*

- Click **OK** to validate.

- Carry out the same operation for the second column (*State*).

Mapping data flows
Using the expression editor

- In the **tMap** output, select the *row2.State* Expression and click the three-dot button to open the **Expression builder** again.

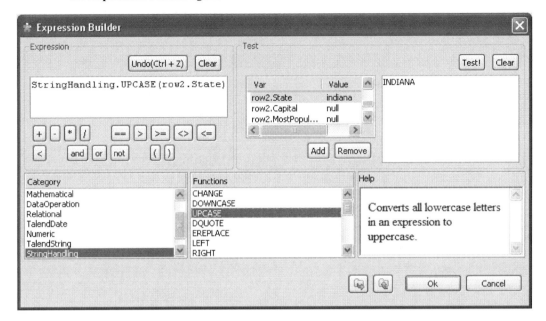

- This time, the `StringHandling` function to be used is `UPCASE`. The complete expression says: `StringHandling.UPCASE(row2.State)`.

- Once again, check that the expression syntax is correct using a dummy **Value** in the **Test** area, e.g.: *indiana*.

- The **Test!** result should display *INDIANA* for this example.

- Click **OK** to validate.

Both expressions now display on the **tMap Expression** field.

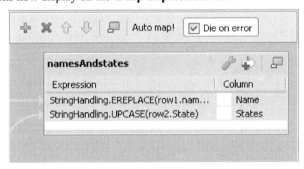

These changes will be carried out along the flow processing. The output of this example is as shown below.

```
Starting job NamesAndStates at 10:02 10/10/2007.
.--------------------------+-------------------.
|              tLogRow_1                       |
|==========================+===================|
|Name                      |States             |
|==========================+===================|
|William_Grant             |IOWA               |
|William_Hoover            |NEW YORK           |
|Grover_Lincoln            |NORTH DAKOTA       |
|Lyndon_Jefferson          |OHIO               |
|Gerald_Hayes              |WASHINGTON         |
|Benjamin_Grant            |MAINE              |
|George_Pierce             |CONNECTICUT        |
|Jimmy_Reagan              |ALASKA             |
|Martin_Hayes              |WASHINGTON         |
|Franklin_Jefferson        |IOWA               |
|Andrew_Nixon              |NEW HAMPSHIRE      |
```

6.6 Mapping the Output setting

On the design workspace, the creation of a Row connection from the **tMap** component to the output components adds Output schema tables in the **Map Editor**.

You can also add an Output schema in your **Map Editor**, using the plus sign from the tool bar of the Output area.

You have as well the possibility to create a join between your output tables. The join on the tables enables you to process several flows separately and unite them in a single output. For more information about the output join tables feature, see *Scenario 7: Mapping with join output tables on page 1488* in the **Talend Open Studio Reference Guide**.

 The join table retrieves the schema of the source table.

When you click the **[+]** button to add an output schema or to make a join between your output tables, a dialog box opens. You have then two options.

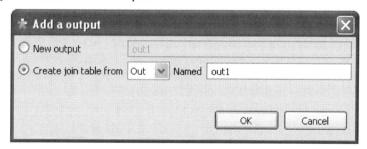

Select...	To...
New output	Add an independent table.
Create join table from	Create a join between output tables. In order to do so, select in the drop down list the table from which you want to create the join. In the **Named** field, type in the name of the table to be created.

Unlike the **Input** area, the order of output schema tables does not make such a difference, as there is no subordination relationship between outputs (of Join type).

Once all connections, hence output schema tables, are created, you can select and organize the output data via drag & drops.

You can drop one or several entries from the **Input** area straight to the relevant output table.

Press **Ctrl** or **Shift**, and click entries to carry out multiple selection.

Or you can drag expressions from the **Var** area and drop them to fill in the output schemas with the appropriate reusable data.

Note that if you make any change to the Input column in the Schema Editor, a dialog prompts you to decide to propagate the changes throughout all Input/Variable/Output table entries, where concerned.

Action	Result
Drag & Drop onto existing expressions.	Concatenates the selected expression with the existing expressions.
Drag & Drop to insertion line.	Inserts one or several new entries at start or end of table or between two existing lines.
Drag & Drop + Ctrl.	Replaces highlighted expression with selected expression.
Drag & Drop + Shift.	Adds to all highlighted expressions the selected fields. Inserts new lines if needed.
Drag & Drop + Ctrl + Shift.	Replaces all highlighted expressions with selected fields. Inserts new lines if needed.

You can add filters and rejections to customize your outputs.

6.6.1 Building complex expressions

If you have complex expressions to build, or advanced changes to be carried out on the output flow, then the Expression Builder interface can help in this task.

Click the **Expression** field of your input or output table to display the three-dot button. Then click this three-dot button to open the **Expression Builder**.

For more information regarding the Expression Builder, see *How to write code using the Expression Builder on page 168*.

6.6.2 Filters

Filters allow you to make a selection among the input fields, and send only the selected fields to various outputs.

Click the plus button at the top of the table to add a filter line.

You can enter freely your filter statements using Perl/Java operators and functions.

Drop expressions from the **Input** area or from the **Var** area to the Filter row entry of the relevant Output table.

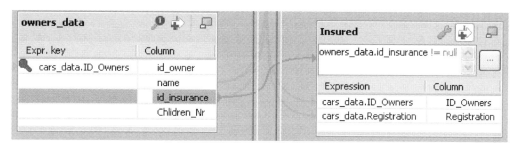

An orange link is then created. Add the required Perl/Java operator to finalize your filter formula.

You can create various filters on different lines. The AND operator is the logical conjunction of all stated filters.

6.6.3 Rejections

Reject options define the nature of an output table.

It groups data which do not satisfy one or more filters defined in the standard output tables. Note that as standard output tables, are meant all non-reject tables.

This way, data rejected from other output tables, are gathered in one or more dedicated tables, allowing you to spot any error or unpredicted case.

The Reject principle concatenates all non Reject tables filters and defines them as an ELSE statement.

Create a dedicated table, click the **tMap settings** button and select **true** in the **Catch output reject** list to define it as Else part of the regular tables.

You can define several Reject tables, to offer multiple refined outputs. To differentiate various Reject outputs, add filter lines, by clicking on the plus arrow button.

Once a table is defined as Reject, the verification process will be first enforced on regular tables before taking in consideration possible constraints of the Reject tables.

Note that data are not exclusively processed to one output. Although a data satisfied one constraint, hence is routed to the corresponding output, this data still gets checked against the other constraints and can be routed to other outputs.

6.6.4 Inner Join Rejection

The Inner Join is a Lookup Join. The Inner Join Reject table is a particular type of Rejection output. It gathers rejected data from the main row table after an Inner Join could not be established.

To define an Output flow as container for rejected Inner Join data, create a new output component on your Job that you connect to the **Map Editor**. Then in the **Map Editor**, click the **tMap settings** button and select **true** in the **Catch lookup inner join reject** list to define this particular Output table as Inner Join Reject table.

Mapping data flows
Mapping the Output setting

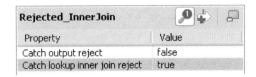

6.6.5 Removing Output entries

To remove Output entries, click the cross sign on the Schema Editor of the selected table.

6.6.6 Handling errors

The **Die on error** option prevent error to be processed. To do so, it stops the Job execution as soon as an error is encountered. The **tMap** component provides this option to prevent processing erroneous data. The **Die on error** option is activated by default in **tMap**.

Deactivating the **Die on error** option will allow you to skip the rows on error and complete the process for error-free rows on one hand, and to retrieve the rows on error and manage them if needed.

To deactivate the **Die on error** option, double-click the **tMap** component on the design workspace to open its **Editor**, and clear the **Die on error** checkbox in the top right hand corner of the editor.

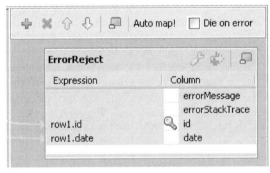

A new table called **ErrorReject** displays on the **tMap** editor output area. This output table automatically comprises two columns : **errorMessage** and **errorStackTrace**, retrieving the message and stack trace of the error encountered during the Job execution. Errors could be unparseable dates, null pointer exceptions, conversion issues, etc.

You can also drag and drop columns (here *id* and *date*) from the input tables to this error reject output table. Those erroneous data can be retrieved with its corresponding error message and be corrected afterward.

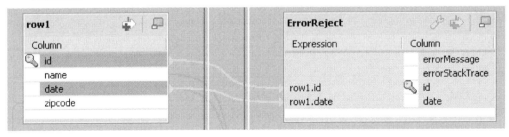

Once the error reject table set, its corresponding flow can be sent to an output component.

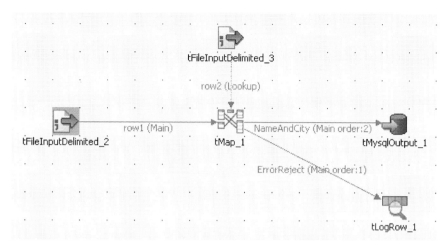

To do so, on the design workspace, right-click the **tMap** component, select **Row** > **ErrorReject** in the menu, and click the corresponding output component, here **tLogRow**.

When you execute the Job, errors are retrieved by the **ErrorReject** flow.

```
Starting job Die_on_error at 17:30 01/09/2010.

java.text.ParseException: Unparseable date: "08 01
1980"|java.lang.RuntimeException:
java.text.ParseException: Unparseable date: "08 01 1980"
    at routines.TalendDate.parseDate(TalendDate.java:503)
    at
doc.die_on_error_0_1.Die_on_error.tFileInputDelimited_2Pro
cess(Die_on_error.java:1409)
    at
doc.die_on_error_0_1.Die_on_error.runJobInTOS(Die_on_error.
java:2262)
    at
doc.die_on_error_0_1.Die_on_error.main(Die_on_error.java:2
160)
Caused by: java.text.ParseException: Unparseable date: "08
01 1980"
    at java.text.DateFormat.parse(Unknown Source)
    at routines.TalendDate.parseDate(TalendDate.java:501)
    ... 3 more
|1|08 01 1980
Job Die_on_error ended at 17:30 01/09/2010. [exit code=0]
```

The result contains the error message, its stack trace, and the two columns, *id* and *date*, dragged and dropped to the **ErrorReject** table, separated by a pipe "|".

6.7 Describing the schema editor

The Schema Editor details all fields of the selected table.

Mapping data flows
Solving memory limitation issues in tMap use

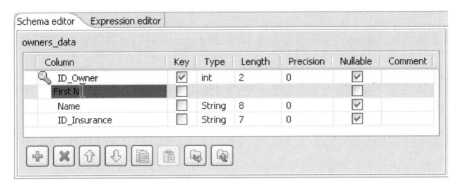

Use the tool bar below the schema table, to add, move or remove columns from the schema.

You can also load a schema from the repository or export it into a file.

Metadata	Description
Column	Column name as defined on the **Map Editor** schemas and on the Input or Output component schemas.
Key	The Key shows if the expression key data should be used to retrieve data through the Join link. If unchecked, the Join relation is disabled.
Type	Type of data. String or Integer. This column should always be defined in a Java version
Length	-1 shows that no length value has been defined in the schema.
Precision	precise the length value if any is defined.
Nullable	Clear this check box if the field value should not be null.
Default	Shows any default value that may be defined for this field.
Comment	Free text field. Enter any useful comment.

 Input metadata and output metadata are independent from each other. You can, for instance, change the label of a column on the output side without the column label of the input schema being changed.

However, any change made to the metadata are immediately reflected in the corresponding schema on the **tMap** relevant (Input or Output) area, but also on the schema defined for the component itself on the design workspace.

A Red colored background shows that an invalid character has been entered. Most special characters are prohibited in order for the Job to be able to interpret and use the text entered in the code. Authorized characters include lower-case, upper-case, figures except as start character.

Browse the mouse over the red field, a tooltip displays the error message.

6.8 Solving memory limitation issues in tMap use

When handling large data sources, including for example, numerous columns, large number of lines or of column types, your system might encounter memory shortage issues that prevent your Job, to complete properly, in particular when using a **tMap** component for your transformation.

Mapping data flows
Solving memory limitation issues in tMap use

A feature has been added (in Java only for the time being) to the **tMap** component, in order to reduce the memory in use for lookup loading. In fact, rather than storing the temporary data in the system memory and thus possibly reaching the memory limitation, the **Store temp data** option allows you to choose to store the temporary data onto a temp directory of your disk instead.

This feature comes as an option to be selected on the Lookup table of the input data in the **tMap** editor.

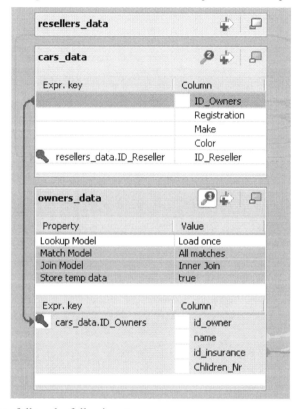

To enable this option, follow the following steps:

- Double-click the **tMap** component in your Job to launch the **tMap** editor
- On the left panel, corresponding to the **Input** and **Lookup** sources, click the **Lookup** table describing the temporary data you want to be loaded onto the disk rather than on the memory.
- Press the **tMap settings** button to display all Lookup table options.
- Select true in the **Store temp data** list to enable the option.
- Click **OK** to validate the change in the **tMap** and come back to the design workspace.

For this option to be fully activated, you also need to set the directory on the disk, where the data will be stored.

Mapping data flows
Handling lookups

- Click the **Component** tab to show the **tMap** component **Basic settings** view.
- On the **Store on disk** area, fill out the **Temp data directory path** field with the full path to the directory where the temporary data should be stored.
- You can use a context variable through the **Ctrl+Space** bar if you set the variable in a Context group in the repository. For more information about contexts, see *How to centralize contexts and variables on page 89*.

At the end of the subjob, the temporary files are cleared.

This way, you limit the use of allocated memory per reference data to be written onto temporary files stored on the disk.

 As writing the main flow onto the disk requires the data to be sorted, note that the order of the output rows cannot be guaranteed.

On the **Advanced settings** view, you can also set a buffer size if need be. Simply fill out the field **Max. buffer size (in Nr of lines)** in order for the data stored on the disk to be splitted into as many files as needed.

6.9 Handling lookups

In order to adapt to the multiple processing types as well as to address performance issues, different types of lookup loading are available in the **tMap** component.

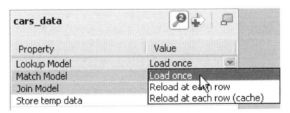

In the lookup table of the input area of the **tMap Editor**, click the **tMap settings** button to explore the list of the loading types available in the **Lookup model** list:

- **Load once**: Default setting. Select this option to load the entire lookup flow before processing the main flow. This is the preferred option if you have a great number of data from your main flow that needs to be requested in your lookup, or if your reference (or lookup) data comes from a file that can be easily loaded.

- **Reload at each row**: At each row, the lookup gets loaded again. This is mainly interesting in Jobs where the lookup volume is large, while the main flow is pretty small. Note that this option allows you to use dynamic variable settings such as where clause, to change/update the lookup flow on the fly as it gets loaded, before the main flow join is processed. This option could be considered as the counter-part of the **Store temp data** option that is available for file lookups.

- **Reload at each row (cache)**: Expressions (in the Lookup table) are assessed and looked up in the cache first. The results of joins that have already been solved, are stored in the cache, in order to avoid loading the same results twice. This option optimizes the processing time and helps improve processing performance of the **tMap** component.

Note that for the time being, you cannot use **Reload at each row (cache)** and **Store temp data** at the same time.

For use cases using these options, see the **tMap** section of the Talend Open Studio Components Reference Guide.

When your lookup is a database table, the best practise is to open the connection to the database in the beginning of your job design in order to optimize performance. For a use case using this option, see *Scenario 6: Advanced mapping with lookup reload at each row (java)* in Talend Open Studio Components Reference Guide.

Mapping data flows
Handling lookups

CHAPTER 7
Managing Metadata

Metadata in Talend Open Studio is definitional data that provides information about or documentation of other data managed within Talend Open Studio.

This chapter provides procedures to create and manage various metadata items that can be used in all your job designs.

Before starting any metadata management processes, you need to be familiar with Talend Open Studio Graphical User Interface (GUI). For more information, see *Talend Open Studio GUI on page 275*.

7.1 Objectives

The **Metadata** folder in the **Repository** tree view stores reusable information on files, databases, and/or systems that you need to build your jobs.

Various corresponding wizards help you store these pieces of information and use them later to set the connection parameters of the relevant input or output components, but you can also store the data description called "schemas" in Talend Open Studio.

Wizards' procedures slightly differ depending on the type of connection chosen.

Click **Metadata** in the **Repository** tree view to expand the folder tree. Each of the connection nodes will gather the various connections you set up.

From Talend Open Studio, you can set up the following, amongst others:

- a DB connection.
- a JDBC schema.
- a file schema.
- an LDAP schema.
- a generic schema.
- a WSDL schema.
- a salesforce schema.

The following sections explain in detail how to set up different connections and schemas.

7.2 Setting up a DB connection

If you often need to connect to database tables of any kind, then you may want to centralize the connection information details in the **Metadata** folder in the **Repository** tree view.

> You can also set up a DB connection the same way by clicking the icon in the **Basic settings** view of all input and output DB components.

7.2.1 Step 1: General properties

The creation procedure is made of two separate but closely related operations. First expand **Metadata** in the **Repository** tree view and right-click **Db Connections** and select **Create connection** on the pop-up menu.

The connection wizard opens up. Fill in the generic Schema properties such as Schema **Name** and **Description**. The **Status** field is a customized field you can define in **Window > Preferences**.

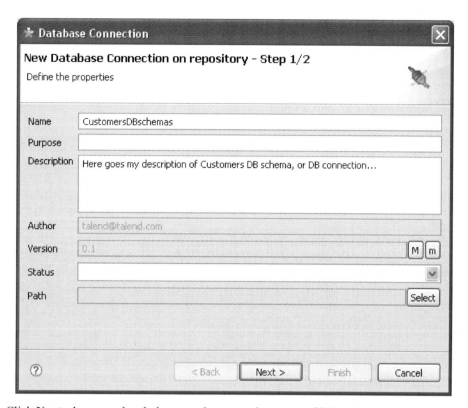

Click **Next** when completed, the second step requires you to fill in DB connection data.

7.2.2 Step 2: Connection

Select the type of the database to which you want to connect and some fields will be available/unavailable according to the DB connection detail requirements.

Managing Metadata
Setting up a DB connection

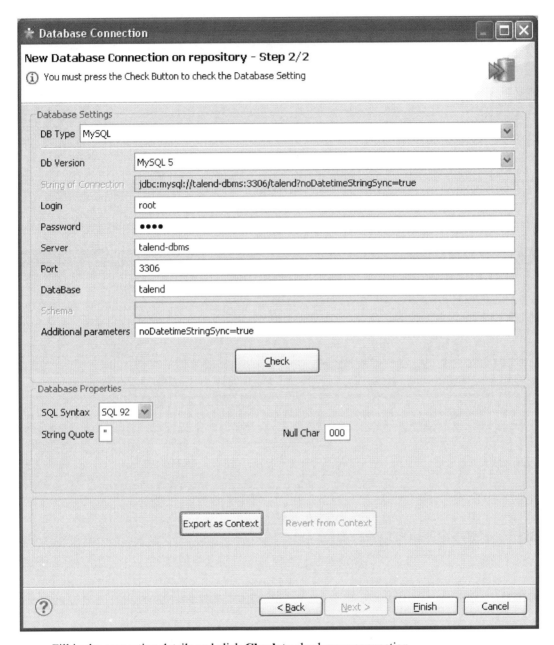

Fill in the connection details and click **Check** to check your connection.

 In order to be able to retrieve all table schemas in the database:
-enter *dbo* in the **Schema** field if you are connecting to MSSQL 2000,
-remove *dbo* from the **Schema** field if you are connecting to MSSQL 2005/2008.

Fill in, if need be, the database properties information. That is all for the first operation on DB connection setup, click **Finish** to validate.

The newly created DB connection is now available in the **Repository** tree view and displays four folders including **Queries** (for SQL queries you save) and **Table schemas** that will gather all schemas linked to this DB connection.

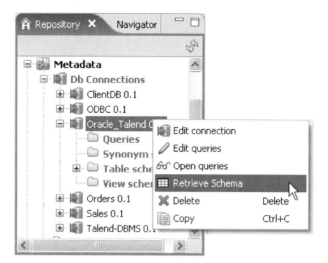

Right-click the newly created connection, and select **Retrieve schema** on the drop-down list in order to load the desired table schema from the established connection.

 An error message will display if there are no tables to retrieve from the selected database or if you do not have the correct rights to access this database.

7.2.3 Step 3: Table upload

When you click **Retrieve Schema**, a new wizard opens up where you can filter and display different objects (tables, views and synonyms) in your database connection.

Managing Metadata
Setting up a DB connection

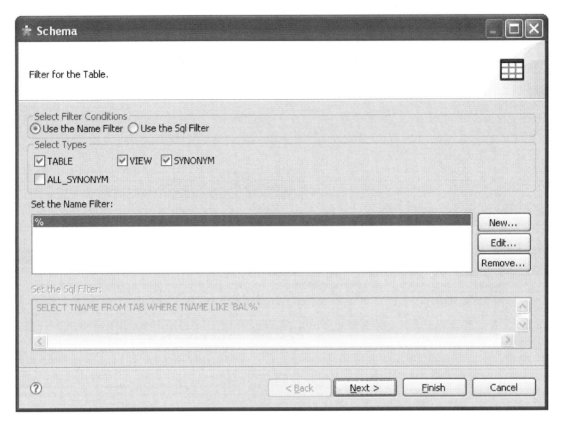

In the **Select Filter Conditions** area, you can filter the database objects using either of the two options: **Set the Name Filter** or **Use the Sql Filter** through filtering on objects names or using SQL queries respectively.

To filter database objects using their names, do the following:

- In the **Select Filter Conditions** area, select the **Use the Name Filter** option.
- In the **Select Types** area, select the check box(es) of the database object(s) you want to filter or display.

 Available options can vary according to the selected database.

- In the **Set the Name Filter** area, click **Edit...** to open the **[Edit Filter Name]** dialog box.
- Enter the filter you want to use in the dialog box. For example, if you want to recuperate the database objects which names start with "A", enter the filter "A%", or if you want to recuperate all database objects which names end with "type", enter "%type" as your filter.
- Click **OK** to close the dialog box.
- Click **Next** to open a new view on the wizard that lists the filtered database objects.

To filter database objects using an SQL query, do the following:

- In the **Select Filter Conditions** area, select the **Use Sql Filter** option.
- In the **Set the Sql Filter** field, enter the SQL query you want to use to filter database objects.

- Click **Next** to open a new view that lists the filtered database objects.

Once you have the filtered list of the database objects (tables, views and synonyms), do the following to load the schemas of the desired objects onto your repository file system:

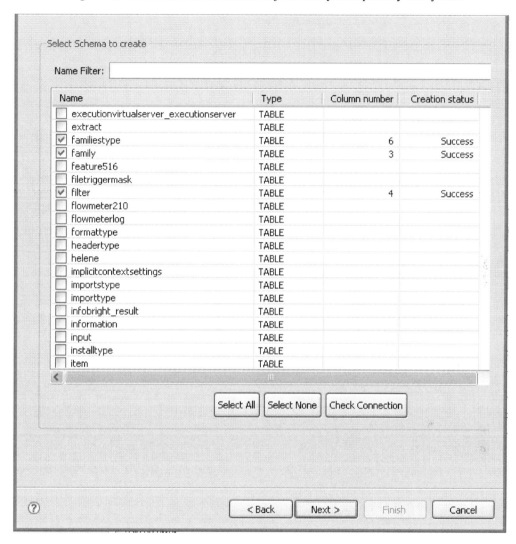

- Select one or more database objects on the list and click **Next** to open a new view on the wizard where you can see the schemas of the selected object.

 If no schema is visible on the list, click the Check connection button below the list to verify the database connection status.

Managing Metadata
Setting up a DB connection

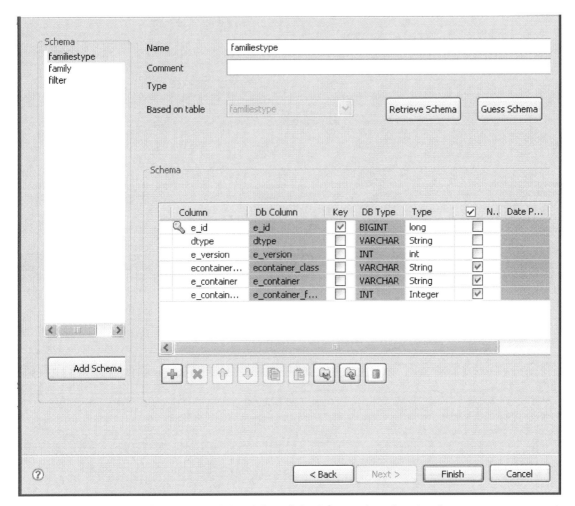

- Modify the schemas if needed and then click **Finish** to close the wizard.

The schemas based on the selected tables are listed under the **Table schemas** folder corresponding to the database connection you created.

 In Java, make sure the data type in the Type column is correctly defined. For more information regarding data types, including date pattern, check out http://java.sun.com/j2se/1.5.0/docs/api/index.html.

7.2.4 Step 4: Schema definition

By default, the schema displayed on the Schema panel is based on the first table selected in the list of schemas loaded (left panel). You can change the name of the schema and according to your needs, you can also customize the schema structure in the schema panel.

Indeed, the tool bar allows you to add, remove or move columns in your schema. In addition, you can load an xml schema from a file or export the current schema as xml.

To retrieve a schema based on one of the loaded table schemas, select the DB table schema name in the drop-down list and click **Retrieve schema**. Note that the retrieved schema then overwrites any current schema and does not retain any custom edits.

Managing Metadata
Setting up an FTP connection

Click **Finish** to complete the DB schema creation. All created schemas display under the relevant **DB connections** node.

7.3 Setting up an FTP connection

If you need to connect to an FTP server regularly, you can centralize the connection information under the **Metadata** node in the **Repository** view.

7.3.1 Step 1: General properties

To create a connection to an FTP server, follow the below steps:

- Expand the **Metadata** node in the **Repository** tree view.

- Right-click **FTP** and select **Create FTP** from the context menu. The connection wizard opens:

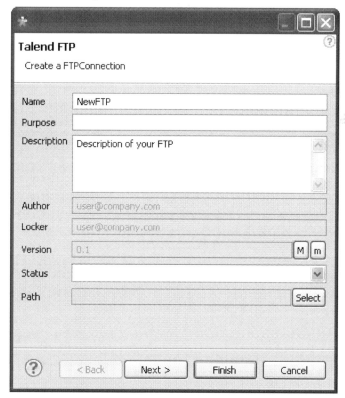

- Enter the generic schema information such as its **Name** and **Description**.

Talend Open Studio 189

Managing Metadata
Setting up an FTP connection

 The status field is a customized field which can be defined in the Preferences dialog box (**Window** > **Preferences**). For further information about setting preferences, see *Setting Talend Open Studio preferences on page 21*.

- When you have finished, click **Next** to enter the FTP server connection information.

7.3.2 Step 2: Connection

In this step we shall define the connection information and parameters.

- Enter your **Username** and **Password** in the corresponding fields.

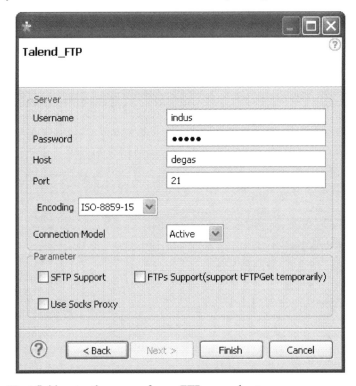

- In the **Host** field, enter the name of your FTP server host.
- Enter the **Port** number in the corresponding field.
- Select the **Encoding** type from the list.
- From the **Connection Model** list, select the connection model you want to use.
  Select **Passive** if you want the FTP server to choose the port connection to be used for data transfer.
  Select **Active** if you want to choose the port yourself.

In the **Parameter** area, select a setting for FTP server usage. For standard usage, there is no need to select an option.

- Select the **SFTP Support** check box to use the SSH security protocol to protect server communications.
  An **Authentication method** appears. Select **Public key** or **Password** according to what you use.

190 Talend Open Studio

- Select the **FTPs Support** chbeck box to protect server communication with the SSL security protocol.

- Select the **Use Socks Proxy** check box if you want to use this option, then enter the proxy information (the host name, port number, username and password).

- Click **Finish** to close the wizard.

All of the connections created appear under the FTP server connection node, in the **Repository** view.

You can drop the connection metadata from the **Repository** onto the design workspace. A dialog box opens in which you can choose the component to be used in your Job.

For further information about how to drop metadata onto the workspace, see *How to drop components from the Metadata node on page 62*.

7.4 Setting up a JDBC schema

For DB table based schemas, the creation procedure is made of two separate but closely related operations. First Right-click **Db Connections** and select **Create connection** on the pop-up menu.

7.4.1 Step 1: General properties

Fill in the schema generic information, such as Schema **Name** and **Description**.

For further information, see *Step 1: General properties on page 182*.

7.4.2 Step 2: Connection

Select the type of Database you want to connect to and fill in the DB connection details.

Managing Metadata
Setting up a JDBC schema

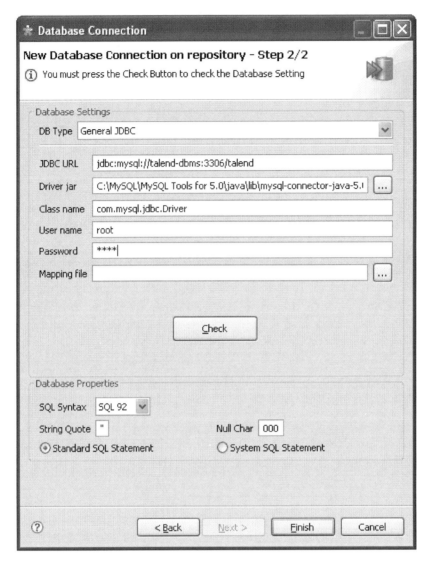

Fill in the connection details below:

- Fill in the **JDBC URL** used to access the DB server.

- In the **Driver jar** field, select the jar driver validating your connection to the database.

- In the **Class name** field, fill in the main class of the driver allowing to communicate with the database.

- Fill in your **User name** and **Password**.

- In the **Mapping File** field, select the mapping allowing the DB Type to match the Java or Perl Type of data on the schema. For example: the DB Type VARCHAR correspond to the String Type for Java and Perl.

 The Mapping files are XML files that you can access via **Window > Preferences > Talend > Metadata of TalendType**.

Click **Check** to check out your connection.

Fill in, if need be, the database properties information. That is all for the first operation on DB connection setup, click **Finish** to validate.

The newly created DB connection is now available in the **Repository** tree view and it displays four folders including **Queries** (for the SQL queries you save) and **Table schemas** that will gather all schemas linked to this DB connection.

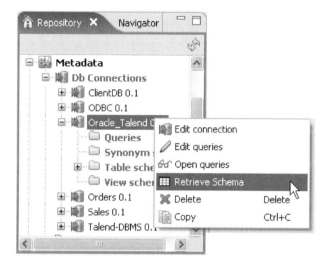

Right-click the newly created connection, and select **Retrieve schema** on the drop-down list.

7.4.3 Step 3: Table upload

A new wizard opens up on the first step window. The List offers all tables present on the DB connection. It can be any type of databases.

Select one or more tables on the list, to load them onto your repository file system. You will base your repository schemas on these tables.

If no schema is visible on the list, click **Check connection**, to verify the DB connection status.

Click **Next**. On the next window, four setting panels help you define the schemas to create.

In Java, make sure the data type is correctly defined. For more information regarding data types, including date pattern, check out http://java.sun.com/j2se/1.5.0/docs/api/index.html.

7.4.4 Step 4: Schema definition

By default, the schema displayed on the Schema panel is based on the first table selected in the list of schemas loaded (left panel). You can change the name of the schema and according to your needs, you can also customize the schema structure in the schema panel.

Indeed, the tool bar allows you to add, remove or move columns in your schema. In addition, you can load an xml schema from a file or export the current schema as xml.

To retrieve a schema based on one of the loaded table schemas, select the DB table schema name in the drop-down list and click **Retrieve schema**. Note that the retrieved schema then overwrites any current schema and doesn't retain any custom edits.

Click **Finish** to complete the DB schema creation. All created schemas display under the relevant **DB connections** node.

7.5 Setting up a SAS connection

Talend Open Studio enables you to configure a connection to a remote SAS system.

7.5.1 Prerequisites

Before carrying on the below procedure to configure your SAS connection, make sure that you retrieve your metadata from the SAS server and export it in XML format.

7.5.2 Step 1: General properties

- In the **Repository** tree view of Talend Open Studio, expand **Metadata** and then right-click **DB Connection**.
- Select Create connection from the contextual menu to open the **[Database Connection]** wizard.
- Fill in schema generic information, such as **Name** and **Description** and click **Next** to open a new view on the wizard.

For further information, see *Step 1: General properties on page 182*.

7.5.3 Step 2: Connection

- In the **DB type** field in the **[Database Connection]** wizard, select **SAS** and fill in the fields that follow with SAS connection information.

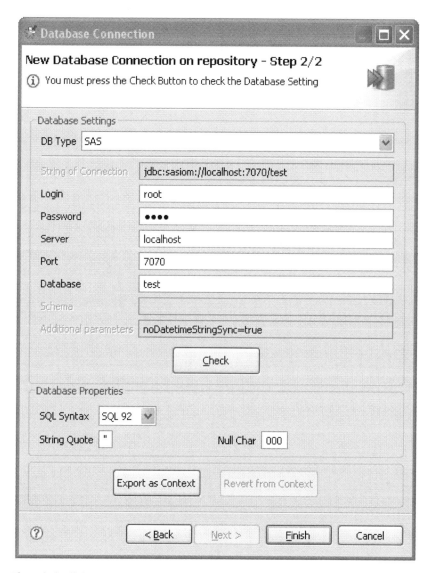

- If needed, click the **Check** tab to verify if your connection is successful.
- If needed, define the properties of the database in the corresponding fields In the **Database Properties** area.
- Click **Finish** to validate your changes and close the wizard.

The newly set connection to the defined database displays under the **DB Connections** folder in the **Repository** tree view. This connection has four sub-folders among which **Table schemas** can group all schemas relative to this connection.

Managing Metadata
Setting up a File Delimited schema

- Right-click the SAS connection you created and then select **Retrieve Schema from SAS** to display all schemas in the defined database under the **Table schemas** sub-folder.

7.6 Setting up a File Delimited schema

File Delimited metadata can be used to define the properties of InputFileDelimited and InputFileCSV components as they are both based on the same structure.

 The file schema creation is very similar for all types of file connections: Delimited, Positional, Regex, Xml, or Ldif.

In the **Repository** tree view, right-click **File Delimited**, and select **Create file delimited** on the pop-up menu.

Unlike the DB connection wizard, the Delimited File wizard gathers both file connection and schema definitions in a four-step procedure.

7.6.1 Step 1: General properties

On the first step, fill in the schema generic information, such as Schema **Name** and **Description**.

For further information, see *Step 1: General properties on page 182*.

7.6.2 Step 2: File upload

Define the **Server** IP address where the file is stored. And click **Browse...** to set the **File path**.

Managing Metadata
Setting up a File Delimited schema

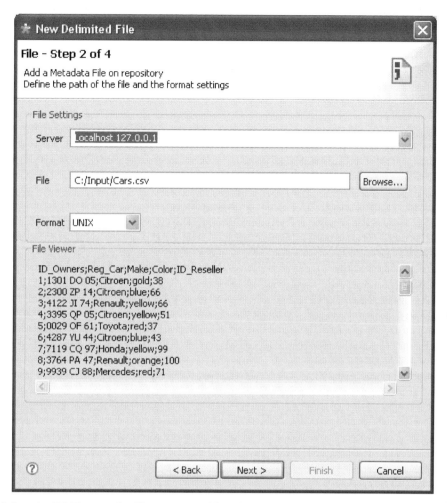

Select the OS **Format** the file was created in. This information is used to prefill subsequent step fields. If the list doesn't include the appropriate format, ignore it.

The **File viewer** gives an instant picture of the file loaded. It allows you to check the file consistency, the presence of header and more generally the file structure.

Click **Next** to proceed to Step3.

7.6.3 Step 3: Schema definition

On this view, you can refine your data description and file settings. Click the squares below, to zoom in and get more information.

Managing Metadata
Setting up a File Delimited schema

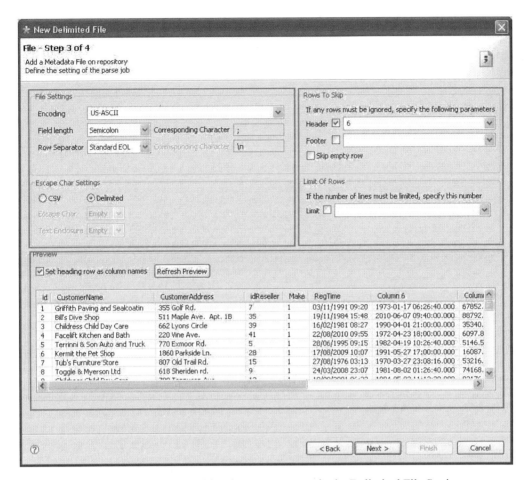

Set the **Encoding**, as well as Field and Row separators in the Delimited File Settings.

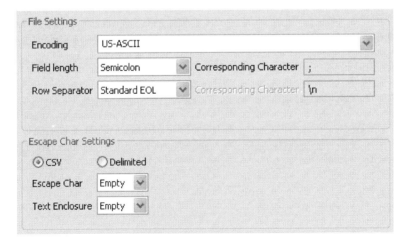

Depending on your file type (csv or delimited), you can also set the Escape and Enclosure characters to be used.

If the file preview shows a header message, you can exclude the header from the parsing. Set the number of header rows to be skipped. Also, if you know that the file contains footer information, set the number of footer lines to be ignored.

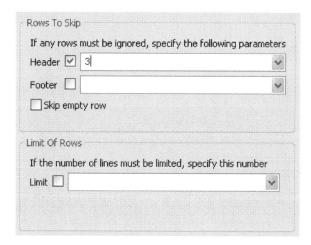

The **Limit of rows** allows you to restrict the extend of the file being parsed.

In the **File Preview** panel, you can view the new settings impact.

Check the **Set heading row as column names** box to transform the first parsed row as labels for schema columns. Note that the number of header rows to be skipped is then incremented by 1.

Click **Refresh** on the preview panel for the settings to take effect and view the result on the viewer.

7.6.4 Step 4: Final schema

The last step shows the Delimited File schema generated. You can customize the schema using the toolbar underneath the table.

Managing Metadata
Setting up a File Positional schema

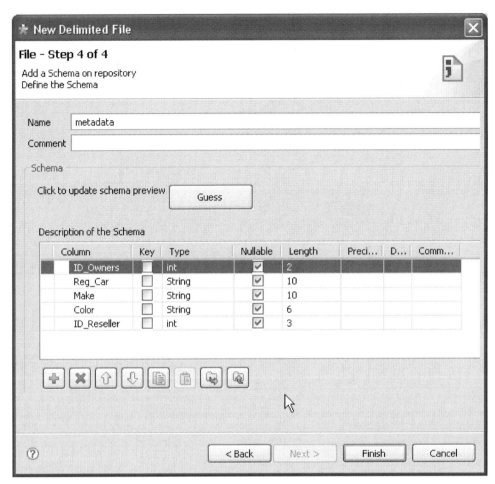

If the Delimited file which the schema is based on has been changed, use the **Guess** button to generate again the schema. Note that if you customized the schema, the **Guess** feature doesn't retain these changes.

Click **Finish**. The new schema displays in the **Repository** tree view, under the relevant **File Delimited** connection node.

For further information about how to drop component metadata onto the workspace, see *How to drop components from the Metadata node on page 62*.

7.7 Setting up a File Positional schema

In the **Repository** tree view, right-click the **File Positional** node and select **Create file positional** on the pop-up menu.

Managing Metadata
Setting up a File Positional schema

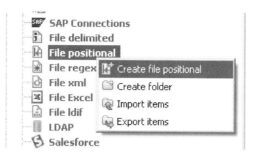

Proceed the same way as for the file delimited connection. Right-click **Metadata** in the **Repository** tree view and select **Create file positional**.

7.7.1 Step 1: General properties

Fill in the schema generic information, such as Schema **Name** and **Description**.

7.7.2 Step 2: Connection and file upload

Then define the positional file connection settings, by filling in the Server IP address and the File path fields.

Like for **Delimited File** schema creation, the format is requested to pre-fill the next step fields. If the file creation OS format is not offered in the list, ignore this field.

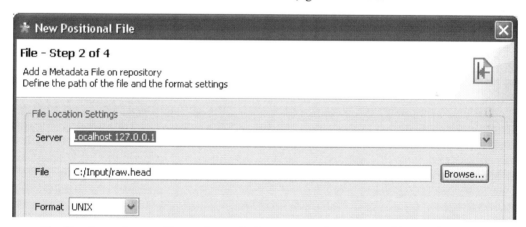

The file viewer shows a file preview and allows you to place your position markers.

Talend Open Studio — 201

Managing Metadata
Setting up a File Positional schema

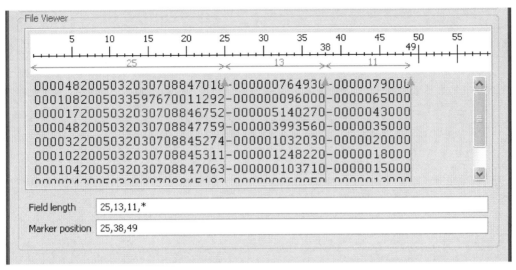

Click the file preview and set the markers against the ruler. The orange arrow helps you refine the position.

The **Field length** field lists a series of figures separated by commas, these are the number of characters between the separators. The asterisk symbol means all remaining characters on the row, starting from the preceding marker position.

The **Marker Position** shows the exact position of the marker on the ruler. You can change it to specify the position precisely.

You can add as many markers as needed. To remove a marker, drag it towards the ruler.

Click **Next** to continue.

7.7.3 Step 3: Schema refining

The next step opens the schema setting window. As for the **Delimited File** schema, you can refine the schema definition by setting precisely the field and row separators, the header message lines and more...

At this stage, the preview shows the file delimited upon the markers' position. If the file contains column labels, select the check box **Set heading row as column names**.

7.7.4 Step 4: Finalising the end schema

Step 4 shows the end schema generated. Note that any character which could be misinterpreted by the program is replaced by neutral characters. Underscores replace asterisks, for example.

You can customize the metadata name (by default, metadata) and edit it using the tool bar.

You can also retrieve or update the Positional File schema by clicking on **Guess**. Note however that any edits to the schema might be lost after "guessing" the file-based schema.

You can drop the metadata defined from the **Repository** onto the design workspace. A dialog box then opens in which you can choose which component to use in your Job.

Managing Metadata
Setting up a File Regex schema

7.8 Setting up a File Regex schema

Regex file schemas are used for files which contain redundant information, such as log files.

Proceed the same way as for the file delimited or positional connection. Right-click **Metadata** in the **Repository** tree view and select **Create file regex**.

7.8.1 Step 1: General properties

Fill in the schema generic information, such as Schema **Name** and **Description**.

7.8.2 Step 2: File upload

Then define the Regex file connection settings, by filling in the Server IP address and the File path fields.

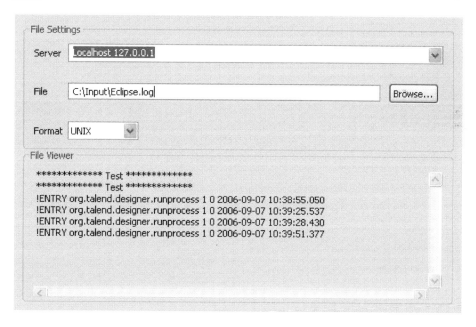

Like for **Delimited File** schema creation, the format is requested for pre-fill purpose of next step fields. If the file creation OS format is not offered in the list, ignore this field.

The file viewer gives an instant picture of the loaded file. Click **Next** to define the schema structure.

7.8.3 Step 3: Schema definition

This step opens the schema setting window. As for the other File schemas, you can refine the schema definition by setting precisely the field and row separators, the header message number of lines and else...

In the **Regular Expression settings** panel, enter the regular expression to be used to delimit the file. (below in Perl)

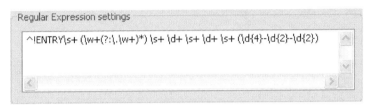

 Make sure to use the correct Regex syntax according to the generation language you use as the syntax is different in Java/Perl, and to include the Regex in single or double quotes accordingly.

Then click **Refresh preview** to take the changes into account. The button changes to **Wait** until the preview is refreshed.

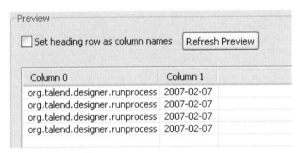

Click **Next** when setting is complete. The last step generates the Regex File schema.

7.8.4 Step 4: Finalizing the end schema

You can add a customized name (by default, metadata) and edit it using the tool bar.

You can also retrieve or update the Regex File schema by clicking on **Guess**. Note however that any edits to the schema might be lost after guessing the file based schema.

Click **Finish**. The new schema displays in the **Repository** tree view under the relevant File regex connection node.

For further information about how to drop component metadata onto the workspace, see *How to drop components from the Metadata node on page 62*.

7.9 Setting up an XML file schema

Centralize your XPath query statements from a defined XML file and gather the values retrieved from it.

This is done in the same way as for the connection of delimited or positional files.

According to the option you select, the wizard helps you create either an input or an output schema. In a Job, the **tFileInputXML** component uses the input schema created to read XML files, whereas **tAdvancedFileOutputXML** uses the output schema created to either write an XML file, or to update an existing XML file.

 Step 1, in which you enter the general properties of the schema to be created, precedes the step at which you set the type of schema as either input or output. It is therefore advisable to enter names which will help you to distinguish between your input and output schemas.

For further information about reading an XML file, see *Setting up an XML schema for an input file on page 205*.
For further information about writing an XML file, see *Setting up an XML schema for an output file on page 211*.

7.9.1 Setting up an XML schema for an input file

This section describes how to define and upload an XML schema for an input file. To define and upload an output file, see *Setting up an XML schema for an output file on page 211*.

Step 1: General properties

In this step, the schema metadata such as the **Name**, **Purpose** and **Description** are set.

- In the **Repository** view, expand the **Metadata** node.
- Right click **File xml**, and select **Create xml file** from the pop-up menu.

- Enter the generic schema information, such as its **Name** and **Description**.

Managing Metadata
Setting up an XML file schema

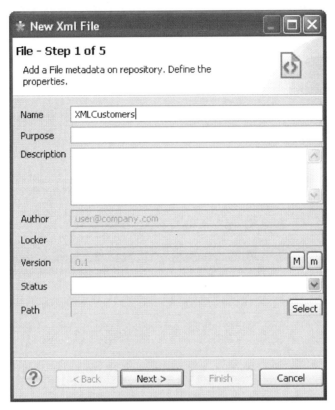

- Click **Next** to select the type of schema.

Step 2: Setting the type of schema (input)

In this step, the type of schema is set as either input or output. For this procedure, the schema of interest is input.

- In the dialog box, select **Input XML**.

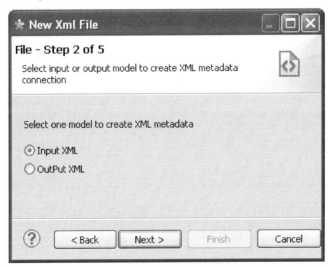

Managing Metadata
Setting up an XML file schema

- Click **Next** to upload the input file.

Step 3: Uploading the input file

This step involves selecting the input file, its encoding type and defining the number of columns on which the XPath query is to be run. You can also preview the structure of the XML file selected.

- Click **[Browse...]** and browse your directory to the XML file to be uploaded. Alternatively, enter the access path to the file.
  The **Schema Viewer** area displays a preview of the XML structure. You can expand and visualize every level of the file's XML structure.

   If you are loading an XSD file, it will be saved in the **Repository**. The metadata will therefore not be affected by the deletion or displacement of the file.

- Enter the **Encoding** type in the corresponding field if the system does not detect it automatically.

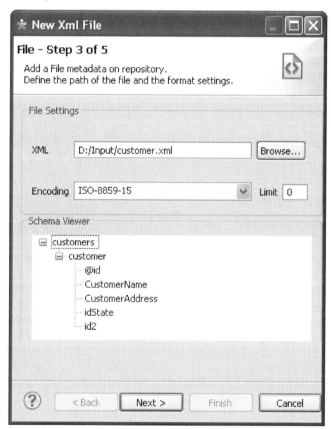

- In the **Limit** field, enter the number of columns on which the XPath query is to be executed, or 0 if you want to run it against all of the columns.

- Click **Next** to define the schema parameters.

Talend Open Studio 207

Step 4: Defining the schema

In this step the schema parameters are set.

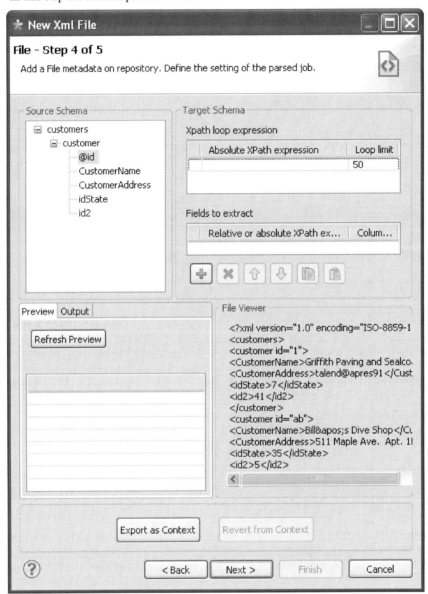

The schema definition window is composed of four views:

View	Descrpition
Source Schema	Tree view of the XML file.
Target Schema	Extraction and iteration information.
Preview	Preview of the target schema.
File viewer	Preview of the brute data.

It is necessary to populate the **XPath loop expression** field with the absolute XPath expression for the node to be iterated upon. There are two ways to do this, either:

- Enter the absolute XPath expression for the node to be iterated upon (Enter the full expression or press **Ctrl+Space** to use the autocompletion list).
  An orange arrow links the node to the corresponding expression.

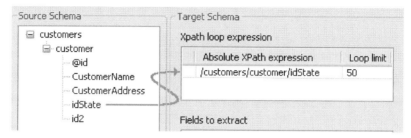

Or

- Drop a node from the tree view under **Source schema** onto the **Absolute XPath expression** field.
  An orange arrow links the node to the corresponding expression.

   The **Xpath loop expression** field is obligatory.

- Enter a **Loop limit** in the corresponding field to limit the number of nodes iterated upon.

Next, it is necessary to define the fields to be extracted. To do so:

- Drop the node(s) of interest from the **Source Schema** tree onto the **Relative or absolute XPath expression**.

   You can select several nodes to drop on the table by pressing **Ctrl** or **Shift** and clicking the nodes of interest. The arrow linking an individual node selected on the **Source Schema** to the **Fields to extract** table are blue in colour. The other ones are gray.

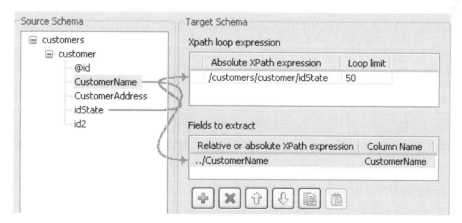

You can add as many columns to be extracted as necessary, delete columns or change the column order using the toolbar:

- Add or delete a column using the ➕ and ✖ buttons.

Managing Metadata
Setting up an XML file schema

- Change the order of the columns using the ⬆ and ⬇ buttons.

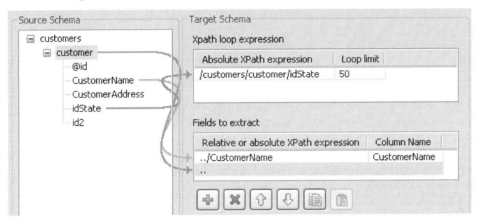

- In the **Column name** fields, enter labels for the columns to be displayed in the schema **Preview** area.

- Click **Refresh preview** to display the schema preview. The fields are consequently displayed in the schema according to the order determined.

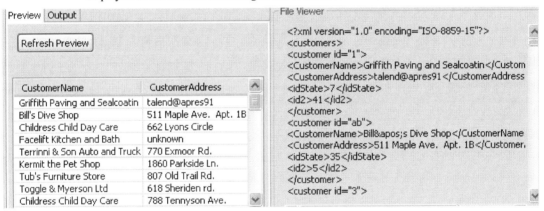

- Click **Next** to finalize the end schema.

Step 5: Finalizing the end schema

The schema generated displays the columns selected from the XML file. You can customize the the schema according to your needs, or reload the original schema using the **Guess** button.

Managing Metadata
Setting up an XML file schema

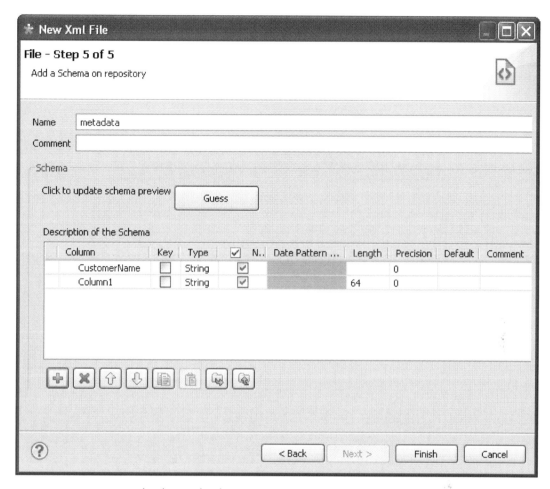

- Click the ⊕ m and ✕ buttons to add or delete selected columns.

- Click the ⬇ and ⬆ buttons to modify the order of the columns.

- Click **Finish**.
  The new schema is added to the **Repository** under the **File xml** node.

7.9.2 Setting up an XML schema for an output file

This section describes how to define and upload an XML schema for an output file. To define and upload an XML schema for an input file, see *Setting up an XML schema for an input file on page 205*.

Step 1: General properties

In this step, the schema metadata such as the **Name**, **Purpose** and **Description** are set.

- In the **Repository** view, expand the **Metadata** node.

- Right click **File XML**, and select **Create XML File** from the pop-up menu.

Managing Metadata
Setting up an XML file schema

- Enter the generic schema information, such as its **Name** and **Description**.

- Click **Next** to set the type of schema.

Step 2: Setting the type of schema (output)

In this step, the type of schema is set as either input or output. For this procedure, the schema of interest is output.

- From the dialog box, select **Output XML**.

Managing Metadata
Setting up an XML file schema

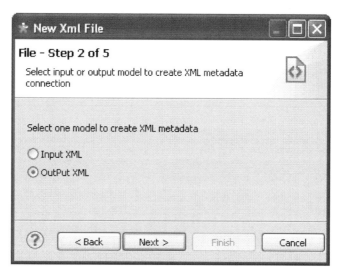

- Click **Next** to define the output file.

Step 3: Defining the output file

You can choose whether to create your file manually or from an existing file. If you choose the **Create manually** option you will have to configure your schema, source and target columns yourself. The file is created in a Job using a an XML output componant such as **tAdvancedFileOutputXML**. In this example, we will create the output file from an existing file.

Managing Metadata
Setting up an XML file schema

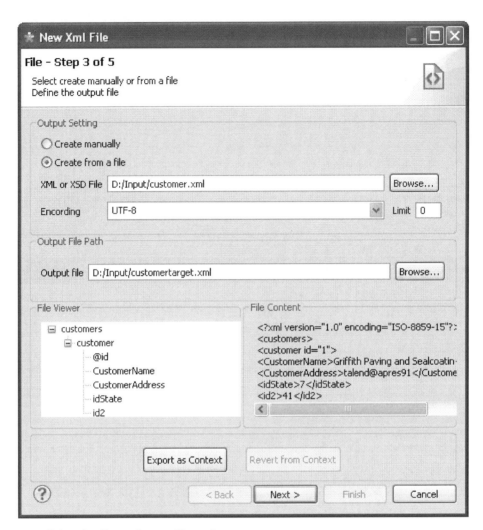

- Select the **Create from a file** option.

- In the **XML or XSD File** field, enter the access path to the XML or XSD file to be uploaded, in which the structure to be applied to the output file is found.

   If you are loading an XSD file, it will be saved in the **Repository**. The metadata will therefore not be affected by the deletion or displacement of the file.

- Enter the **Encoding** type in the corresponding field if the system doesn't detect it automatically.

- In the **Limit** field, enter the number of columns on which the XPath query is to be executed, or enter 0 if you want it to be run against all of the columns.

- In the **Output File** field, in the **Output File Path** zone, browse to or enter the path to the output file. If the file doesn't exist as yet, it will be created during the execution of a Job using a **tAdvancedFileOutputXML** component. If the file already exists, it will be overwritten.

- The **File Viewer** zone displays a preview of the XML structure.

Managing Metadata
Setting up an XML file schema

- Click **Next** to define the schema.

Step 4: Defining the schema

In the **Linker Target** zone you must define the element on which to run a loop. To do this:

- Right click on the element of choice and select **Set As Loop Element** from the contextual menu.

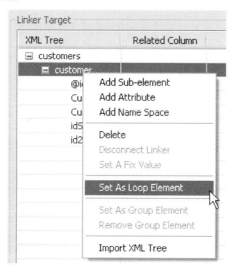

Next, you have to map the columns, according to your needs.

 You can select and drop several fields at a time, using the **Ctrl + Shift** technique to make multiple selections, therefore making mapping faster. You can also make multiple selections for right-click operations.

To do so:

- Drop the source columns from the **Linker Source** area onto the target columns in the **Linker Target** area.
  A dialog box opens in which you must choose one of three possible operations. Either:

- Select **Create as sub-element of target node**.

Or

- Select **Create as attribute of target node** if you want to add a node to an element. This node will be considered to be an attribute of the element.

Or

- Select **Add linker to target node** if you want to store the value of the source schema in the corresponding XML tag.

Talend Open Studio 215

Managing Metadata
Setting up an XML file schema

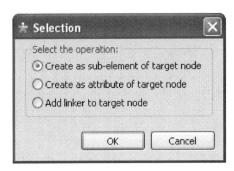

- In this example, select the **Create as sub-element as target node** option. Click **OK** to validate the choice.

- A blue arrow links the columns mapped.

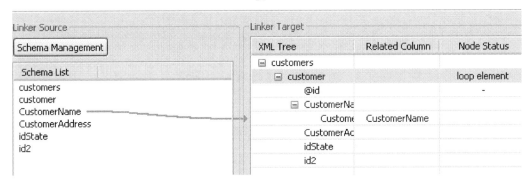

- Click **Next** to finalize the end schema.

Step 5: Finalizing the end schema

Step 5 displays the end schema generated.

Managing Metadata
Setting up a File Excel schema

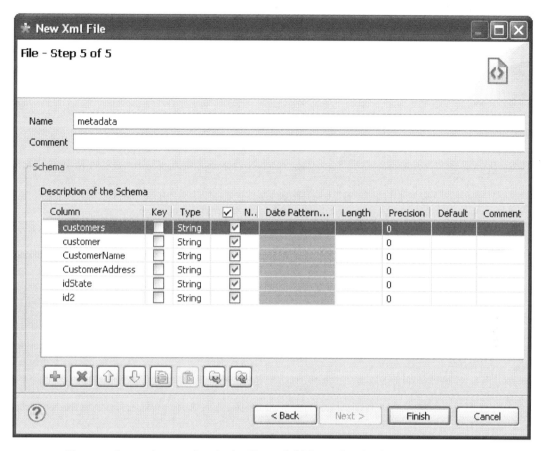

You can change the metadata in the **Name** field (*metadata*, by default), add a **Comment** in the corresponding field and make further modifications using the toolbar, for example:

- Add or delete a column using the ![+] and ![x] buttons.
- Change the order of the columns using the ![up] and ![down] buttons.
- Click **Finish** to finalize creation of the XML output file.
- Click **Finish** to finalize creation of the XML output file.
  The new schema appears in the Repository, under the corresponding **File xml** node.

7.10 Setting up a File Excel schema

In the **Repository** tree view, right-click **File Excel** tree node, and select **Create file Excel** on the pop-up menu.

Managing Metadata
Setting up a File Excel schema

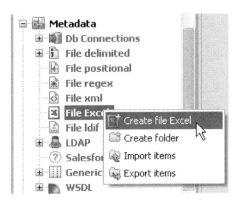

Then proceed the same way as for the file delimited connection.

7.10.1 Step 1: General properties

Fill in the schema general information, such as Schema **Name** and **Description**.

7.10.2 Step 2: File upload

Browse to the file to upload and fill out the **File** field.

 You can upload all types of Excel files including *..xlsx* of Excel 2007.

Managing Metadata
Setting up a File Excel schema

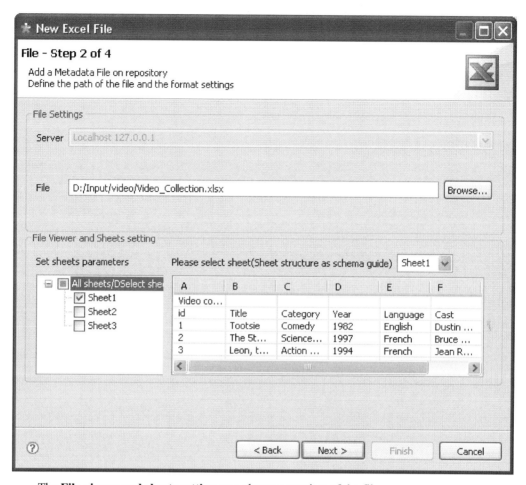

The **File viewer and sheets setting** area shows a preview of the file.

In the **Set sheets parameters list**, select the dialog box next to the sheet you want to upload. By default the file preview displays the Sheet1.

Select another sheet on the drop-down list, if need be and check that the file is properly read on the preview table.

Click **Next** to continue.

7.10.3 Step 3: Schema refining

The next step opens the schema setting window.

Managing Metadata
Setting up a File Excel schema

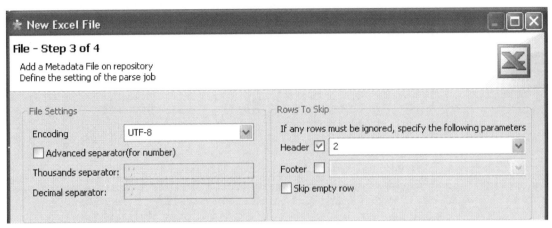

The same way as for the File Delimited schema procedure, you can set precisely the separator, the rows that should be skipped as they are header or footer.

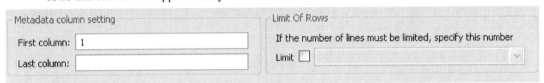

You can fill out the **First column** and **Last column** fields, to set precisely the columns to be read in the file. You can need to skip column A for example as it may not contain proper data to be processed.

Also check the **Set heading row as column names** to take into account the heading names. Make sure you press **Refresh** to be able to view the change in the preview table.

Then click **Next** to continue.

7.10.4 Step 4: Finalising the end schema

Step 4 shows the end schema generated. Note that any character which could be misinterpreted by the program is replaced by neutral characters, like underscores replace asterisks.

You can add a customized name (by default, metadata) and make edits to it using the tool bar.

You can also retrieve or update the Excel File schema by clicking on **Guess**. Note however that any custom edits to the schema might thus be lost using this feature.

Click **Finish**. The new schema displays in the **Repository** tree view under the relevant File Excel connection node.

7.11 Setting up a File LDIF schema

LDIF files are directory files described by attributes. File LDIF metadata centralize these LDIF-type files and their attribute description.

Proceed the same way as for other file connections. Right-click **Metadata** in the **Repository** tree view and select **Create file Ldif**.

 Make sure that you installed the relevant module as described in the Installation guide. For more information, check out http://talendforge.org/wiki/doku.php.

7.11.1 Step 1: General properties

On the first step, fill in the schema generic information, such as Schema name and description.

7.11.2 Step 2: File upload

Then define the Ldif file connection settings by filling in the **File path** field.

Managing Metadata
Setting up a File LDIF schema

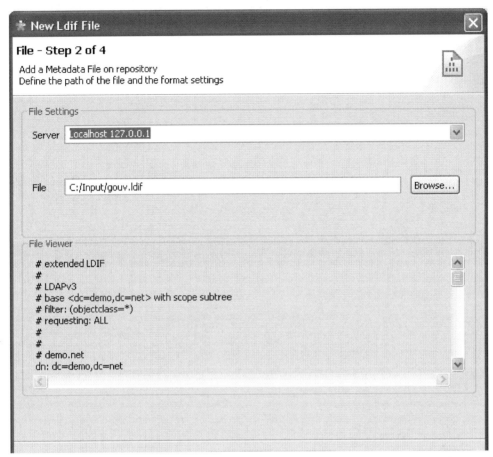

 The connection functionality to a remote server is not operational yet for the LDIF file collection.

The File viewer provides a preview of the file's first 50 rows.

7.11.3 Step 3: Schema definition

The list of attributes of the description file displays on the top of the panel. Select the attributes you want to extract from the LDIF description file, by selecting the relevant check boxes.

Managing Metadata
Setting up an LDAP schema

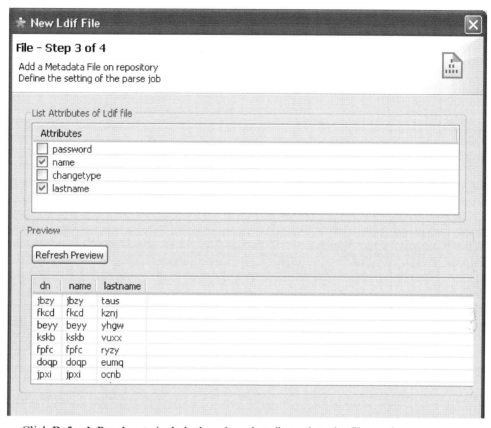

Click **Refresh Preview** to include the selected attributes into the file preview.

 DN is omitted in the list of attributes as this key attribute is automatically included in the file preview, hence in the generated schema.

7.11.4 Step 4: Finalising the end schema

The schema generated shows the columns of the description file. You can customize it upon your needs and reload the original schema using the **Guess** button.

Click **Finish**. The new schema displays in the **Repository** tree view under the relevant Ldif file connection node.

7.12 Setting up an LDAP schema

In the **Repository** tree view, right-click the **LDAP** tree node, and select **Create LDAP schema** on the pop-up menu.

Managing Metadata
Setting up an LDAP schema

Unlike the DB connection wizard, the LDAP wizard gathers both file connection and schema definition in a four-step procedure.

7.12.1 Step 1: General properties

On the first step, fill in the schema generic information, such as Schema **Name** and **Description**.

For further information, see *Step 1: General properties on page 182*.

7.12.2 Step 2: Server connection

Fill the connection details.

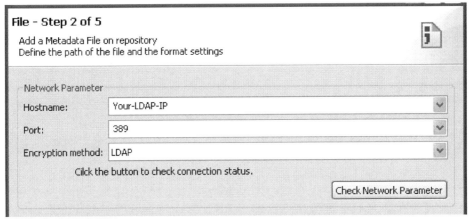

Then check your connection using **Check Network Parameter** to verify the connection and activate the **Next** button.

Field	Description
Host	LDAP Server IP address
Port	Listening port to the LDAP directory
Encryption method	**LDAP**: no encryption is used **LDAPS**: secured LDAP **TLS**: certificate is used

Click **Next** to validate this step and continue.

7.12.3 Step 3: Authentication and DN fetching

In this view, set the authentication and data access mode.

Managing Metadata
Setting up an LDAP schema

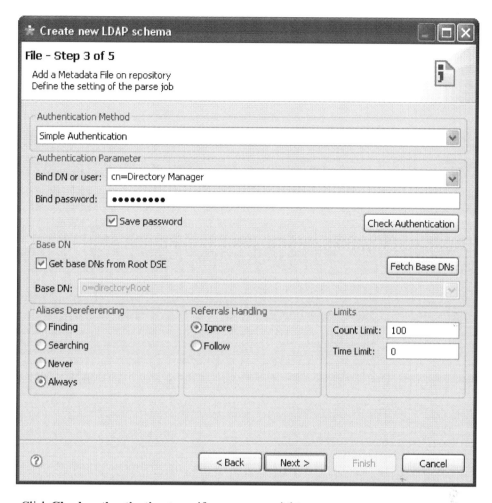

Click **Check authentication** to verify your access rights.

Field	Description
Authentication method	**Simple authentication**: requires **Authentication Parameters** field to be filled in **Anonymous authentication**: does not require authentication parameters
Authentication Parameters	**Bind DN or User**: login as expected by the LDAP authentication method **Bind password**: expected password **Save password**: remembers the login details.
Get Base DN from Root DSE / Base DN	Path to user's authorized tree leaf **Fetch Base DNs** button retrieves the DN automatically from Root.

Managing Metadata
Setting up an LDAP schema

Field	Description
Alias Dereferencing	**Never** allows to improve search performance if you are sure that no aliases is to be dereferenced. By default, Always is to be used. **Always**: Always dereference aliases **Never**: Never dereferences aliases. **Searching**:Dereferences aliases only after name resolution. **Finding**: Dereferences aliases only during name resolution
Referral Handling	Redirection of user request: **Ignore**: does not handle request redirections **Follow**:does handle request redirections
Limit	Limited number of records to be read

Click **Fetch Base DNs** to retrieve the DN and click the **Next** button to continue.

7.12.4 Step 4: Schema definition

Select the attributes to be included in the schema structure.

Add a filter if you want selected data only.

Managing Metadata
Setting up an LDAP schema

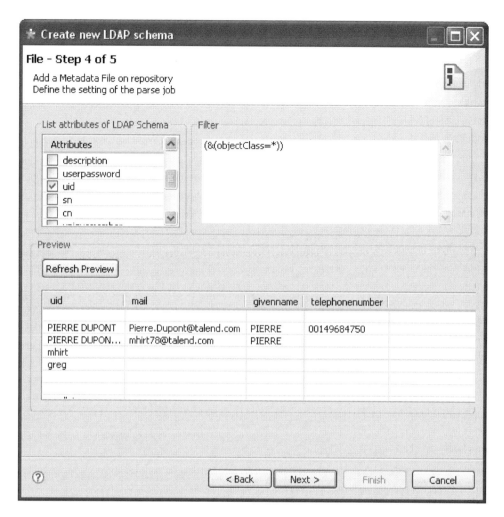

Click **Refresh Preview** to display the selected column and a sample of the data.

Then click **Next** to continue.

7.12.5 Step 5: Finalising the end schema

The last step shows the LDAP schema generated. You can customize the schema using the toolbar underneath the table.

Managing Metadata
Setting up a Salesforce schema

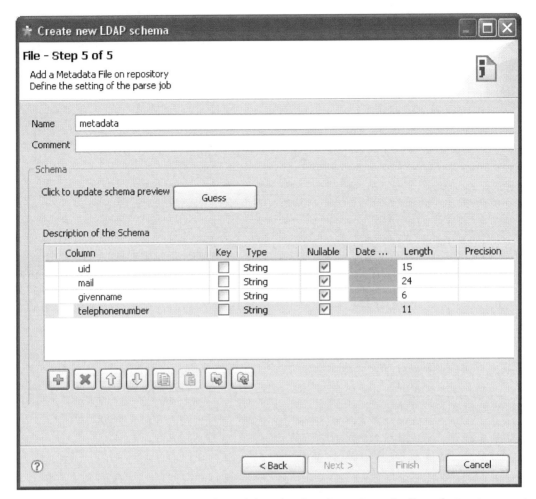

If the LDAP directory which the schema is based on has changed, use the **Guess** button to generate again the schema. Note that if you customized the schema, your changes won't be retained after the **Guess** operation.

Click **Finish**. The new schema displays in the **Repository** tree view under the relevant LDAP connection node.

7.13 Setting up a Salesforce schema

In the **Repository** tree view, right-click the **Salesforce** tree node, and select **Create Salesforce schema** on the pop-up menu.

Then proceed the same way as for any other metadata connection.

7.13.1 Step 1: General properties

Fill in the schema general information, such as Schema **Name** and **Description**.

7.13.2 Step 2: Connection to a Salesforce account

The Salesforce Web service URL displays by default in the **Web service URL** field.

- Enter your **User name** and **Password** in the corresponding fields to connect to your Salesforce account through the salesforce webservice.
- From the **Standard objects** list, select the object you want to access and get the schema from.
- In the **Standard objects** list, select the standard or personalized object you want to access and get the schema from.
- Click **Check Login** to verify that you can connect without issue.
- Click **Next** to continue.

7.13.3 Step 3: Schema refining

The next step opens the schema setting window based on the Module you selected in Step 2.

Managing Metadata
Setting up a Salesforce schema

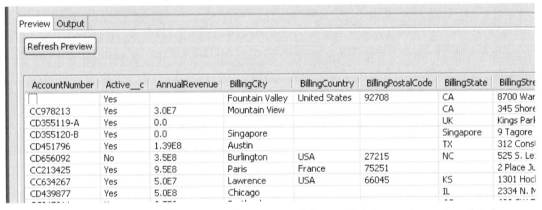

In the **Browse data column and set query condition** area, you can narrow down the selection and filter displayed data. To do that, type in the column you want to filter on and the value you want to drill down to in the **Query Condition** field.

The columns in the **Column** list are listed in alphabetical order. Select the **order the fields** check box to list them randomly.

Click **Refresh Preview**, if you entered a query condition, so that the preview gets updated accordingly. By default, the preview shows all columns of the selected module.

Then click **Next** to continue.

7.13.4 Step 4: Finalising the end schema

Step 4 shows the final generated schema.

You can add a customized name (by default, metadata) and make edits to the schema using the tool bar.

Managing Metadata
Setting up a Generic schema

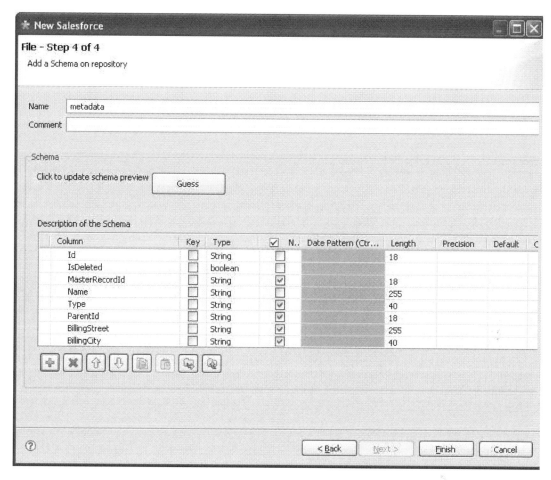

You can also retrieve or update the Salesforce schema by clicking **Guess**. Note however, that any changes or customization of the schema might be lost using this feature.

Click **Finish**. The new schema displays in the **Repository** tree view under the relevant File Excel connection node.

You can drop the metadata defined from the **Repository** onto the design workspace. A dialog box opens in which you can choose to use either a **tSalesforceInput** or **tSalesforceOutput** component in your Job.

7.14 Setting up a Generic schema

Talend Open Studio allows you to create any schema from scratch if none of the specific metadata wizards matches your need or if you don't have any source file to take the schema from. The creation procedure is made of two steps.

First right-click **Generic Schema** in the **Repository** tree view and select **Create generic schema**.

7.14.1 Step 1: General properties

A connection wizard opens up. Fill in the generic Schema properties such as Schema **Name** and **Description**. The **Status** field is a customized field you can define in **Window > Preferences**.

Click **Next** when completed.

7.14.2 Step 2: Schema definition

There is no default schema displaying as there is no source to take it from.

- You can give a name to the schema or use the default name (metadata) and add a comment if you feel like.

- Then, customize the schema structure in the schema panel, based on your needs.

- Indeed, the tool bar allows you add, remove or move columns in your schema. Also, you can load an xml schema or export the current schema as xml.

- Click **Finish** to complete the generic schema creation. All created schemas display under the relevant **Generic Schemas** connection node.

7.15 Setting up a Web Service schema

In Talend Open Studio you can save your Web Service connections in the **Repository**.

7.15.1 Setting up a simple schema

This section describes how to define a Web Service schema.

Step 1: General properties

This step illustrates how to define the file's general properties.

- In the **Repository**, expand the **Metadata** node.

- Right-click **Web Service** and select **Create Web Service schema** from the context menu list.

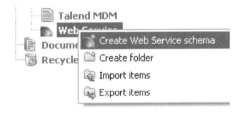

- Enter the generic schema information such as its **Name** and **Description**.

Managing Metadata
Setting up a Web Service schema

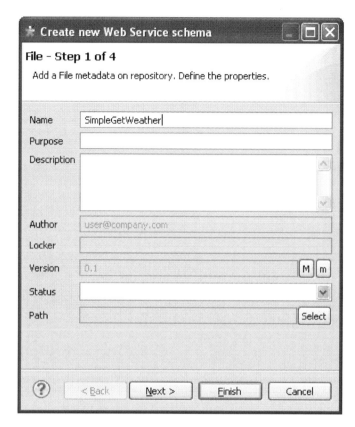

- Click **Next** to select the schema type in step 2.

Step 2: URI and method definition.

This step involves the definition of the URI and other parameters required to obtain the desired values.

Managing Metadata
Setting up a Web Service schema

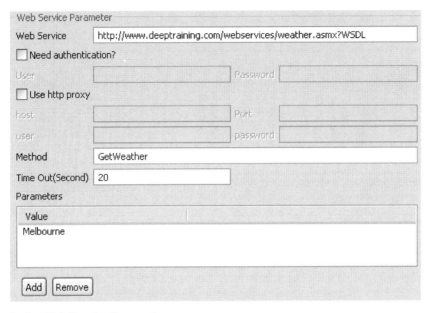

In the **Web Service Parameter** zone:

- Enter the URI which will transmit the desired values, in the **Web Service** field.
- If necessary, select the **Need authentication?** check box and then enter your authentication information in the **User** and **Password** fields.
- If you use an http proxy, select the **Use http proxy** check box and enter the information required in the **host**, **Port**, **user** and **password** fields.
- Enter the **Method** name in the corresponding field.
- In the **Value** table, **Add** or **Remove** values as desired, using the corresponding buttons.
- Click **Refresh Preview** to check that the parameters have been entered correctly.

In the **Preview** tab, the values to be transmitted by the Web Service method are displayed, based on the parameters entered.

Step 3: Finalizing the end schema

You can modify the schema name (*metadata*, by default) and modify the schema itself using the tool bar.

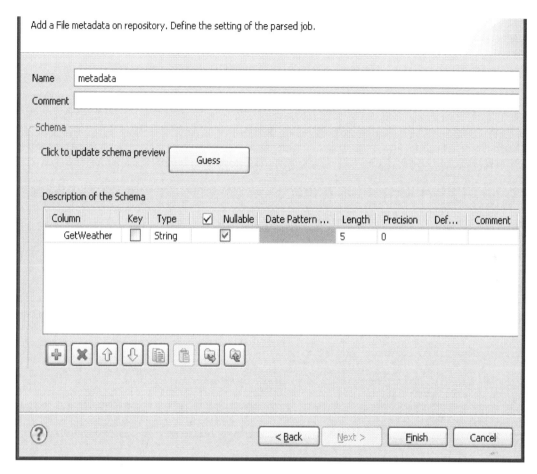

- Add or delete columns using the ✚ and ✖ buttons.
- Modify the order of the columns using the ⬆ and ⬇ buttons.
- Click **Finish**.
  The new schema is added to the **Repository** under the **Web Service** node.

7.16 Setting up an MDM connection

Talend Open Studio enables you to centralized the details of one or more MDM connections under the **Metadata** folder in the **Repository** tree view. You can then use any of these established connections to connect to the MDM server.

Managing Metadata
Setting up an MDM connection

> You can also set up an MDM connection the same way by clicking the icon in the **Basic settings** view of the **tMDMInput** and **tMDMOutput** components. For more information, see the *Talend MDM components* chapter in the Talend Open Studio Components Reference Guide.

According to the option you select, the wizard helps you create an input XML, an output XML or a receive XML schema. Later, in a **Talend** Job, the **tMDMInput** component uses the defined input schema to read master data stored in XML documents, **tMDMOutput** uses the defined output schema to either write master data in an XML document on the MDM server, or to update existing XML documents and finally the **tMDMReceive** component uses the defined XML schema to receive an MDM record in XML from MDM triggers and processes.

7.16.1 Step 1: Setting up the connection

To establish an MDM connection, complete the following:

- In the **Repository** tree view, expand **Metadata** and right-click **Talend MDM**.
- Select **Create MDM** on the contextual menu.
  The connection wizard displays.

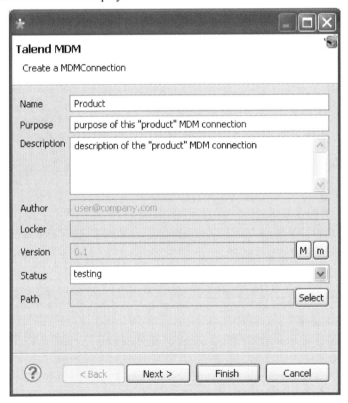

- Fill in the connection properties such as **Name**, **Purpose** and **Description**. The **Status** field is a customized field that can be defined. For more information, see *Status settings on page 39*.

- Click **Next** to proceed to the next step.

236 Talend Open Studio

- Fill in the connection details including the authentication information to the MDM server and then click **Check** to check the connection you have created.
  A dialog box displays to confirm if your connection is successful.

- Click **OK** to close the confirm dialog box and then **Next** to proceed to the next step.

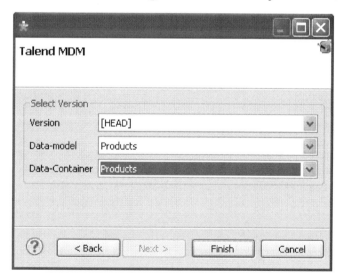

- From the **Version** list, select the master data version on the MDM server to which you want to connect.

- From the **Data-Model** list, select the data model against which the master data is validated.

- From the **Data-Container** list, select the data container that holds the master data you want to access.

Managing Metadata
Setting up an MDM connection

- Click **Finish** to validate your changes and close the dialog box.

The newly created connection is listed under **Talend MDM** under the **Metadata** folder in the **Repository** tree view.

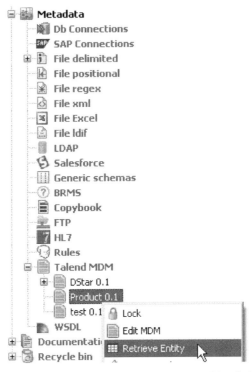

You need now to retrieve the XML schema of the business entities linked to this MDM connection.

7.16.2 Step 2: Defining MDM schema

Defining Input MDM schema

This section describes how to define and download an input MDM XML schema. To define and download an output MDM XML schema, see *Defining output MDM schema on page 243*.

To set the values to be fetched from one or more entities linked to a specific MDM connection, complete the following:

- In the **Repository** tree view, expand **Metadata** and right-click the MDM connection for which you want to retrieve the entity values.

- Select **Retrieve Entity** from the contextual menu.
  A dialog box displays.

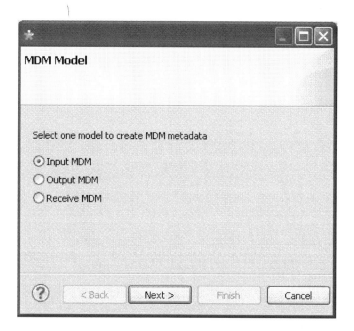

- Select the **Input MDM** option in order to download an input XML schema and then click **Next** to proceed to the following step.

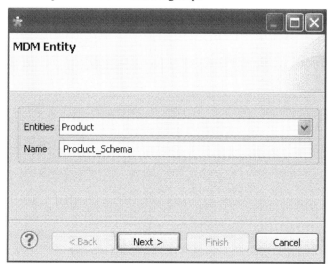

- From the **Entities** field, select the business entity (XML schema) from which you want to retrieve values.
  The name displays automatically in the **Name** field.

   You are free to enter any text in this field, although you would likely put the name of the entity from which you are retrieving the schema.

- Click **Next** to proceed to the next step.

Managing Metadata
Setting up an MDM connection

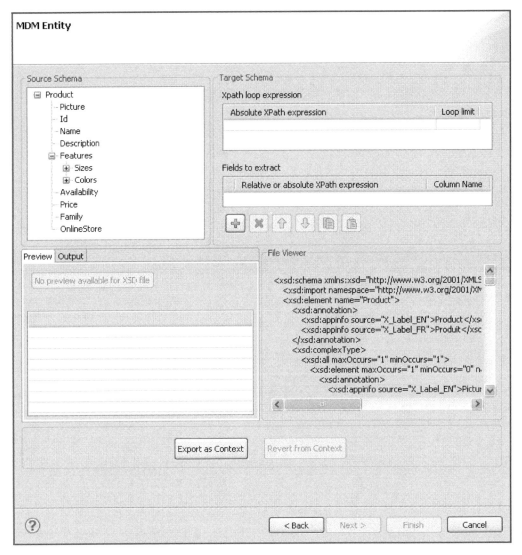

 The schema of the entity you selected display in the **Source Schema** panel.

Here, you can set the parameters to be taken into account for the XML schema definition.

The schema dialog box is divided into four different panels as the following:

Panel	Description
Source Schema	Tree view of the uploaded entity.
Target schema	Extraction and iteration information.
Preview	Target schema preview.
File viewer	Raw data viewer.

- In the **Xpath loop expression** area, enter the absolute xpath expression leading to the XML structure node on which to apply the iteration. Or, drop the node from the source schema to the target schema Xpath field. This link is orange in color.

The **Xpath loop expression** field is compulsory.

- If required, define a **Loop limit** to restrict the iteration to a number of nodes.

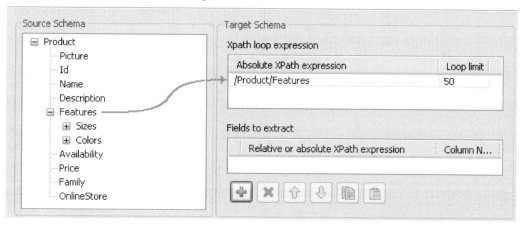

In the above capture, we use *Features* as the element to loop on because it is repeated within the *Product* entity as the following:

```
<Product>
    <Id>1</Id>
    <Name>Cup</Name>
    <Description/>
    <Features>
        <Feature>Color red</Feature>
        <Feature>Size maxi</Feature>
    <Features>
    ...
</Product>
<Product>
    <Id>2</Id>
    <Name>Cup</Name>
    <Description/>
    <Features>
        <Feature>Color blue</Feature>
        <Feature>Thermos</Feature>
    <Features>
    ...
</Product>
```

By doing so, the **tMDMInput** component that uses this MDM connection will create a new row for every item with different feature.

- To define the fields to extract, drop the relevant node from the source schema to the **Relative or absolute XPath expression** field.

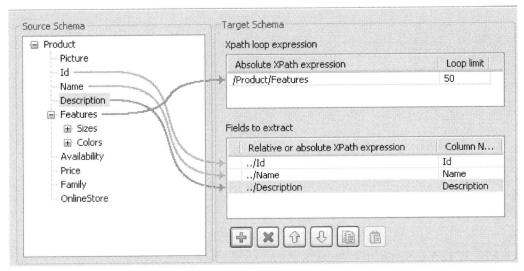

 Use the plus sign to add rows to the table and select as many fields to extract as necessary. Press the **Ctrl** or the **Shift** keys for multiple selection of grouped or separate nodes and drop them to the table.

- If required, enter a name to each of the retrieved columns in the **Column name** field.

   You can prioritize the order of the fields to extract by selecting the field and using the up and down arrows. The link of the selected field is blue, and all other links are grey.

- Click **Finish** to validate your modifications and close the dialog box.

The newly created schema is listed under the corresponding MDM connection in the **Repository** tree view.

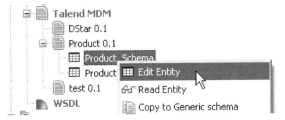

To modify the created schema, complete the following:

- In the **Repository** tree view, expand **Metadata** and **Talend MDM** and then browse to the schema you want to modify.

- Right-click the schema name and select **Edit Entity** from the contextual menu. A dialog box displays.

Managing Metadata
Setting up an MDM connection

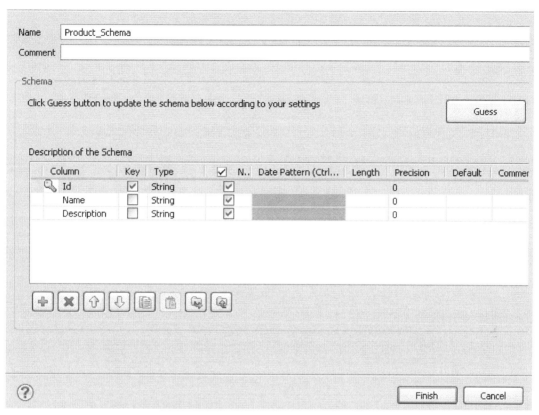

- Modify the schema as needed.
  You can change the name of the schema according to your needs, you can also customize the schema structure in the schema panel. The tool bar allows you to add, remove or move columns in your schema.

- Click **Finish** to close the dialog box.
  The MDM input connection (**tMDMInput**) is now ready to be dropped in any of your Jobs.

Defining output MDM schema

This section describes how to define and download an output MDM XML schema. To define and download an input MDM XML schema, see *Step 1: Setting up the connection on page 236*.

To set the values to be written in one or more entities linked to a specific MDM connection, complete the following:

- In the **Repository** tree view, expand **Metadata** and right-click the MDM connection for which you want to write the entity values.

- Select **Retrieve Entity** from the contextual menu.
  A dialog box displays.

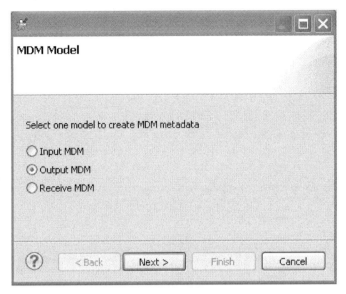

- Select the **Output MDM** option in order to define an output XML schema and then click **Next** to proceed to the following step.

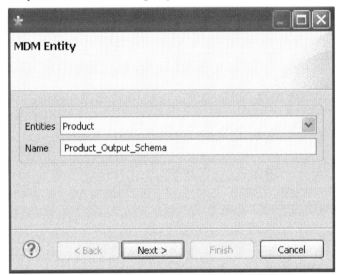

- From the **Entities** field, select the business entity (XML schema) in which you want to write values.
  The name displays automatically in the **Name** field.

   You are free to enter any text in this field, although you would likely put the name of the entity from which you are retrieving the schema.

- Click **Next** to proceed to the next step.

Managing Metadata
Setting up an MDM connection

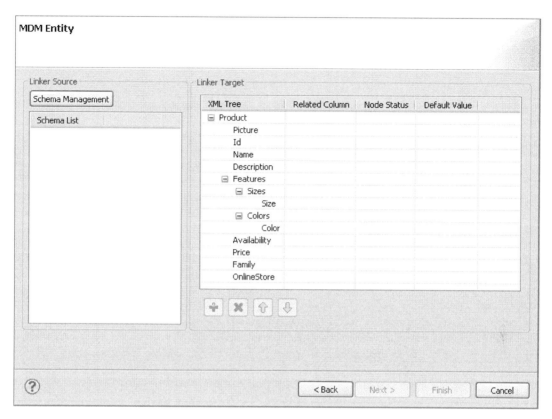

 The schema of the entity you selected display in the **Linker Target** panel.

Here, you can set the parameters to be taken into account for the XML schema definition.

- Click **Schema Management** to display a dialog box.
- Click the plus button to add lines and define the XML schema you want to write in the selected entity.

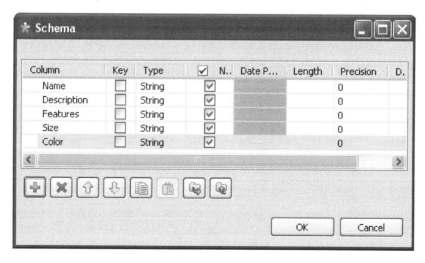

Talend Open Studio   245

Managing Metadata
Setting up an MDM connection

Your **Linker Source** schema must corresponds to the **Linker Target** schema, i.e define the elements in which you want to write values.

- Click **OK** to close the dialog box.
  The defined schema displays under **Schema list**.

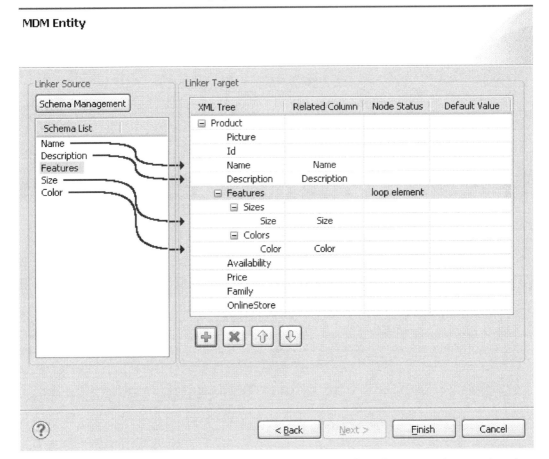

- To define the fields to write, drop the relevant nodes from the source schema to those in the target schema.

   You can select and drop several nodes at a time, using the **Ctrl + Shift** technique, therefore making mapping faster. You can also make multiple selections for all right-click operations on the nodes in the **Linker target** panel.

- In the **Linker Target** panel, right-click the element you want to define as a loop element and select **Set as loop element**. This will restrict the iteration to one or more nodes.

By doing so, the **tMDMOutput** component that uses this MDM connection will create a new row for every item with different feature.

 You can prioritize the order of the fields to write by selecting the field and using the up and down arrows.

- Click **Finish** to validate your modifications and close the dialog box.

The newly created schema is listed under the corresponding MDM connection in the **Repository** tree view.

246   Talend Open Studio

Managing Metadata
Setting up an MDM connection

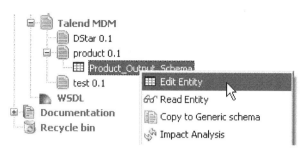

To modify the created schema, complete the following:

- In the **Repository** tree view, expand **Metadata** and **Talend MDM** and then browse to the schema you want to modify.

- Right-click the schema name and select **Edit Entity** from the contextual menu.
  A dialog box displays.

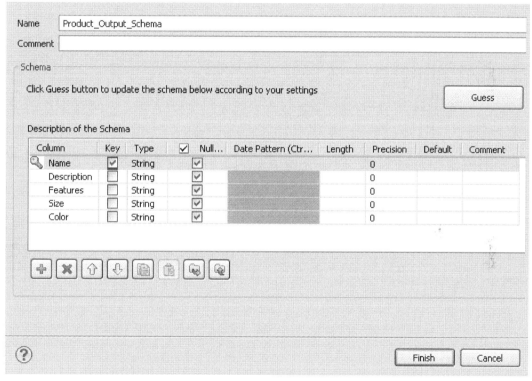

- Modify the schema as needed.
  You can change the name of the schema according to your needs, you can also customize the schema structure in the schema panel. The tool bar allows you to add, remove or move columns in your schema.

- Click **Finish** to close the dialog box.
  The MDM output connection (**tMDMOutput**) is now ready to be dropped in any of your Jobs.

Talend Open Studio

Defining Receive MDM schema

This section describes how to define a receive MDM XML schema based on the MDM connection.

To set the XML schema you want to receive in accordance with a specific MDM connection, complete the following:

- In the **Repository** tree view, expand **Metadata** and right-click the MDM connection for which you want to retrieve the entity values.

- Select **Retrieve Entity** from the contextual menu.
  A dialog box displays.

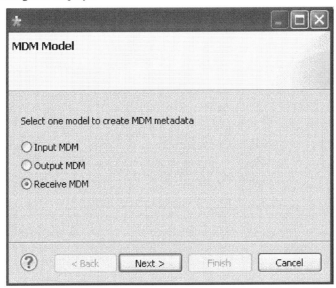

- Select the **Receive MDM** option in order to define a receive XML schema and then click **Next** to proceed to the following step.

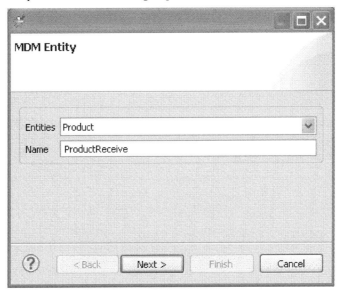

Managing Metadata
Setting up an MDM connection

- From the **Entities** field, select the business entity (XML schema) according to which you want to receive the XML schema.
  The name displays automatically in the **Name** field.

   You can enter any text in this field, although you would likely put the name of the entity according to which you want to receive the XML schema.

- Click **Next** to proceed to the next step.

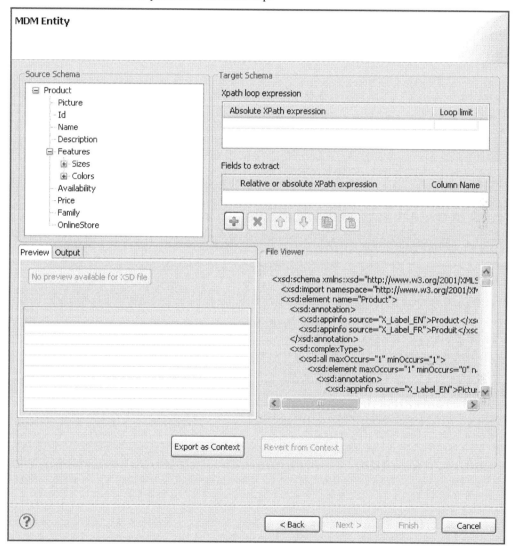

 The schema of the entity you selected display in the **Source Schema** panel.

Here, you can set the parameters to be taken into account for the XML schema definition.

The schema dialog box is divided into four different panels as the following:

Panel	Description
Source Schema	Tree view of the uploaded entity.

Managing Metadata
Setting up an MDM connection

Panel	Description
Target schema	Extraction and iteration information.
Preview	Target schema preview.
File viewer	Raw data viewer.

- In the **Xpath loop expression** area, enter the absolute xpath expression leading to the XML structure node on which to apply the iteration. Or, drop the node from the source schema to the target schema Xpath field. This link is orange in color.

 The **Xpath loop expression** field is compulsory.

- If required, define a **Loop limit** to restrict the iteration to one or more nodes.

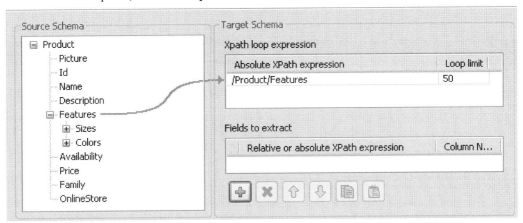

In the above capture, we use *Features* as the element to loop on because it is repeated within the *Product* entity as the following:

```
<Product>
    <Id>1</Id>
    <Name>Cup</Name>
    <Description/>
    <Features>
        <Feature>Color red</Feature>
        <Feature>Size maxi</Feature
    <Features>
    ...
</Product>
<Product>
    <Id>2</Id>
    <Name>Cup</Name>
    <Description/>
    <Features>
        <Feature>Color blue</Feature>
        <Feature>Thermos</Feature>
    <Features>
    ...
</Product>
```

By doing so, the **tMDMReceive** component that uses this MDM connection will create a new row for every item with different feature.

- To define the fields to receive, drop the relevant node from the source schema to the **Relative or absolute XPath expression** field.

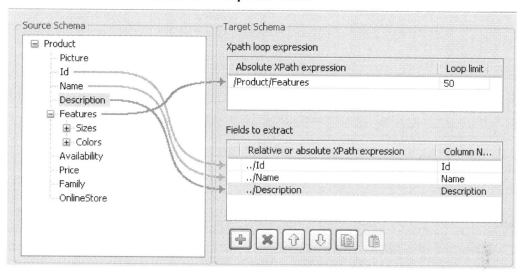

 Use the plus sign to add rows to the table and select as many fields to extract as necessary. Press the **Ctrl** or the **Shift** keys for multiple selection of grouped or separate nodes and drop them to the table.

- If required, enter a name to each of the received columns in the **Column name** field.

 You can prioritize the order of the fields you want to receive by selecting the field and using the up and down arrows. The link of the selected field is blue, and all other links are grey.

- Click **Finish** to validate your modifications and close the dialog box.

The newly created schema is listed under the corresponding MDM connection in the **Repository** tree view.

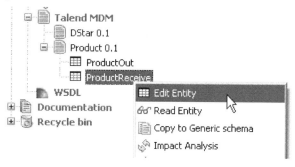

To modify the created schema, complete the following:

- In the **Repository** tree view, expand **Metadata** and **Talend MDM** and then browse to the schema you want to modify.

- Right-click the schema name and select **Edit Entity** from the contextual menu. A dialog box displays.

Managing Metadata
Exporting Metadata as context

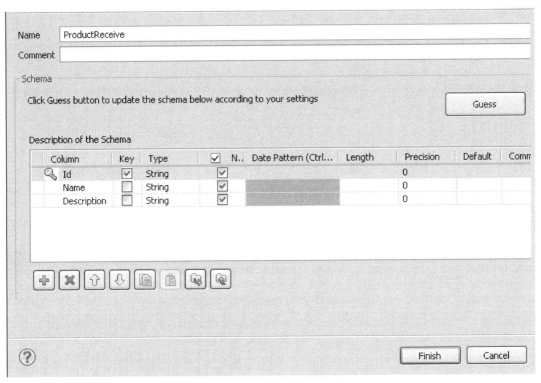

- Modify the schema as needed.
  You can change the name of the schema according to your needs, you can also customize the schema structure in the schema panel. The tool bar allows you to add, remove or move columns in your schema.

- Click **Finish** to close the dialog box.
  The MDM receive connection (**tMDMReceive**) is now ready to be dropped in any of your Jobs.

7.17 Exporting Metadata as context

For every Metadata connection (either File or Database), you can export the connection details as a Context.

- On the last step or second last step of the wizard, click **Export as Context**.
- The Context creation 2-step wizard launches.
- On Step 1, fill out a name for the Context. By default the name of the Metadata entry is proposed.
- Click Next.
- On Step 2, the automatically created context variables are displaying on the three tab table. Check out that the variable values showing on the Values tab are correctly set.
- Click **Finish** to validate the creation.

CHAPTER 8
Managing routines

This chapter defines the routines, along with user scenarios, and explains how to create your own routines or how to customize the system routines. The chapter also gives an overview of the main routines and use cases of them. To have an overview of the most commonly used routines and other use cases, see *System routines* Appendix.

Before starting any data integration processes, you need to be familiar with Talend Open Studio Graphical User Interface (GUI). For more information, see *Talend Open Studio GUI on page 275*.

8.1 What are routines

Routines are fairly complex Java or Perl functions, generally used to factorize code. They therefore optimize data processing and improve Job capacities.

You can also use the **Repository** tree view to store frequently used parts of code or extract parts of existing company functions, by calling them via the routines. This factorization makes it easier to resolve any problems which may arise and allows you to update the code used in multiple jobs quickly and easily.

On top of this, certain system routines adopt the most common Java methods, using the **Talend** syntax. This allows you to escalate Java errors in the studio directly, thereby facilitating the identification and resolution of problems which may arise as your integration processes evolve with **Talend**.

There are two types of routines:

- System routines: a number of system routines are provided. They are classed according to the type of data which they process: numerical, string, date...
- User routines: these are routines which you have created or adapted from existing routines.

You do not need any knowledge of the Java language to create and use **Talend** routines.

All of the routines are stored under **Code** > **Routines** in the **Repository** tree view.

For further information concerning the system routines, see *Accessing the System Routines on page 254*.

For further information about how to create user routines, see *How to create user routines on page 257*.

You can also set up routine dependancies on Jobs. To do so, simply right click a Job on the **Repository** tree view and select **Set up routine dependancies**. In the dialog box which opens, all routines are set by default. You can use the tool bar to remove routines if required.

8.2 Accessing the System Routines

To access the system routines, click on **Code** > **Routines** > **system**. The routines or functions are classed according to their usage.

The **system** folder and its content are read only.

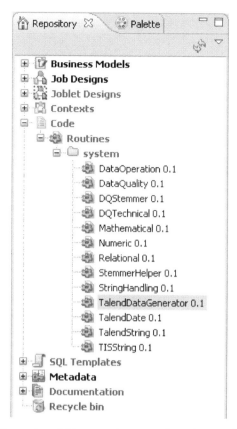

Each class or category in the system folder contains several routines or functions. Double click on the class that you want to open.

All of the routines or functions within a class are composed of some descriptive text, followed by the corresponding code (Java or Perl, according to your project language). In the Routines view, you can use the scrollbar to browse the different routines. Or alternatively:

- Click **Ctrl + O** in the routines view.
  A dialog box displays a list of the different routines in the category.

- Click the routine of interest.
  The view jumps to the section comprising the routine's descriptive text and corresponding code.

 The syntax of routine call statements is case sensitive.

For more information about the most common Java routines, see *System routines* Appendix.

8.3 Customizing the system routines

If the system routines are not adapted to your specific needs, you can customize them by copying and pasting the content in a user routine, then modify the content accordingly.

To customize a system routine

Managing routines
Managing user routines

- First of all, create a user routine by following the steps outlined in the section entitled *How to create user routines on page 257*. The routine opens in the workspace, where you shall find a basic example of a routine.
- Then, under **Code** > **Routines** > **system**, select the class of routines which contains the routine(s) you want to customize.
- Double click on the class which contains the relevant routine to open it in the workspace.
- Use the **Outline** panel on the bottom left of the studio to locate the routine from which you want to copy all or part of the content

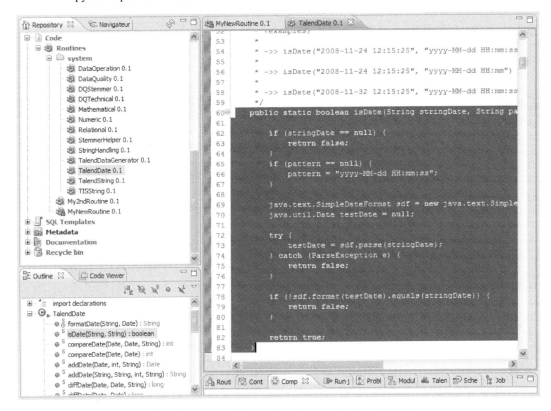

- In the workspace, select all or part of the code and copy it using **Ctrl+C**
- Click on the tab to access your user routine and paste the code by pressing **Ctrl+V**.
- Modify the code as required and press **Ctrl+S** to save it.

We advise you to use the descriptive text (in blue) to detail the input and output parameters. This will make your routines easier to maintain and reuse.

8.4 Managing user routines

Talend Open Studio allows you to create user routines, to modify them or to modify system routines, in order to fill your specific needs.

8.4.1 How to create user routines

You can create your own routines according to your particular factorization needs. Like the system routines, the user routines are stored in the **Repository** tree view under **Code** > **Routines**. You can add folders to help organize your routines and call them easily in any of your Jobs.

To create a new user routine, complete the following:

- In the **Repository** tree view, expand **Code** to display the **Routines** folder.

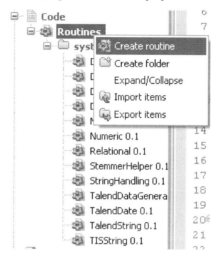

- Right-click on **Routines** and select **Create routine**.

- The **[New routine]** dialog box opens. Enter the information required to create the routine, ie., its name, description...

- Click **Finish** to proceed to the next step.

Managing routines
Managing user routines

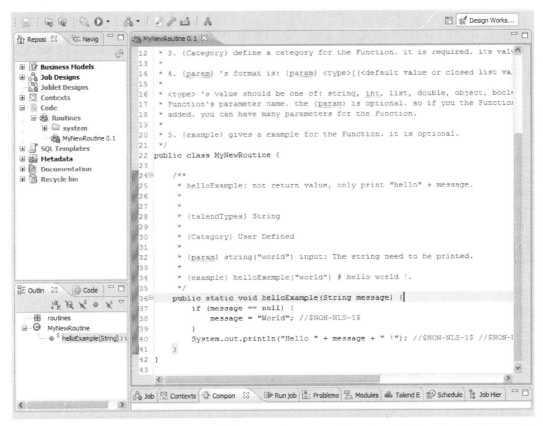

The newly created routine appears in the **Repository** tree view, directly below the **Routines** node. The routine editor opens to reveal a model routine which contains a simple example, by default, comprising descriptive text in blue, followed by the corresponding code.

We advise you to add a very detailed description of the routine. The description should generally include the input and output parameters you would expect to use in the routine, as well as the results returned along with an example. This information tends to be useful for collaborative work and the maintenance of the routines.

The following example of code is provided by default:
```
public static void helloExample(String message) {
      if (message == null) {
         message = "World"; //$NON-NLS-1$
      }
      System.out.println("Hello " + message + " !");
```

- Modify or replace the model with your own code and press **Ctrl+S** to save the routine. Otherwise, the routine is saved automatically when you close it.

You can copy all or part of a system routine or class and use it in a user routine by using the **Ctrl+C** and **Ctrl+V** commands, then adapt the code according to your needs. For further information about how to customize routines, see*Customizing the system routines on page 255*.

258   Talend Open Studio

8.4.2 How to edit user routines

You can modify the user routines whenever you like.

 The **system** folder and all of the routines held within are read only.

To edit your user routines:

- Right click on the routine you want to edit and select **Edit Routine**.
- The routine opens in the workspace, where you can modify it.
- Once you have adapted the routine to suit your needs, press **Ctrl+S** to save it.

If you want to reuse a system routine for your own specific needs, please see the section entitled *Customizing the system routines*.

8.4.3 How to edit user routine libraries

You can edit the library of any of the user routines by importing external .jar files for the selected routine. These external library files will be listed, like modules, in the **Modules** view in your current Studio. For more information on the **Modules** view, see *How to install external modules on page 108*.

The .jar file of the imported library will be also listed in the library file of your current Studio.

To edit a user routine library, complete the following:

- In the **Repository** tree view, expand **Code** > **Routines**.
- Right-click the user routine you want to edit its library and then select **Edit Routine Library**.
  The **[Import External Library]** dialog box displays.

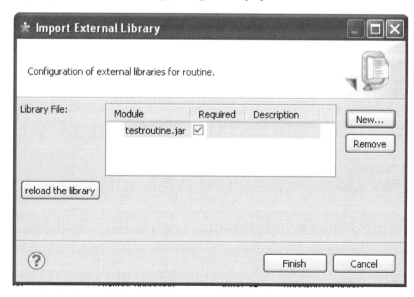

- Click **New** to open a new dialog box where you can import the external library.

You can delete any of the already imported routine files if you select the file in the **Library File** list and click the **Remove** button.

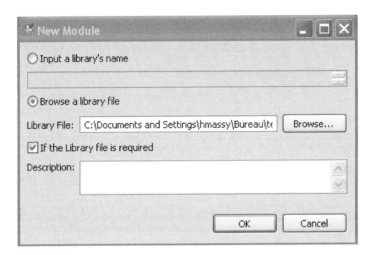

- Enter the name of the library file in the **Input a library's name** field followed by the file format (.jar), or

- Select the **Browse a library file** option and click browse to set the file path in the corresponding field.

- If required, enter a description in the **Description** field and then click **OK** to confirm your changes.
  The imported library file is listed in the **Library File** list in the **[Import External Library]** dialog box.

- Click **Finish** to close the dialog box.
  The library file is imported into the library folder of your current Studio and also listed in the **Module** view of the same Studio.
  For more information about the **Modules** view, see *How to install external modules on page 108*.

8.5 Calling a routine from a Job

Pre-requisite: You must have at least one Job created, in order to run a routine. For further information regarding how to create a job, see *How to create a Job on page 58* of the Talend Open Studio User Guide.

You can call any of your user and system routines from your Job components in order to run them at the same time as your Job.

To access all the routines saved in the **Routines** folder in the **Repository** tree view, press **Ctrl + Espace** in any of the fields in the **Basic settings** view of any of the **Talend** components used in your Job and select the one you want to run.

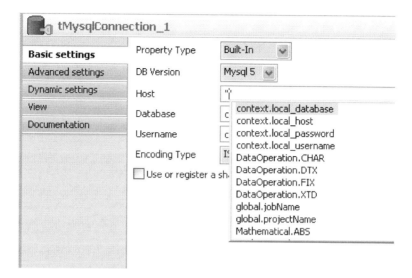

Alternatively, you can call any of these routines by indicating the relevant class name and the name of the routine, followed by the expected settings, in any of the **Basic settings** fields in the following way:

`<ClassName>.<RoutineName>.`

8.6 Use case: Creating a file for the current date

This scenario describes how to use a routine. The Job uses just one component, which calls a system routine.

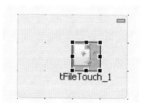

- In the **Palette**, click on **File** > **Management**, then drop a **tFileTouch** component onto the workspace. This component allows you to create an empty file.

- Double click on the component to open its **Basic settings** view in the **Component** tab.

- In the **FileName** field, enter the path to access your file, or click on **[...]** and browse the directory to locate the file.

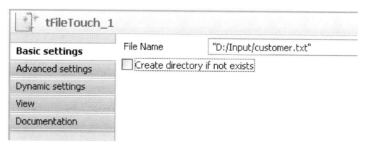

- Close the double inverted commas around your file extension as follows: "D:/Input/customer".txt.
- Add the plus symbol (+) between the closing inverted commas and the file extension.
- Press **Ctrl+espace** to open a list of all of the routines.
- In the auto-completion list which appears, select *TalendDate.getDate* to use the **Talend** routine which allows you to obtain the current date.
- Modify the format of the date provided by default, if required.
- Enter the plus symbol (+) next to the *getDate* variable to complete the routine call.
- Place double inverted commas around the file extension.

 If you are working on windows, the ":" between the hours and minutes and between the minutes and seconds must be removed.

- Press **F6** to run the Job.
- The **FileTouch** component creates an empty file with the days date, retrieved upon execution of the *GetDate* routine called.

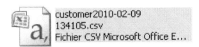

CHAPTER 9
Using SQL templates

SQL templates are groups of pre-defined query arguments that run in the ELT mode. This chapter explains the ELT mode, defines the SQL templates and provides user scenarios to explain how to use the SQL templates or how to create your own ones.

Before starting any data integration processes, you need to be familiar with Talend Open Studio Graphical User Interface (GUI). For more information, see *Talend Open Studio GUI on page 275*.

9.1 What is ELT

Extract, Load and Transform (ELT) is a data manipulation process in database usage, especially in data warehousing. Different from the traditional ETL (Extract, Transform, Load) mode, in ELT, data is extracted, loaded into the database and then is transformed where it sits in the database, prior to use. This data is migrated in bulk according to the data set and the transformation process occurs after the data has been loaded into the targeted DBMS in its raw format. This way, less stress is placed on the network and larger throughput is gained.

However, the ELT mode is certainly not optimal for all situations, for example,

- As SQL is less powerful than Java, the scope of available data transformations is limited.
- ELT requires users that have high proficiency in SQL tuning and DBMS tuning.
- Using ELT with Talend Open Studio, you cannot pass or reject one single row of data as you can do in ETL. For more information about row rejection, see section *Row connection on page 82*.

Based on the advantages and disadvantages of ELT, the SQL templates are designed as the ELT facilitation requires.

9.2 Introducing Talend SQL templates

SQL is a standardized query language used to access and manage information in databases. Its scope includes data query and update, schema creation and modification, and data access control. Talend Open Studio provides a range of SQL templates to simplify the most common tasks. It also comprises a SQL editor which allows you to customize or design your own SQL templates to meet less common requirements.

These SQL templates are used with the components from the **Talend** ELT component family including **tELT**, **tELTFilterColumns**, **tELTCommit**, **tELTFilterRows**, **tELTRollback** and **tELTAggregate**. These components execute the selected SQL statements. Using the UNION, EXCEPT and INTERSECT operators, you can modify data directly on the DBMS without using the system memory.

Moreover, with the help of these SQL templates, you can optimize the efficiency of your database management system by storing and retrieving your data according to the structural requirements.

Talend Open Studio provides the following types of SQL templates under the **SQL templates** node in the **Repository** tree view:

- System SQL templates: They are classified according to the type of database for which they are tailored.
- User-defined SQL templates: these are templates which you have created or adapted from existing templates.

More detailed information about the SQL templates is presented in the below sections.

For further information concerning the components from the ELT component family, see *ELT components on page 961* in the *Talend Open Studio Components Reference Guide*.

 As most of the SQL templates are tailored for specific databases, if you change database in your system, it is inevitable to switch to or develop new templates for the new database.

9.3 Managing Talend SQL templates

Talend Open Studio enables you via the **SQL Templates** folder in the **Repository** tree view to use system or user-defined SQL templates in the Jobs you create in the Studio using the ELT components.

The below sections show you how to manage these two types of SQL templates.

9.3.1 Types of system SQL templates

This section gives detail information related to the different types of the pre-defined SQL templates.

Even though the statements of each group of templates vary from database to database, according to the operations they are intended to accomplish, they are also grouped on the basis of their types in each folder.

The below table provides these types and their related information.

Name	Function	Associated components	Required component parameters
Aggregate	Realizes aggregation (sum, average, count, etc.) over a set of data.	tELTAggregate	Database name Source table name Target table name
Commit	Sends a Commit instruction to RDBMS	tELT tELTAggregate tELTCommit tELTFilterColumns tELTFilterRows tELTRollback	Null
Rollback	Sends a Rollback instruction to RDBMS.	tELT tELTAggregate tELTCommit tELTFilterColumns tELTFilterRow tELTRollback	Null
DropSourceTable	Removes a source table.	tELT tELTAggregate tELTFilterColumns tELTRow	Table name (when use tELT) Source table name
DropTargetTable	Removes a target table	tELTAggregate tELTFilterColumns tELTRow	Target table name
FilterColumns	Selects and extracts a set of data from given columns in RDBMS.	tELTAggregate tELTFilterColumns tELTRows	Target table name (and schema) Source table name (and schema)
FilterRow	Selects and extracts a set of data from given rows in RDBMS.	tELTFilterRow	Target table name (and schema) Source table name (and schema) Conditions

9.3.2 How to access a system SQL template

To access a system SQL template, expand the **SQL Templates** node in the **Repository** tree view.

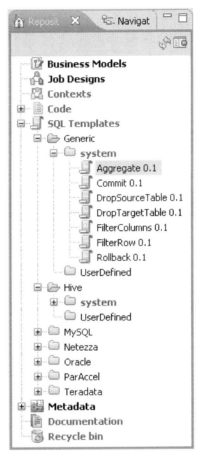

Each folder contains **system** sub-folders containing pre-defined SQL statements, as well as a **UserDefined** folder in which you can store SQL statements that you have created or customized.

Each system folder contains several types of SQL templates, each designed to accomplish a dedicated task.

Apart from the **Generic** folder, the SQL templates are grouped into different folders according to the type of database for which they are to be used. The templates in the **Generic** folder are standard, for use in any database. You can use these as as a basis from which you can develop more specific SQL templates than those defined in Talend Open Studio.

 The **system** folders and their content are read only.

From the **Repository** tree view, proceed as follows to open an SQL template:

- In the **Repository** tree view, expand **SQL Templates** and browse to the template you want to open.

- Double click the class that you want to open, for example, *aggregate* in the **Generic** folder. The *aggregate* template view displays in the workspace.

Using SQL templates
Managing Talend SQL templates

```
1  <%
2      EXTRACT(__GROUPBY__);
3      EXTRACT(__OPERATION__);
4      String operation = "";
5      boolean flag=false;
6      for(int i=0; i < __OPERATION_INPUT_COLUMN__.length; i++){
7        if(flag){
8          operation += ",";
9        }else{
10         flag=true;
11       }
12       operation += (__OPERATION_FUNCTION__[i] + "(" + __OPERATION_INPU
13     }
14
15  %>
16
17  INSERT INTO <%=__TABLE_NAME_TARGET__%> (<%=StringUtils.list(__OPERATI
18  SELECT <%= operation %>, <%= StringUtils.list(__GROUPBY_INPUT_COLUMN_
19  GROUP BY <%=StringUtils.list(__GROUPBY_INPUT_COLUMN__, ",", "", "") %
```

You can read the predefined *aggregate* statements in the template view. The parameters, such as TABLE_NAME_TARGET, operation, are to be defined when you design related Jobs. Then the parameters can be easily set in the associated components, as mentioned in the previous section.

- Everytime you click or open an SQL template, its corresponding property view displays at the bottom of the studio. Click the *aggregate* template, for example, to view its properties as presented below:

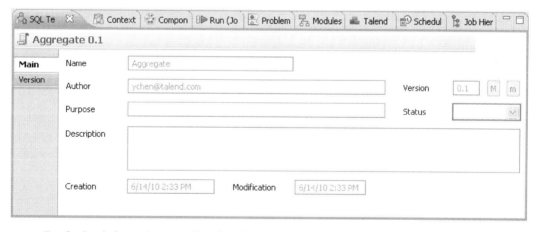

For further information regarding the different types of SQL templates, see *Types of system SQL templates on page 265*

For further information about how to use the SQL templates with the associated components, see *A use case of system SQL Templates on page 269*.

9.3.3 How to create user-defined SQL templates

As the transformation you need to accomplish in ELT may exceed the scope of what the given SQL templates can achieve, **Talend Open Studio** allows you to develop your own SQL templates according to some writing rules. These SQL templates are stored in the **User-defined** folders grouped according to the database type in which they will be used.

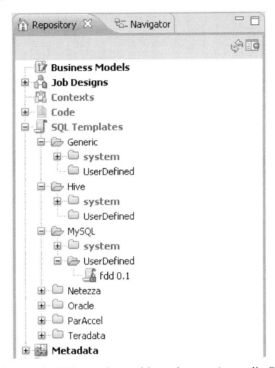

For more information on the SQL template writing rules, see Appendix *SQL template writing rules on page 299*.

To create a user-defined SQL template:

- In the **Repository** tree view, expand **SQL Templates** and then the category you want to create the SQL template in.

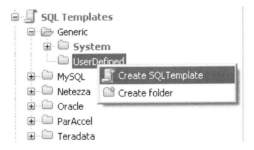

- Right-click **UserDefined** and select **Create SQL Template** to open the **[SQL Templates]** wizard.

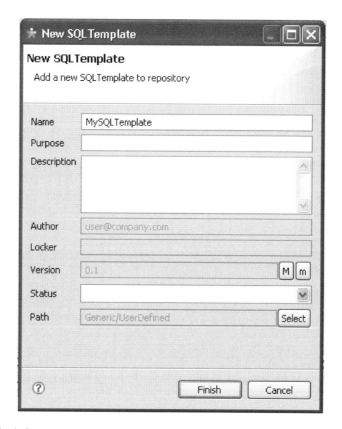

- Enter the information required to create the template and click **Finish** to close the wizard. The name of the newly created template appears under **UserDefined** in the **Repository** tree view. Also, an SQL template editor opens on the design workspace, where you can enter the code for the newly created template.

For further information about how to create a user-defined SQL template and how to use it in a job, see *Scenario: Iterating on DB tables and deleting their content using a user-defined SQL template* in the Talend Open Studio Components Reference Guide.

9.3.4 A use case of system SQL Templates

As there are many common, standardized SQL statements, Talend Open Studio allows you to benefit from various system SQL templates.

This section presents you with a use case that takes you through the steps of using Mysql system templates in a Job that:

- opens a connection to a Mysql database.
- collects data grouped by specific value(s) from a database table and writes aggregated data in a target database table.
- deletes the source table where the aggregated data comes from.
- reads the target database table and lists the Job execution result.

To connect to the database and aggregate the database table columns:

Using SQL templates
Managing Talend SQL templates

- Drop the following components from the **Palette** onto the design workspace: **tMysqlconnection**, **tELTAggregae**, **tELTCommit**, and **tMysqlInput, tLogrow**.
- Right-click **tMysqlconnection** and from the contextual menu, select **Trigger > OnComponentOk** to connect **tMysqlconnection** to **tELTAggregate**.
- Connect **tELTAggregate**, **tELTCommit** and **tMysqlInput** using **OnComponentOk** links.
- Connect **tMysqlInput** to **tLogRow** using an **Main > Row** link.

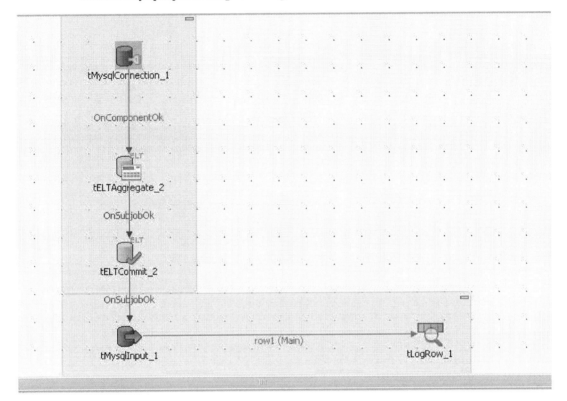

- In the design workspace, select **tMysqlConnection** and click the **Component** tab to define the component basic settings.
- In the **Basic settings** view, set the database connection details manually.

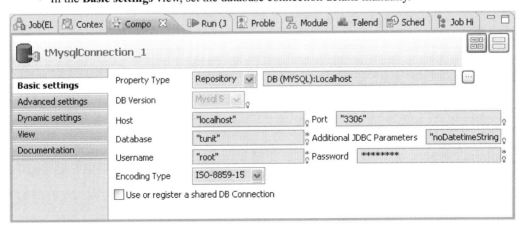

270   Talend Open Studio

Using SQL templates
Managing Talend SQL templates

- In the design workspace, select **tELTAggregate** and click the **Component** tab to define its basic settings.

- On the **Database type** list, select the relevant database.

- On the **Component list**, select the relevant database connection component if more than one connection is used.

- Enter the names for the database, source table, and target table in the corresponding fields and click the three-dot button next to **Edit schema** to define the data structure in the source and target tables.

The source table schema consists of three columns: *First_Name, Last_Name* and *Country*. The target table schema consists of two columns: *country* and *total*. In this example, we want to group citizens by their nationalities and count citizen number in each country. To do that, we define the **Operations** and **Group by** parameters accordingly.

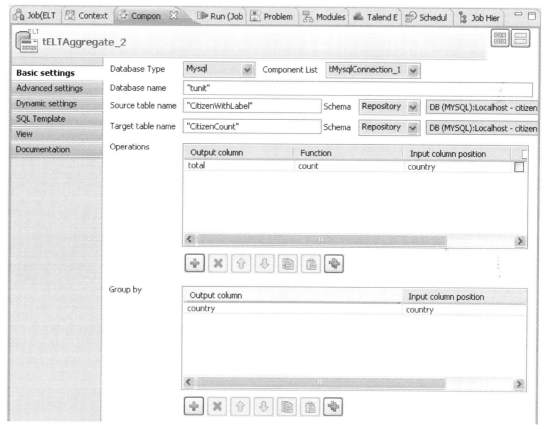

- In the **Operations** table, click the plus button to add one or more lines and then click in the **Output column** line to select the output column that will hold the counted data.

- Click in the **Function** line and select the operation to be carried on.

- In the **Group by** table, click the plus button to add one or more lines and then click in the **Output column** line to select the output column that will hold the aggregated data.

- Click the **SQL template** tab to open the corresponding view.

Talend Open Studio 271

Using SQL templates
Managing Talend SQL templates

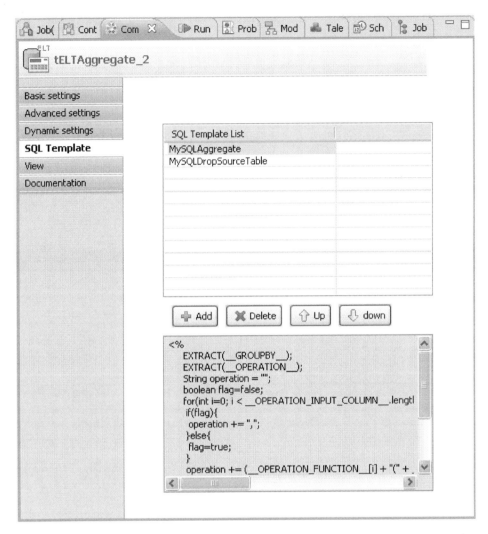

- Click the plus button twice under the **SQL template list** table to add two SQL templates.

- Click on the first SQL template row and select the *MySQLAggregate* template from the drop-down list. This template generates codes to aggregate data according to the configuration in the **Basic settings** view.

- Do the same to select the *MySQLDropSourceTable* template for the second SQL template row. This template generates codes to delete the source table where the data to be aggregated comes from.

 To add new SQL templates to an ELT component for execution, you can simply drop the templates of your choice either onto the component in the design workspace, or onto the component's **SQL template list** table.

The templates set up in the SQL template list table have priority over the parameters set in the Basic settings view and are executed in a top-down order. So in this use case, if you only select MySQLDropSourceTable from the list, the source table will be deleted prior to aggregation, meaning that nothing will be aggregated.

272 Talend Open Studio

- In the design workspace, select **tELTCommit** and click the **Component** tab to define its basic settings.
- On the **Database type** list, select the relevant database.
- On the **Component list**, select the relevant database connection component if more than one connection is used.
- In the design workspace, select **tMysqlInput**, and click the **Componnent** tab to define its basic settings.

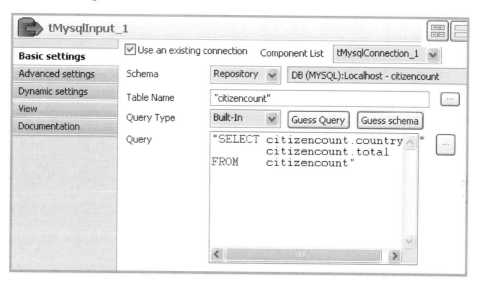

- Select the **Use an existing connection** check box to use the database connection that you have defined on the **tMysqlConnection** component.
- To define the schema, select **Repository** and then click the three-dot button to choose the database table whose schema is used. In this example, the target table holding the aggregated data is selected.
- In the **Table Name** field, type in the name of the table you want to query. In this example, the table is the one holding the aggregated data.
- In the **Query** area, enter the query statement to select the columns to be displayed.
- Save your Job and press **F6** to execute it.
  The source table is deleted.

Using SQL templates
Managing Talend SQL templates

```
Starting job ELTYudong at 02:43 24/05/2010.

[statistics] connecting to socket on port 3918
[statistics] connected
.-------+-----.
|   tLogRow_1  |
|=------+----=|
|country|total|
|=------+----=|
|Canada |2030 |
|China  |2012 |
|France |2009 |
|Japan  |1925 |
|USA    |2024 |
'-------+-----'

[statistics] disconnected
Job ELTYudong ended at 02:43 24/05/2010. [exit code=0]
```

A two-column table *citizencount* is created in the database. It groups citizens according to their nationalities and gives their total count in each country.

APPENDIX A
Talend Open Studio GUI

This appendix describes the Graphical User Interfaces (GUI) of Talend Open Studio.

Main window

A.1 Main window

Talend Open Studio main window is the interface from which you manage all types of data integration processes.

The Talend Open Studio multi-panel window is divided into:

- menu bar,
- toolbar,
- **Repository** tree view,
- design workspace,
- Palette,
- various configuration views in a tab system, for any of the elements in the data integration Job designed in the workspace,
- **Outline view** and **Code Viewer**.

The figure below illustrates Talend Open Studio main window and its panels and views.

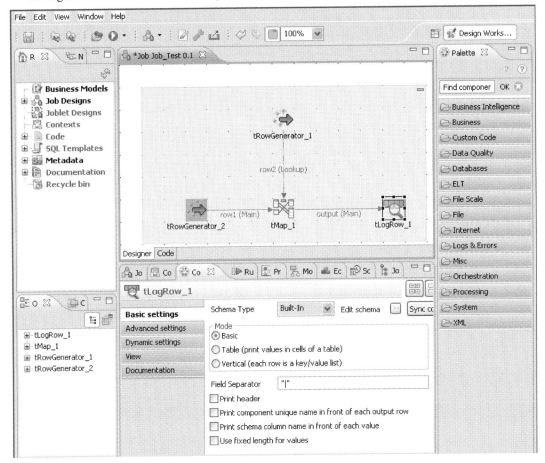

The various panels and their respective features are detailed hereafter.

A.2 Menu bar and Toolbar

At the top of the Talend Open Studio main window, various menus and a quick access toolbar gather **Talend** commonly features along with some Eclipse functions.

A.2.1 Menu bar of Talend Open Studio

Talend Open Studio's menus include:

- some standard functions, such as **Save**, **Print**, **Exit**, which are to be used at the application level.
- some Eclipse native features to be used mainly at the design workspace level as well as specific Talend Open Studio functions.

The table below describes menus and menu items available to you on the menu bar of Talend Open Studio.

 The menus on the menu bar differ slightly according to what you are working with: a Business Model or a Job.

Menu	Menu item	Description
File	**Close**	Closes the current open view on the Studio design workspace.
	Close All	Closes all open views on the Studio design workspace.
	Save	Saves any changes done in the current open view.
	Save as	Saves any changes done without changing the current open view. For more information, see *Saving a Business Model on page 54*
	Save All	Saves any changes done in all open views.
	Print	.Unavailable option.
	Switch project	Closes the current session and launches another one to enable you to open a different project in the Studio.
	Edit project properties	Opens a dialog box where you can customize the settings of the current project. For more information, see *Customizing project settings on page 31*
	Import	Opens a wizard that helps you to import different types of resources (files, items, preferences, XML catalogs, etc.) from different sources.
	Export	Opens a wizard that helps you to export different types of resources (files, items, preferences, breakpoints, XML catalogs, etc.) to different destinations.
	Exit	Closes The Studio main window.
	Open File	Opens a file from within the Studio.

Menu bar and Toolbar

Menu	Menu item	Description
Edit	Undo Move Node	Undoes the last action done in the Studio design workspace.
	Redo	Redoes the last action done in the Studio design workspace.
	Cut	Cuts selected object in the Studio design workspace.
	Copy	Copies the selected object in the Studio design workspace.
	Paste	Pastes the previously copied object in the Studio design workspace.
	Delete	Deletes the selected object in the Studio design workspace.
	Select All	Selects all components present in the Studio design workspace.
View	Zoom In	Obtains a larger image of the open Job.
	Zoom Out	Obtains a smaller image of the open Job.
	Grid	Displays grid in the design workspace. All items in the open Job are snapped to it.
	Snap to Geometry	Enables the Snap to Geometry feature.
Window	Perspective	Opens different perspectives corresponding to the different items in the list.
	Show View...	Opens the [Show View] dialog box which enables you to display different views on the Studio.
	Maximize Active View or Editor...	Maximizes the current perspective.
	Preferences	Opens the [Preferences] dialog box which enables you to set your preferences. For more information about preferences, see *Setting Talend Open Studio preferences on page 21*
Help	Welcome	Opens a welcoming page which has links to Talend Open Studio documentation and **Talend** practical sites.
	Help Contents	Opens the Eclipse help system documentation.
	About Talend Open Studio	Displays: -the software version you are using -detailed information on your software configuration that may be useful if there is a problem -detailed information about plug-in(s) -detailed information about Talend Open Studio features.
	Export logs	Opens a wizard that helps you to export all logs generated in the Studio and system configuration information to an archived file.
	Software Updates	**Find and Install...**: Opens the [Install/Update] wizard that helps searching for updates for the currently installed features, or searching for new features to install.
		Manage Configuration...: Opens the [Product Configuration] dialog box where you can manage Talend Open Studio configuration.

A.2.2 Toolbar of Talend Open Studio

The toolbar contains icons that provide you with quick access to the commonly used operations you can perform from Talend Open Studio main window.

 The icons on the toolbar differ slightly according to what you are working with: a Business Model or a Job.

The table below describes the toolbar icons and their functions.

Name	Icon	Description
Save		Saves current job design.
Save as		Saves as another new Job.
Export items		Exports repository items to an archive file, for deploying outside Talend Open Studio. Instead if you intend to import the exported element into a newer version of Talend Open Studio or of another workstation, make sure the source files are included in the archive.
Import items		Imports repository items from an archive file into your current Talend Open Studio. For more information regarding the import/export items feature, see *How to import items on page 127*.
Find a specific job		Displays the relevant dialog box that enables you to open any Job listed in the **Repository** tree view.
Run job		Executes the Job currently shown on the design space. For more information about job execution, see *How to run a Job on page 71*.
Create		Launches the relevant creation wizard. Through this menu, you can create any repository item including Business models, Job Designs, contexts, routines and metadata entries.
Project settings		Launches the **[Project Settings]** dialog box. From this dialog box, you can add a description to the current Project and customize the **Palette** display. For more information., see *Customizing project settings on page 31*.
Detect and update all jobs		Searches for all updates available for your Jobs.
Export Talend projects		Launches the **[Export Talend projects]** wizard. For more information about project export, see *How to export a project on page 19*

A.3 Repository tree view

The **Repository** tree view gathers all the technical items that can be used either to describe business models or to design Jobs. It gives access to any item including **Business Models**, **JobDesigns**, as well as reusable routines or documentation.

The Repository centralizes and stores all necessary elements for any job design and business modeling contained in a project.

The figure below illustrates the elements stored in the Repository.

Repository tree view

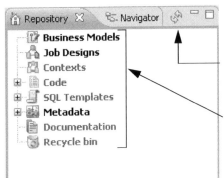

The refresh button allows you to update the tree view with the last changes made.

The Repository tree view stores all your data (BMs, JDs, SQL templates) and metadata (Routines, DB/File connections, any meaningful Documentation and so on).

The table below describes the nodes in the **Repository** tree view.

Node	Description
Business Models	Under the **Business Models** folder, are grouped all business models of the project. Double-click the name of the model to open it on the design workspace. For more information, see *Designing a Business Model on page 43*.
Job Designs	The **Job Designs** folder shows the tree view of the designed Jobs for the current project. Double-click the name of the Job to open it on the design workspace. For more information, see *Designing a data integration Job on page 57*.
Contexts	The **Context** folder groups files holding the contextual variables that you want to reuse in various Jobs, such as filepaths or DB connection details. For more information, see *How to centralize contexts and variables on page 89*.
Code	The **Code** folder is a library that groups the routines available for this project and other pieces of code that could be reused in the project. Click the relevant tree entry to expand the appropriate code piece. For more information, see *Designing a data integration Job on page 57*.
SQL Templates	The **SQL Templates** folder groups all system SQL templates and gives the possibility to create user-defined SQL templates. For more information, see *How to use the SQL Templates on page 101*.
Metadata	The **Metadata** folder bundles files holding redundant information you want to reuse in various Jobs, such as schemas and property data. For more information, see *Managing Metadata on page 181*.
Documentation	The **Documentation** folder gathers all types of documents, of any format. This could be, for example, specification documents or a description of technical format of a file. Double-click to open the document in the relevant application. For more information, see *How to generate HTML documentation on page 150*.

Node	Description
Recycle bin	The **Recycle bin** groups all elements deleted from any folder in the **Repository** tree view.
	💡 The deleted elements are still present on your file system, in the recycle bin, until you right-click the recycle bin icon and select **Empty Recycle bin**
	💡 Expand the recycle bin to view any folders, subfolders or elements held within. You can action an element directly from the recycle bin, restore it or delete it forever by clicking right and selecting the desired action from the list.

A.4 Design workspace

The design workspace is Talend Open Studio's flowcharting editor, where both business models and job designs can be laid out.

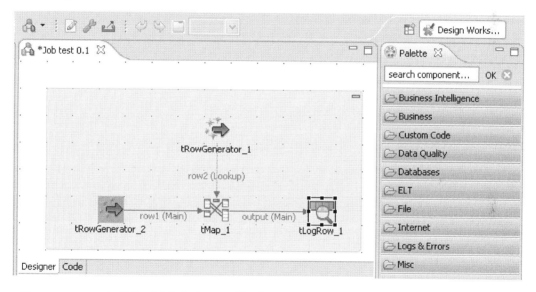

You can open and edit both job designs and business models, in this single graphical editor. Active designs display in a easily accessible tab system.

A **Palette** is docked at the top of the design workspace to help you draw the model corresponding to your workflow needs.

A.5 Palette

From the **Palette**, depending on whether you are designing a Job or modeling a Business Model, you can drop technical components or shapes, branches and notes to the design workspace. You can define and format them using the various tools offered in the **Business Model** view for the Business Models and in the **Component** view for the Job.

Related topics:

- *Designing a Business Model on page 43.*
- *Designing a data integration Job on page 57.*
- *How to change the Palette layout and settings on page 77.*

A.6 Configuration tabs

The configuration tabs are located in the lower half of the design workspace. Each tab opens a view that displays the properties of the selected element in the design workspace. These properties can be edited to change or set the parameters related to a particular component or to the Job as a whole.

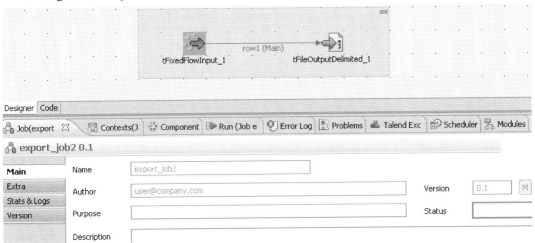

The **Component**, **Run Jobs**, **Problems** and **Error Log** views gather all information relative to the graphical elements selected in the design workspace or the actual execution of the open Job.

The **Modules** and **Scheduler** tabs are located in the same tab system as the **Component**, **Logs** and **Run Job** tabs. Both views are independent from the active or inactive Jobs open on the design workspace.

 You can show more tabs in this tab system and directly open the corresponding view if you select **Window > Show view** and then, in the open dialog box, expand any node and select the element you want to display.

The sections below describe the view of each of the configuration tabs.

View	Description
Component	This view details the parameters specific to each component of the Palette. To build a Job that will function, you are required to fill out the necessary fields of this **Component** view for each component forming your Job. For more information about the **Component** view, see *How to define component properties on page 65*.
Run Job	This view obviously shows the current job execution. It becomes a log console at the end of an execution. For details about job execution, see *How to run a Job on page 71*.

Configuration tabs

View	Description
Error Log	This view is mainly used for job execution errors. It shows the history of warnings or errors occurring during job executions. 💡 The log tab has also an informative function for Perl/Java component operating progress, for example. **Error Log** tab is hidden by default. As for any other view, go to **Window > Show views**, then expand **PDE Runtime** node and select **Error Log** to display it on the tab system.
Modules	This view shows if a module is necessary and required for the use of a referenced component. Checking the **Modules** view helps to verify what modules you have or should have to run smoothly your Jobs. For more information, see *How to install external modules on page 108*.
Scheduler	This view enables you to schedule a task that will launch periodically the Job you select via the crontab program. For more information, see *How to launch a Job periodically on page 110*.
Job view	The **Job** view displays various information related to the open Job on the design workspace. This view has the following tabs:

	Main tab	This tab displays basic information about the Job opened on the design workspace, i.e. its name, author, version number, etc. The information is read-only. To edit it you have to close your Job, right-click its label on the **Repository** tree view and click **Edit properties** on the drop-down list
	Extra tab	This tab displays extra parameters including multi thread and implicit context loading features. For more information, see *How to use the features in the Extra tab on page 121*.
	Stats/Log tab	This tab allows you to enable/disable the statistics and logs for the whole Job. You can already enable these features for every single component of your Job by simply using and setting the relevant components: **tFlowMeterCatcher**, **tStatCatcher**, **tLogCatcher**. For more information about these components, see *tFlowMeterCatcher*, *tLogCatcher* and *tStatCatcher* in the Talend Open Studio Components Reference Guide. In addition, you can now set these features for the whole active Job (i.e. all components of your Job) in one go, without using the Catcher components mentioned above. This way, all components get tracked and logged in the File or Database table according to your setting. You can also set the current setting as preference by clicking the relevant button. For more details about the Stats & Logs automation, see *How to automate the use of statistics & logs on page 120*.
	Version tab	This tab displays the different versions of the Job opened on the design workspace and their creation and modification dates.

Talend Exchange	This view enables you to access a list of all community components in **Talend Exchange** that are compatible with your current version of Talend Open Studio and are not yet installed in your **Palette**. You can then download these components to use them later in the job designs you carry out in the Studio. For more information, see *How to download external community components on page 106*.

View	Description
Problems	This view displays the messages linked to the icons docked at a components in case of problem, for example when part of its setting is missing. Three types of icons/messages exist: **Error**, **Warning** and **Infos**. For more information, see *Warnings and error icons on components on page 115*.
Job Hierarchy	This view displays a tree folder showing the child Job(s) of the parent Job selected. To show this view, right-click the parent Job in the **Repository** tree view and select **Open Job Hierarchy** on the drop-down list. You can also show this view in the **Window > Show view...** combination where you can select **Talend > Job Hierarchy**. You can see **Job Hierarchy** only if you create a parent Job and one or more child Job(s) via the **tRunJob** component. For more information about **tRunJob**, see *tRunJob* in the Talend Open Studio Components Reference Guide.
Properties	When inserting a shape in the design workspace, the **Properties** view offers a range of formatting tools to help you customizing your business model and improve its readability.

A.7 Outline and code summary panel

This panel is located below the **Repository** tree view. It displays detailed information about the open Job or Business Model in the design workspace.

The Information panel is composed of two tabs, **Outline** and **Code Viewer**, which provide information regarding the displayed diagram (either Job or Business Model) and also the generated code.

For more information, see *How to display the code or the outline of your Job on page 117*.

A.8 Shortcuts and aliases

Below is a table gathering all keyboard shortcuts currently in use:

Shortcut	Operation	Context
F2	Shows **Component** settings view	Global application
F4	Shows **Run Job** view	Global application
F6	Runs current Job or shows **Run Job** view if no Job is open.	Global application
Ctrl + F2	Shows **Module** view	Global application
Ctrl + F3	Shows **Problems** view	Global application
Ctrl + H	Shows the **Designer** view of the current Job	Global application
Ctrl + G	Shows the **Code** view of the current Job	Global application
Ctrl + R	Restores the initial **Repository** view	From **Repository** view
Ctrl + Shift + F3	Synchronizes components perljet templates and associated java classes	Global application
Ctrl + Shift + J	Opens a Job	Global application (In Windows)
F7	Switches to **Debug** mode	From **Run Job** view
F5	Refreshes the **Repository** view	From **Repository** view

Shortcut	Operation	Context
F8	Kills current Job	From **Run Job** view
F5	Refreshes **Modules** install status	From **Modules** view
Ctrl+L	Execute SQL queries	**Talend** commands (in Windows)
Ctrl+Space bar	Access global and user-defined variables. It can be error messages or line number for example, depending on the component selected.	From any component field in **Job** or **Component** views

Shortcuts and aliases

APPENDIX B
Theory into practice: Job example

This chapter aims at users of Talend Open Studio who seek a real-life use case to help them take full control over the product. This chapter comes as a complement of the Talend Open Studio Components Reference Guide.

B.1 Introducing the scenario

To illustrate the way Talend Open Studio operates, find below a real-life example scenario. In this scenario, we will load a MySQL table with a file, that gets transformed on the fly. Then in a further step, we will select the data to be loaded using a dynamic filter.

Before actually starting the Job, let's inspect the input data and the expected output data.

 This scenario is provided in Java, but the same Job can be carried out in a Perl project, with significant differences in the way transformations are phrased.

B.1.1 Input data

Our input file, the data of which will be loaded into the database table, lists clients from all over the State of California.

The file structure usually called **Schema** in Talend Open Studio includes the following columns:

- First name
- Last name
- Address
- City

B.1.2 Output data

We want to load into the database, California clients living in a couple of Counties only: Orange and Los Angeles counties.

The table structure is slightly different, therefore the data expected to be loaded into the DB table should have the following structure:

- `Key` (key, Type: Integer)
- `Name` (Type: String, max. length: 40)
- `Address` (Type: String, max.length: 40)
- `County` (Type: String, max. length:40)

In order to load this table, we will need to use the following mapping process:

The `Key` column is fed with an auto-incremented integer.

The `Name` column is filled out with a concatenation of first and last names.

The `Address` column data comes from the equivalent Address column of the input file, but supports a upper-case transformation before the loading.

The `County` column is fed with the name of the County where the city is located using a reference file which will help filtering Orange and Los Angeles counties' cities.

B.1.3 Reference data

As only Orange and Los Angeles counties data should be loaded into the database, we need to map cities of California with their respective county, in order to filter only Orange and Los Angeles ones.

To do so, we will use a reference file, listing cities that are located in Orange and Los Angeles counties such as:

City	County
Agoura Hills	Los Angeles
Alhambra	Los Angeles
Aliso Viejo	Orange
Anaheim	Orange
Arcadia	Los Angeles

The reference file in this Job is named *LosAngelesandOrangeCounties.txt*.

B.2 Translating the scenario into a Job

In order to implement this scenario, let's break down the Job into four steps.

- Step 1: Creation of the Job, configuration of the input file parameters, and reading of the input file,
- Step 2: Mapping of data and transformations,
- Step 3: Definition of the reference file parameters, relevant mapping using the **tMap** component, and selection of inner join mode,
- Step 4: Redirection of the output into a MySQL table.

B.2.1 Step 1: Job creation, input definition, file reading

After launching Talend Open Studio, you need to create a connection to the local repository. To do so, click "..." to the right of **Connection**.

In the **User Email** field, type in your email (!) then click **OK**.

Then click the **Demo** button and select Java to import the DEMO JAVA project jobs. This operation will need a while to complete but will give you access to dozen of job examples, illustrating the main functionalities of Talend Open Studio.

Then click **OK** to launch the Studio. And click the link **Start using** Talend Open Studio **now!** to access directly the main window.

The window is divided into several areas:

- To the left: the **Repository** tree view that holds Jobs, Business Models, Metadata, shared Code, Documentation and so on.
- In the center: the **Editor** (main Design area)
- At the bottom: **Component** and **Job** tabs

- To the right: the **Palette** of business or technical components depending on the software tool you are using within Talend Open Studio.

To the left of the Studio, the **Repository** tree view that gives an access to:

- The **Business Modeler**: For more information, see *Modeling a Business Model on page 46*.
- The **Job Designer**: For details about this part, see *Getting started with a basic job design on page 58*.
- The **Metadata Manager**: For details about this part, see *How to centralize the Metadata items on page 88*.

To create the Job, right-click **Job Designs** in the **Repository** tree view and select **Create Job**.

In the dialog box displaying then, only the first field (**Name**) is required. Type in **California1** and click **Finish**.

An empty Job then opens on the main window and the **Palette** of technical components (by default, to the right of the Studio) comes up showing a dozen of component families such as: **Databases**, **Files**, **Internet**, **Data Quality** and so on, hundreds of components are already available.

To read the file *California_Clients*, let's use the **tFileInputDelimited** component. This component can be found in the **File/Input** group of the **Palette**. Click this component then click to the left of the design workspace to place it on the design area.

Let's define now the reading properties for this component: File path, column delimiter, encoding... To do so, let's use the **Metadata Manager**. This tool offers numerous wizards that will help us to configure parameters and allow us to store these properties for a one-click re-use in all future Jobs we may need.

As our input file is a delimited flat file, let's select **File Delimited** on the right-click list of the **Metadata** folder in the **Repository** tree view. Then select **Create file delimited**. A wizard dedicated to delimited file thus displays:

- At Step1, only the **Name** field is required: simply type in **California_clients** and go to the next Step.
- At Step2, select the input file (California_Clients.csv) via the **Browse...** button. Immediately an extract of the file shows on the Preview, at the bottom of the screen so that you can check its content. Click **Next**.
- At Step3, we will define the file parameters: file encoding, line and column delimiters... As our input file is pretty standard, most default values are fine. The first line of our file is a header containing column names. To retrieve automatically these names, click **Set heading row as column names** then click **Refresh Preview**. And click **Next** to the last step.
- At Step4, each column of the file is to be set. The wizard includes algorithms which guess types and length of the column based on the file first data rows. The suggested data description (called schema in Talend Open Studio) can be modified at any time. In this particular scenario, they can be used as is.

There you go, the **California_clients** metadata is complete!

We can now use it in our input component. Select the **tFileInputDelimited** you had dropped on the design workspace earlier, and select the **Component** view at the bottom of the window.

Select the vertical tab **Basic settings**. In this tab, you'll find all technical properties required to let the component work. Rather than setting each one of these properties, let's use the Metadata entry we just defined.

Select **Repository** as **Property type** in the list. A new field shows: **Repository**, click "..." button and select the relevant Metadata entry on the list: **California_clients**. You can notice now that all parameters get automatically filled out.

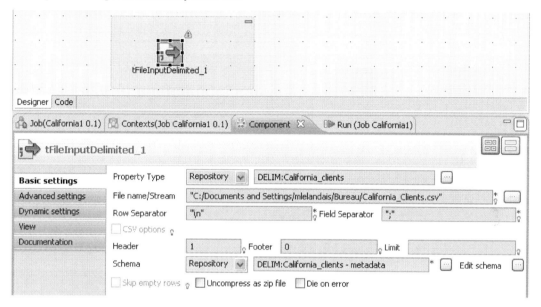

At this stage, we will terminate our flow by simply sending the data read from this input file onto the standard output (StdOut).

To do so, add a **tLogRow** component (from the **Logs & Errors** group).

To link both components, right-click the input component and select **Row/Main**. Then click the output component: **tLogRow**.

This Job is now ready to be executed. To run it, select the **Run** tab on the bottom panel.

Enable the statistics by selecting the **Statistics** check box in the **Advanced Settings** vertical tab of the **Run** view, then run the Job by clicking **Run** in the **Basic Run** tab.

Translating the scenario into a Job

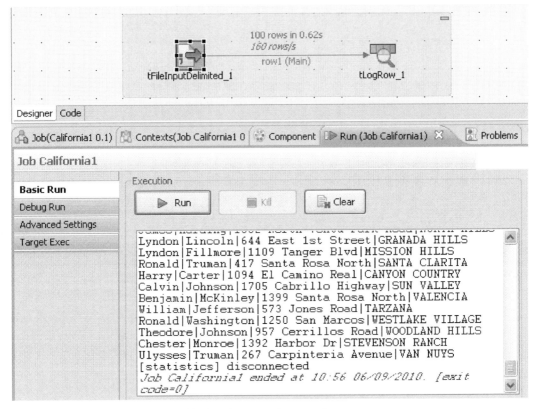

The content of the input file display thus onto the console.

B.2.2 Step 2: Mapping and transformations

We will now enrich our Job to include on-the-fly transformations. To implement these transformation, we need to add a **tMap** component to our Job. This component is multiple and can handle:

- multiple inputs and outputs
- search for reference (simple, cartesian product, first, last match...)
- join (inner, outer)
- transformations
- rejections
- and more...

Remove the link that binds together the job's two components via a right-click the link, then **Delete** option. Then place the **tMap** of the **Processing** component group inbetween before linking the input component to the **tMap** as we did it previously.

Eventually to link the **tMap** to the standard output, right-click the **tMap** component, select **Row/*New Output* (Main)** and click the **tLogRow** component. Type in *out1* in the dialog box to implement the link. Logically, a message box shows up (for the back-propagation of schemas), ignore it by clicking on **No**.

Now, double-click the **tMap** to access its interface.

To the left, you can see the schema (description) of your input file (*row1*). To the right, your output is for the time being still empty (*out1*).

Drop the *Firstname* and *Lastname* columns to the right, onto the *Name* column as shown on the screen below. Then drop the other columns *Address* and *City* to their respective line.

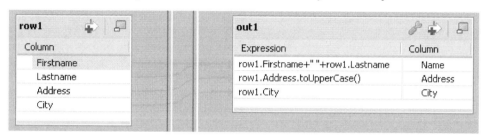

Then carry out the following transformations on each column:

- Change the Expression of the *Name* column to `row1.Firstname + " " + row1.LastName`. Concatenate the *Firstname* column with the *Lastname* column following strictly this syntax (in Java), in order for the columns to display together in one column.

- Change the Expression of the *Address* column to `row1.Address.toUpperCase()` which will thus change the address case to upper case.

 These transformations are stated in Java for this Job and would require a different syntax if you use them in a Perl project.

Then remove the *Lastname* column from the *out1* table and increase the length of the remaining columns. To do so, go to the **Schema Editor** located at the bottom of the tMap editor and proceed as follows:

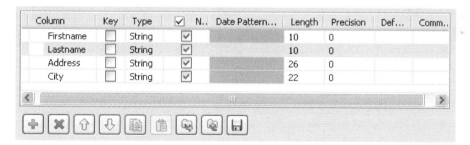

- Select the column to be removed from the schema, and click the cross icon.
- Select the column of which you need increase the length size.
- Type in the length size you intend in the length column. In this example, change the length of every remaining column to 40.

 As the first name and the last name of a client is concatenated, it is necessary to increase the length of the name column in order to match the full name size.

No transformation is made onto the *City* column. Click **OK** to validate the changes and close the Map editor interface.

Translating the scenario into a Job

If you run your Job at this stage (via the **Run** view as we did it before), you'll notice the changes that you defined are implemented.

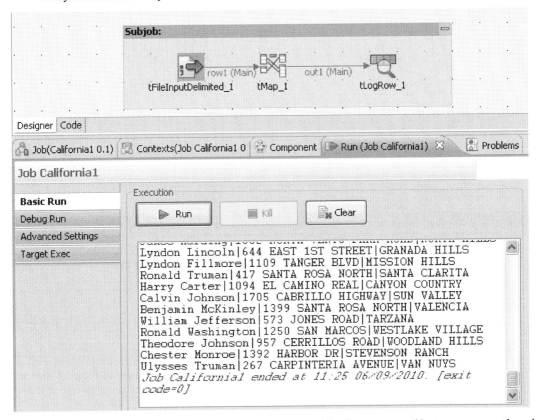

For example, the Address case has been to upper case and the first names and last names are gathered together in the same column.

B.2.3 Step 3: Reference file definition, re-mapping, inner join mode selection

Define the Metadata corresponding to the *LosAngelesandOrangeCounties.txt* file just the way we did it previously for *California_clients* file, using the wizard.

At Step1 of the wizard, name this metadata entry: *LA_Orange_cities*.

Then drop this newly created metadata to the top of the design area to create automatically a reading component pointing to this metadata.

Then link this component to the **tMap** component.

Translating the scenario into a Job

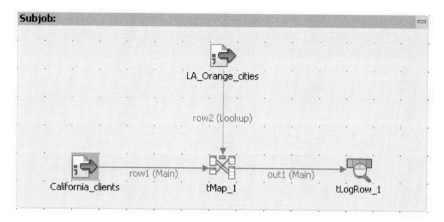

Double-click again on the **tMap** component to open its interface. Note that the reference input table (*row2*) corresponding to the LA and Orange county file, shows to the left of the window, right under your main input (*row1*).

Now let's define the join between the main flow and the reference flow. In this use case, the join is pretty basic to define as the *City* column is present in both files and the data match perfectly. But even though this was not the case, we could have carried out operations directly at this level to establish a link among the data (padding, case change...)

To implement the join, drop the *City* column from your first input table onto the *City* column of your reference table. A violet link then displays, to materialize this join.

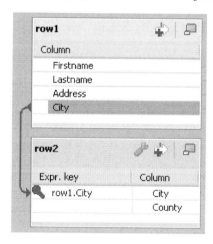

Now, we are able to use the *County* column from the reference table in the output table (out1).

Talend Open Studio 295

Translating the scenario into a Job

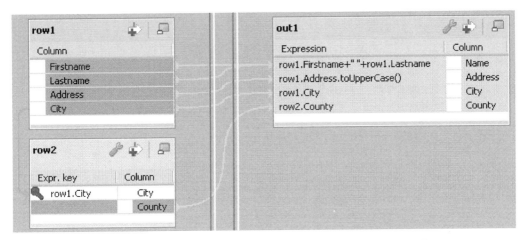

Eventually, click the **OK** button to validate your changes, and run the new Job.

The following output should display on the console.

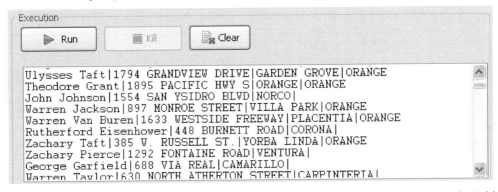

As you can notice, the last column is only filled out for *Los Angeles* and *Orange* counties' cities. For all other lines, this column is empty. The reason for this is that by default, the **tMap** implements a left outer join mode. If you want to filter your data to only display lines for which a match is found by the **tMap**, then open again the **tMap**, click the **tMap settings** button and select the **Inner Join** in the **Join Model** list on the reference table (*row2*).

B.2.4 Step 4: Output to a MySQL table

Our Job works perfectly! To finalize it, let's direct the output flow to a MySQL table.

To do so, let's first create the Metadata describing the connection to the MySQL database. Double-click Metadata/MySQL/DemoMySQL in the referential (on the condition that you imported the Demo project properly). This opens the Metadata wizard.

On Step2 of the wizard, type in the relevant connection parameters. Check the validity of this connection by clicking on the **Check** button. Eventually, validate your changes, by clicking on **Finish**.

Drop this metadata to the right of the design workspace, while maintaining the **Ctrl** key down, in order to create automatically a **tMysqlOutput** component.

Remove the **tLogRow** component from your Job.

Reconnect the out1 output flow from the **tMap** to the new component **tMysqlOutput** (Right-click/Row/out1):

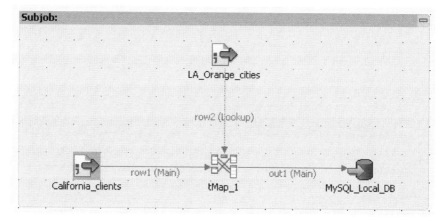

On the **Basic Settings** tab of this component:

- Type in *LA_Orange_Clients* in the **Table** field, in order to name your target table which will get created on the fly.
- Select the **Drop table if exists and create** option or on the **Action on table** field.
- Click **Edit Schema** and click the **Reset DB type** button (DB button on the tool bar) in order to fill out automatically the DB type if need be.

Run again the Job. The target table should be automatically created and filled with data in less a a second!

In this scenario, we did use only four different components out of hundreds of components available in the **Palette** and grouped according to different categories (databases, Web service, FTP and so on)!

And more components, this time created by the community, are also available on the community site (talendforge.org).

For more information regarding the components, check out Talend Open Studio Components Reference Guide.

APPENDIX C
SQL template writing rules

This chapter describes the rules applied for the creation of SQL templates. It aims to help users of SQL templates in Talend Open Studio to understand and develop the SQL templates for more customized usage.

These rules provide details that you have to respect when writing the template statement, a comment line or the different relevant syntaxes.

These rules helps to use the SQL code in specific use cases, such as to access the various parameters defined in components.

C.1 SQL statements

An SQL statement can be any valid SQL statement that the related JDBC is able to execute. The SQL template code is a group of SQL statements. The basic rules to write an SQL statement in the SQL template editor are:

- An SQL statement must end with ;.
- An SQL statement can span lines. In this case, no line should be ended with ; except the last one.

C.2 Comment lines

A comment line starts with # or --. Any line that starts with # or -- will be ignored in code generating.

 There is no exception to the lines in the middle part of a SQL statement or within the `<%... %>` syntax.

C.3 The `<%...%>` syntax

This syntax can span lines. The following list points out what you can do with this syntax and what you should pay attention to.

- You can define new variables, use Java logical code like `if`, `for` and `while`, and also get parameter values.
  For example, if you want to get the *FILE_NAME* parameter, use the code as follows:

```
<%
String filename = __FILE_NAME__ ;
%>
```

- This syntax cannot be used within an SQL statement. In other words, It should be used between two separated SQL statements.
  For example, the syntax in the following code is valid.

```
#sql sentence
DROP TABLE temp_0;
<%
#loop
for(int i=1; i<10; i++){
%>
#sql sentence
DROP TABLE temp_<%=i %>;
<%
}
%>
#sql sentence
DROP TABLE temp_10;
```

In this example, the syntax is used between two separated SQL templates: `DROP TABLE temp_0;` and `DROP TABLE temp_<%=i%>;`.

The SQL statements are intended to remove several tables beginning from *temp_0*. The code between `<%` and `%>` generate a sequence of number in loop to identify tables to be removed and close the loop after the number generation.

- Within this syntax, the `<%=...%>` or `</.../>` syntax should not be used.

`<%=...%>` and `</.../>` are also syntax intended for the SQL templates. The below sections describe related information.

> Parameters that the SQL templates can access with this syntax are simple. They are often used for connection purpose and can be easily defined in components, such as TABLE_NAME, DB_VERSION, SCHEMA_TYPE, etc.

C.4 The `<%=...%>` syntax

This syntax cannot span lines and is used for SQL statement. The following list points out what you can do with this syntax and what you should pay attention to.

- This syntax can be used to generate any variable value, and also the value of any existing parameter.
- No space char is allowed after `<%=`.
- Inside this syntax, the `<%...%>` or `</.../>` syntax should not be used.

The statement written in the below example is a valid one.

```
#sql sentence
DROP TABLE temp_<%= TABLE_NAME %>;
```

The code is used to remove the table defined through an associated component.

For more information about what components are associated with the SQL templates, see chapter *Using SQL templates on page 263*.

For more information on the `<%...%>` syntax, see section *The <%...%> syntax on page 300*.

For more information on the `</.../>` syntax, see the following section.

> Parameters that the SQL templates can access with this syntax are simple. They are often used for connection purpose and can be easily defined in components, such as TABLE_NAME, DB_VERSION, SCHEMA_TYPE, etc.

C.5 The `</.../>` syntax

This syntax cannot span lines. The following list points out what you can do with this syntax and what you should pay attention to.

- It can be used to generate the value of any existing parameter. The generated value should not be enclosed by quotation marks.
- No space char is allowed after `</` or before `/>`.
- Inside this syntax, the `<%...%>` or `<%=...%>` syntax should not be used.

The statement written in the below example is a valid one.

```
#sql sentence
DROP TABLE temp_</TABLE_NAME/>;
```

The statement identifies the *TABLE_NAME* parameter and then removes the corresponding table.

For more information on the <%...%> syntax, see section *The <%...%> syntax on page 300*.

For more information on the <%=...%> syntax, see section *The <%=...%> syntax on page 301*.

The following sections present more specific code used to access more complicated parameters.

 Parameters that the SQL templates can access with this syntax are simple. They are often used for connection purpose and can be easily defined in components, such as *TABLE_NAME, DB_VERSION, SCHEMA_TYPE*, etc.

C.6 Code to access the component schema elements

Component schema elements are presented on a schema column name list (delimited by a dot "."). These elements are created and defined in components by users.

The below code composes an example to access some elements included in a component schema. In the following example, the *ELT_METADATA_SHEMA* variable name is used to get the component schema.

```
<%
String query = "select ";
SCHEMA(__ELT_METADATA_SHEMA__);
for (int i=0; i < __ELT_METADATA_SHEMA__.length ; i++) {
query += (__ELT_METADATA_SHEMA__[i].name + ",");
}
query += " from " + __TABLE_NAME__;
%>
<%=query %>;
```

In this example, and according to what you want to do, the __ELT_METADATA_SHEMA__[i].name code can be replaced by __ELT_METADATA_SHEMA__[i].dbType, __ELT_METADATA_SHEMA__[i].isKey, __ELT_METADATA_SHEMA__[i].length or __ELT_METADATA_SHEMA__[i].nullable to access the other fields of the schema column.

The extract statement is SCHEMA(__ELT_METADATA_SHEMA__);. In this statement, ELT_METADATA_SHEMA is the variable name representing the schema parameter to be extracted. The variable name used in the code is just an example. You can change it to another variable name to represent the schema parameter you already defined.

 Make sure that the name you give to the schema parameter does not conflict with any name of other parameters.

For more information on component schema, see *Basic Settings tab on page 65*.

C.7 Code to access the component matrix properties

The component matrix properties are created and changed by users according to various data transformation purposes. These properties are defined by tabular parameters, for example, the *operation* parameters or *groupby* parameters that users can define through the **tELTAggregate** component.

To access these tabular parameters that are naturally more flexible and complicated, two approaches are available:

- The `</.../>` approach:

`</.../>` is one of the syntax used by the SQL templates. This approach often needs hard coding for every parameter to be extracted.

For example, a new parameter is created by user and is given the name *NEW_PROPERTY*. If you want to access it by using `</NEW_PROPERTY/>`, the below code is needed.

```
else if (paramName.equals("NEW_PROPERTY")) {
List<Map<String, String>> newPropertyTableValue = (List<Map<String, String>>)
ElementParameterParser.getObjectValue(node, "__NEW_PROPERTY__");
for (int ii = 0; ii <newPropertyTableValue.size(); ii++) {
Map<String, String> newPropertyMap =newPropertyTableValue.get(ii);
realValue += ...;//append generated codes
......
}
}
```

- The `EXTRACT(__GROUPBY__);` approach:

The below code shows the second way to access the tabular parameter *(GROUPBY)*.

```
<%
String query = "insert into " + __TABLE_NAME__ + "(id, name, date_birth) select sum(id), name, date_birth from cust_teradata group by";
EXTRACT(__GROUPBY__);
for (int i=0; i < __GROUPBY_LENGTH__ ; i++) {
query += (__GROUPBY_INPUT_COLUMN__[i] + " ");
}
%>
<%=query %>;
```

When coding the statements, respect the rules as follows:

- The extract statement must use `EXTRACT(__GROUPBY__);`. Upcase should be used and no space char is allowed. This statement should be used between `<%` and `%>`.

- Use `__GROUPBY_LENGTH__`, in which the parameter name is followed by `_LENGTH`, to get the line number of the tabular *GROUPBY* parameters you define in the **Groupby** area on a **Component** view. It can be used between `<%` and `%>` or `<%=` and `%>`.

- Use code like `__GROUPBY_INPUT_COLUMN__[i]` to extract the parameter values. This can be used between `<%` and `%>` or between `<%=` and `%>`.

- In order to access the parameter correctly, do not use the identical name prefix for several parameters. For example in the component, avoid to define two parameters with the names `PARAMETER_NAME` and `PARAMETER_NAME_2`, as the same prefix in the names causes erroneous code generation.

Code to access the component matrix properties

APPENDIX D
System routines

This appendix gives you an overview of the most commonly used routines, along with use cases. In this Appendix, routines follow the order in which they display in the **Repository**. They are grouped according to their types. Each type is detailed in a different section.

For more information on how to define routines, to access to system routines or to manage system or user routines, see *Managing routines*.

Before starting any data integration processes, you need to be familiar with Talend Open Studio Graphical User Interface (GUI). For more information, see *Talend Open Studio GUI on page 275*.

D.1 Numeric Routines

Numeric routines allow you to return whole or decimal numbers in order to use them as settings in one or more Job components. To add numeric IDs, for instance.

To access these routines, double click on the **Numeric** category, in the **system** folder. The Numeric category contains several routines, notably sequence, random and decimal (convertImpliedDecimalFormat):

Routine	Description	Syntax
sequence	Returns an incremental numeric ID.	`Numeric.sequence("Parameter name", start value, increment value)`
resetSequence	Creates a sequence if it doesn't exist and attributes a new start value.	`Numeric.resetSequence (Sequence Identifier, start value)`
removeSequence	Removes a sequence.	`Numeric.RemoveSequence (Sequence Identifier)`
random	Returns a random whole number between the maximum and minimum values.	`Numeric.random(minimum start value, maximum end value)`
convertImpliedDecimalFormat	Returns a decimal with the help of an implicit decimal model.	`Numeric.convertImpliedDecimalFormat("Target Format", value to be converted)`

D.1.1 How to create a Sequence

The **sequence** routine allows you to create automatically incremented IDs, using a **tJava** component:

```
System.out.println(Numeric.sequence("s1",1,1));
System.out.println(Numeric.sequence("s1",1,1));
```

The routine generates and increments the ID automatically:

```
[statistics] connecting to socket on port 3360
[statistics] connected
1
2
```

D.1.2 How to convert an Implied Decimal

It is easy to use the **convertImpliedDecimalFormat** routine, along with a **tJava** component, for example:

```
System.out.println(Numeric.convertImpliedDecimalFormat("9V99","123"));
```

The routine automatically converts the value entered as a parameter according to the format of the implied decimal provided:

D.2 Relational Routines

```
[statistics] connecting to socket on port 3360
[statistics] connected
1
2
```

Relational routines allow you to check affirmations based on booleans.

To access these routines, double click on the **Relational** class under the **system** folder. The Relational class contains several routines, notably:

Routine	Description	Syntax
ISNULL	Checks if the variable provided is a null value	`Relational.ISNULL(variable to be checked)`

To check a Relational Routine, you can use the **ISNULL** routine, along with a **tJava** component, for example:

```
System.out.println(Relational.ISNULL(null));
```

In this example, the test result is displayed in the **Run** view:

```
Starting job test_routine at 14:14 04/02/2010.

[statistics] connecting to socket on port 3375
[statistics] connected
true
[statistics] disconnected
Job test_routine ended at 14:14 04/02/2010. [exit code=0]
```

D.3 StringHandling Routines

The **StringHandling** routines allow you to carry out various kinds of operations and tests on alphanumeric expressions, based on Java methods.

To access these routines, doubleclick on **StringHandling** under the system folder. The **StringHandling** class includes the following routines:

Routine	Description	Syntax
ALPHA	checks whether the expression is arranged in alphabetical order. Returns the true or false boolean accordingly.	`StringHandling.ALPHA("string to be checked")`
IS_ALPHA	checks whether the expression contains alphabetical characters only, or otherwise. Returns the true or false boolean accordingly.	`StringHandling.IS_ALPHA("string to be checked")`

StringHandling Routines

Routine	Description	Syntax
CHANGE	replaces an element of a string with a defined replacement element and returns the new string.	`StringHandling.CHANGE("string to be checked", "string to be replaced","replacement string")`
COUNT	Returns the number of times a substring occurs within a string.	`StringHandling.COUNT("string to be checked", "substring to be counted")`
DOWNCASE	converts all uppercase letters in an expression into lowercase and returns the new string.	`StringHandling.DOWNCASE("string to be converted")`
UPCASE	converts all lowercase letters in an expression into uppercase and returns the new string.	`StringHandling.UPCASE("string to be converted")`
DQUOTE	encloses an expression in double quotation marks.	`StringHandling.DQUOTE("string to be enclosed in double quotation marks")`
INDEX	returns the position of the first character in a specified substring, within a whole string. If the substring specified doesn't exist in the whole string, the value – 1 is returned.	`StringHandling.INDEX("string to be checked", "substring specified")`
LEFT	specifies a substring which corresponds to the first n characters in a string	`StringHandling.LEFT("string to be checked", number of characters)`
RIGHT	specifies a substring which corresponds to the last n characters in a string.	`StringHandling.RIGHT("chaîne à vérifier", number of characters)`
LEN	calculates the length of a string.	`StringHandling.LEN("string to check")`
SPACE	generates a string consisting of a specified number of blank spaces.	`StringHandling.SPACE(number of blank spaces to be generated)`
SQUOTE	encloses an expression in single quotation marks.	`StringHandling.SQUOTE("string to be enclosed in single quotation marks")`
STR	generates a particular character a the number of times specified.	`StringHandling.STR('character to be generated', number of times)`
TRIM	deletes the spaces and tabs before the first non-blank character in a string and after the last non-blank character, then returns the new string	`StringHandling.TRIM("string to be checked")`
BTRIM	deletes all the spaces and tabs after the last non-blank character in a string and returns the new string.	`StringHandling.BTRIM("string to be checked")`
FTRIM	deletes all the spaces and tabs preceding the first non-blank character in a string.	`StringHandling.FTRIM("string to be checked")`

D.3.1 How to store a string in alphabetical order

It is easy to use the ALPHA routine along with a **tJava** component, to check whether a string is in alphabetical order:

```
System.out.println(StringHandling.ALPHA("abcdefg"));
```

The check returns a boolean value.

```
Starting job test_routine at 14:29 04/02/2010.
[statistics] connecting to socket on port 3469
[statistics] connected
true
```

D.3.2 How to check whether a string is alphabetical

It is easy to use the **IS_ALPHA** routine along with a **tJava** component, to check whether the string is alphabetical:

```
System.out.println(StringHandling.IS_ALPHA("ab33cd"));
```

The check returns a boolean value.

```
Starting job routine1 at 11:45 23/02/2010.
[statistics] connecting to socket on port 3892
[statistics] connected
false
[statistics] disconnected
Job routine1 ended at 11:45 23/02/2010. [exit code=0]
```

D.3.3 How to replace an element in a string

It is easy use the **CHANGE** routine along with a **tJava** component, to replace one element in a string with another:

```
System.out.println(StringHandling.CHANGE("hello world!","world","guy"));
```

La routine replaces the old element with the new element specified.

```
hello guy!
```

D.3.4 How to check the position of a specific character or substring, within a string

The **INDEX** routine is easy to use along with a **tJava** component, to check whether a string contains a specified character or substring:

```
System.out.println(StringHandling.INDEX("hello world!", "hello"));
System.out.println(StringHandling.INDEX("hello world!", "world"));
System.out.println(StringHandling.INDEX("hello world!", "!"));
System.out.println(StringHandling.INDEX("hello world!", "?"));
```

The routine returns a whole number which indicates the position of the first character specified, or indeed the first character of the substring specified. Otherwise, -1 is returned if no occurrences are found.

```
Starting job routine1 at 15:47 24/02/2010.
[statistics] connecting to socket on port 4027
[statistics] connected
0
6
11
-1
[statistics] disconnected
Job routine1 ended at 15:47 24/02/2010. [exit code=0]
```

D.3.5 How to calculate the length of a string

The **LEN** routine is easy to use, along with a **tJava** component, to check the length of a string:

```
System.out.println(StringHandling.LEN("hello world!"));
```

The check returns a whole number which indicates the length of the chain, including spaces and blank characters.

```
12
```

D.3.6 How to delete blank characters

The **FTRIM** routine is easy to use, along with a **tJava** component, to delete blank characters from the start of a chain:

```
System.out.println(StringHandling.FTRIM("   Hello world   !"));
```

The routine returns the string with the blank characters removed from the beginning.

```
Starting job routine1 at 16:14 24/02/2010.
[statistics] connecting to socket on port 3790
[statistics] connected
Hello world   !
[statistics] disconnected
Job routine1 ended at 16:14 24/02/2010. [exit code=0]
```

D.4 TalendDataGenerator Routines

The **TalendDataGenerator** routines are functions which allow you to generate sets of test data. They are based on fictitious lists of first names, second names, addresses, towns and States provided by **Talend**. These routines are generally used when developing Jobs, using a **tRowGenerator**, for example, to avoid using production or company data.

To access the routines, double click on **TalendDataGenerator** under the **system** folder:

Routine	Description	Syntax
getFirstName	returns a first name taken randomly from a fictitious list.	`TalendDataGenerator.getFirstName()`

Routine	Description	Syntax
getLastName	returns a random surname from a fictitious list.	`TalendDataGenerator.getLastName()`
getUsStreet	returns an address taken randomly from a list of common American street names.	`TalendDataGenerator.getUsStreet()`
getUsCity	returns the name of a town taken randomly from a list of American towns.	`TalendDataGenerator.getUsCity()`
getUsState	returns the name of a State taken randomly from a list of American States.	`TalendDataGenerator.getUsState()`
getUsStateId	returns an ID randomly taken from a list of IDs attributed to American States.	`TalendDataGenerator.getUsStateId()`

 No entry parameter is required as **Talend** provides the list of fictitious data.

You can customize the fictitious data by modifying the **TalendGeneratorRoutines**. For further information on how to customize routines, see *Customizing the system routines on page 255*.

D.4.1 How to generate fictitious data

It is easy to use the different functions to generate data randomly. Using a **tJava** component, you can, for example, create a list of fictitious client data using functions such as **getFirstName**, **getLastName**, **getUSCity**:

```
System.out.println(TalendDataGenerator.getFirstName());
System.out.println(TalendDataGenerator.getLastName());
System.out.println(TalendDataGenerator.getUsCity());
System.out.println(TalendDataGenerator.getUsState());
System.out.println(TalendDataGenerator.getUsStateId());
System.out.println(TalendDataGenerator.getUsStreet());
```

The set of data taken randomly from the list of fictitious data is displayed in the **Run** view:

```
Starting job test_routine at 14:44 04/02/2010.

[statistics] connecting to socket on port 3907
[statistics] connected
Jimmy
Arthur
Des Moines
Wyoming
UT
Milpas Street
[statistics] disconnected
Job test_routine ended at 14:44 04/02/2010. [exit code=0]
```

D.5 TalendDate Routines

The TalendDate routines allow you to carry out different kinds of operations and checks concerning the format of Date expressions.

To access these routines, double click on TalendDate under the **system** folder:

Routine	Description	Syntax
formatDate	returns a date string which corresponds to the format specified.	`TalendDate.formatDate("date format - eg.: yyyy-MM-dd HH:mm:ss", Date() to be formatted)`
isDate	checks whether the date string corresponds to the format specified. Returns the boolean value true or false according to the outcome.	`TalendDate.isDate(Date() to be checked, "format of the date to be checked - eg.: yyyy-MM-dd HH:mm:ss")`
compareDate	compares all or part of two dates according to the format specified. Returns 0 if the dates are identical, 1 if the first date is older than the second and -1 if it is more recent than the second	`TalendDate.compareDate(Date date1, Date date2, "format to be compared - eg.: yyyy-MM-dd")`
addDate	adds n days, n months, n hours, n minutes or n seconds to a Java date and returns the new date. The Date format is: "yyyy", "MM", "dd", "HH", "mm", "ss" or "SSS".	`TalendDate.addDate("String date initiale", "format Date - eg.: yyyy/MM/dd", whole n,"format of the part of the date to which n is to be added - eg.:yyyy").`
diffDate	returns the difference between two dates in terms of days, months, years, minutes or seconds according to the comparison parameter specified.	`TalendDate.diffDate(Date1(), Date2(), "format of the part of the date to be compared - eg.:yyyy")`
getFirstDayOfMonth	changes the date of an event to the first day of the current month and returns the new date.	`TalendDate.getFirstDayMonth(Date)`
getLastDayOfMonth	changes the date of an event to the last day of the current month and returns the new date.	`TalendDate.getLastDayMonth(Date)`
setDate	modifies part of a date according to the part and value of the date specified and the format specified.	`TalendDate.setDate(Date, whole n, "format of the part of the date to be modified - eg.:yyyy")`
formatDateLocale	changes a date into a date/hour string according to the format used in the target country	`TalendDate.formatDateLocale("format target", java.util.Date date, "language or country code")`
parseDate	changes a string into a Date. Returns a date in the standard format.	`TalendDate.parseDate("format date of the string to be parsed", "string in the format of the date to be parsed")`

Routine	Description	Syntax
parseDateLocale	parses a string according to a specified format and extracts the date. Returns the date according to the local format specified.	`TalendDate.parseDateLocale("date format of the string to be parsed", "String in the format of the date to be parsed", "code corresponding to the country or language")`
getDate	returns the current date and hour in the format specified (optional). This string can contain fixed character strings or variables linked to the date. By default, the string is returned in the format, DD/MM/CCYY.	`TalendDate.getDate("Format of the string - ex: CCYY-MM-DD")`
getCurrentDate	returns the current date. No entry parameter is required.	`TalendDate.getCurrentDate()`
getRandomDate	returns a random date, in the ISO format.	`TalendDate.getRandomDate("Chaîne de caractère de type Date", String minDate, String maxDate)`

D.5.1 How to format a date

The **formatDate** routine is easy to use, along with a **tJava** component:

```
System.out.println(TalendDate.formatDate("dd-MM-yyyy", new Date()));
```

The current date is initialized according to the pattern specified by the `new date()` Java `function` and is displayed in the **Run** view:

```
Starting job routine1 at 17:28 25/02/2010.
2010-02-25 17:28:07
Job routine1 ended at 17:28 25/02/2010. [exit code=0]
```

D.5.2 How to check a Date

It is easy to use the **isDate** routine, along with a **tJava** component to check if a date expression is in the format specified:

```
System.out.println(TalendDate.isDate("2010-02-09 00:00:00","yyyy-MM-dd HH:mm:ss"));
```

A boolean is returned in the **Run** view:

```
Starting job routine1 at 17:36 25/02/2010.
true
Job routine1 ended at 17:36 25/02/2010. [exit code=0]
```

D.5.3 How to compare Dates

It is easy to use the **formatDate** routine, along with a **tJava** component to check if the current date is more recent than a specific date, according to the format specified.

```
System.out.println(TalendDate.compareDate(new Date(),
TalendDate.parseDate("yyyy-MM-dd", "2010/11/24"), "yyyy-MM-dd"));
```

The current date is initialized by the Java function `new date()` and the value -1 is displayed in the **Run** view to indicate that the current date precedes the reference date.

```
Starting job routine1 at 18:09 25/02/2010.
-1
Job routine1 ended at 18:09 25/02/2010. [exit code=0]
```

D.5.4 How to configure a date

It is easy to use the **setDate** routine, along with a **tJava** component to change the year of the current date, for example:

```
System.out.println(TalendDate.formatDate("yyyy/MM/dd HH:mm:ss",new Date()));
System.out.println(TalendDate.setDate(new Date(),2011,"yyyy"));
```

The current date, followed by the new date are displayed in the **Run** view:

```
Starting job routine1 at 18:03 26/02/2010.
2010/02/26 18:03:14
Sat Feb 26 18:03:14 CET 2011
Job routine1 ended at 18:03 26/02/2010. [exit code=0]
```

D.5.5 How to parse a Date

It is easy to use the **parseDate** routine, along with a **tJava** component to change a date string from one format into another Date format, for example:

```
System.out.println(TalendDate.parseDate("yyyy-MM-dd HH:mm:ss",
"1979-10-20 19:00:59"));
```

The string is changed and returned in the Date format:

```
Starting job routine1 at 11:58 01/03/2010.
Sat Oct 20 19:00:59 CET 1979
Job routine1 ended at 11:58 01/03/2010. [exit code=0]
```

D.5.6 How to format the Current Date

It is easy to use the **getDate** routine, along with a **tJava** component, to retrieve and format the current date according to a specified format, for example:

```
System.out.println(TalendDate.getDate("CCYY-MM-DD"));
```

The current date is returned in the specified format (optional):

```
Starting job routine1 at 10:58 02/03/2010.
2010-03-02
Job routine1 ended at 10:58 02/03/2010. [exit code=0]
```

D.6 TalendString Routines

The **TalendString** routines allow you to carry out various operations on alphanumerical expressions.

To access these routines, double click on **TalendString** under the **system** folder. The **TalendString** class contains the following routines:

Routine	Description	Syntax
replaceSpecialCharForXML	returns a string from which the special characters (eg.:: <, >, &...) have been replaced by equivalent XML characters.	`TalendString.replaceSpecialCharForXML("string containing the special characters - eg.: Thelma & Louise")`
checkCDATAForXML	identifies characters starting with <![CDATA[and ending with]]> as pertaining to XML and returns them without modification. Transforms the strings not identified as XML in a form which is compatible with XML and returns them.	`TalendString.checkCDATAForXML("string to be parsed")`
talendTrim	parses the entry string and removes the filler characters from the start and end of the string according to the alignment value specified: -1 for the filler characters at the end of the string, 1 for those at the start of the string and 0 for both. Returns the trimmed string.	`TalendString.talendTrim("string to be parsed", "filler character to be removed", character position)`
removeAccents	removes accents from a string and returns the string without the accents.	`TalendString.removeAccents("String")`
getAsciiRandomString	generates a random string with a specific number of characters	`TalendString.getAsciiRandomString(whole number indicating the length of the string)`

D.6.1 How to format an XML string

It is easy to run the **replaceSpecialCharForXML** routine along with a **tJava** component, to format a string for XML:

```
System.out.println(TalendString.replaceSpecialCharForXML("Thelma & Louise"));
```

In this example, the "&" character is replaced in order to make the string XML compatible:

```
Starting job routine1 at 15:48 02/03/2010.

Thelma &amp; Louise
Job routine1 ended at 15:48 02/03/2010. [exit code=0]
```

D.6.2 How to trim a string

It is easy to use the **talendTrim** routine, along with a **tJava** component to remove the string padding characters from the start and end of the string:

```
System.out.println(TalendString.talendTrim("**talend open studio****", '*', -1));
System.out.println(TalendString.talendTrim("**talend open studio****", '*', 1));
System.out.println(TalendString.talendTrim("**talend open studio****", '*', 0));
```

The star characters are removed from the start, then the end of the string and then finally from both ends:

```
Starting job routine1 at 14:19 02/03/2010.

**talend open studio
talend open studio****
talend open studio
Job routine1 ended at 14:19 02/03/2010. [exit code=0]
```

D.6.3 How to remove accents from a string

It is easy to use the **removeAccents** routine, along with a **tJava** component, to replace the accented characters, for example:

```
System.out.println(TalendString.removeAccents("sâcrebleü!"));
```

The accented characters are replaced with non-accented characters:

```
Starting job routine1 at 16:02 02/03/2010.

sacrebleu!
Job routine1 ended at 16:02 02/03/2010. [exit code=0]
```

A

Activate/Deactivate 126
Advanced Settings 68
    Measuring data flows 68
Advanced settings 68
Appearance 50
Assignment table 53

B

Basic settings 65
Breakpoint 73
Built-in
    Variable 89
Built-in schema 66
Business Model 45
Business Modeler 45
Business Models
    Creating 45
    Opening 44
Business models 44
    Connecting shapes 47
    Copying/Pasting 54
    Creating 44
    Deleting 54
    Modeling 46
    Moving 54
    Objectives 44
    Renaming 54
    Saving 54

C

Centralizing context 89
Centralizing items 88
Changing workspace 11
Code & outline 117
Code Viewer 117, 118, 284
Code viewer 284
Componens
    Dynamic settings 68
Component 61, 81, 282
    Advanced Settings 68
    Basic settings 65
    basic settings 65
    External 22
    view tab 70
Components
    Advanced settings 68
    Basic settings 65
    Connecting 64

Connection types 81
    documentation 70
    Dropping 61
    Dynamic settings 68
    filter connections 83
    lookup connections 82
    main connections 82
    Properties 65
    rejects connections 83
    row connections 82
    Start 114
    uniques/duplicates connections 84
    View 70
Components properties 65
Configuration tabs
    Modules view 108
    Schedular view 110
Connecting
    Local repository 10
Connecting components 64
Connecting to the studio 10
Connection
    Iterate 84
    Link 85
    Lookup 82
    Main 82
    Output 82
    Reject 82
    Row 82
    Trigger 84
Context 72

D

Data analytics 2
Data integration 1
Debug mode 73
Delimited 196
Deploying a job 151
document a job 150
Documentation 70
Duplicates 84
Dynamic settings 68

E

Edit Schema 66
ErrorReject 83
Errors & warnings 115
Execution monitoring 3
Export

example 132
Export job
  autonomous 131
  JBoss ESB 136
  petals ESB 137
  webservice 132
Export to ESB 138
Exporting metadata 252
Expression Builder 168
Expression editor
  access 166
  use case 168
External modules 108
Extra 121

F
File XML
  Loop limit 241, 250
FilePositional 200
FileRegex 203
Find jobs 122

G
Graphical workspace 44, 281
Grid 51
GUI
  Main window 276
  Menus 277
  Palette 281
  Repository 279
  Toolbar 279
  Workspace 281
Gui
  Code viewer 284
  Job configuration tabs 282
  Job outline 284

H
Hash key 159

I
Importing
  Items 127
Importing job samples 16
Inner join 162
Inner Join Reject 162
Input MDM connection 238
Installing components 107
Item

Importing 127
Iterate 84

J
Job
  activate 126
  code & outline 117
  color 118
  component properties 65
  connect components 64
  context parameters 144
  create 58
  create folder 60
  Creating 58
  deactivate 126
  deploy 151
  drop components (palette) 61
  drop components (repository) 62
  edit document 151
  errors & warnings 115
  export items 142
  export script (java) 129
  export script (perl) 140
  HTML document 150
  import items 127
  note 116
  Opening/Creating 58
  run 71
  Running 71, 72, 74, 100
  version 149
Job dependencies 145
Job design 58
Job Designer
  Panels 80
Job designing 57
Job Designs 59
Job outline 284
Job Settings
  Extra tab 121
  Stats & Logs tab 120
Job version 149
Job view 120
Jobs
  Versioning 149

K
Key 159
Keyboard shortcuts 284

L
Launching the studio 6
LDIFfile 221
Link 85
Logs 81, 282

M
Main properties 54
Main row 82
Main window 276
Managing installed components 107
Mapper 84
Mapping flows 102
Measuring data flows 68
Menus 277
Metadata 88
    DB Connection schema 182, 191, 236
    Dropping Components 62
    FileDelimited schema 196
    FileLDIF Schema 221
    FilePositional schema 200
    FileRegex schema 203
    XML File Schema 204
Metadata manager 88
Model
    Arranging 49, 50
    Assigning 53
    Commenting 49
    Deleting 54
Modeler 45
Multiple Input/Output 84

N
Notes 116

O
Object 46
Open
    local project 18
Operational integration 2
Outline 117, 118, 284
Outline panel 117
Output 83
Output MDM connection 243

P
Palette 46, 49, 61, 77, 281
    find jobs 122
    hide/show 77

Moving 77
Note 49
Note attachment 49
position 77
search components 63
Select 49
Showing 77
Zoom 49
Palette favorite 78
Palette layout 79
Palette settings 77
Panel position 80
Postjob component 112
Preferences
    code 25
    components 22, 80
    debug&execution 23
    language 23
    Libraries 29
    Perl&Java 21
    schema 28
    Special characters 27
    SQL builder 28
    type conversion 30
Prejob component 112
Primary Key 159
Problems 81, 282
Project
    creating 14
    deleting 18
    exporting 19
    importing 17
    opening 18
Project settings 31
Projects 13
Properties 46, 50, 281
    Comment 71
    Main 54
    Rulers & Grid 51

Q
Query
    SQLBuilder 102

R
Receive MDM connection 248
Recycle bin 54
Regular Expressions 204
Reject row 82

Rejects 83
Relationship 47
    Bidirectional 48
    Directional 48
    Simple 48
Repository 14, 58, 88, 279
    detect dependencies 147
    detect Job dependencies 145
    edit item 145
    update jobs 146
Repository items
    Assigning 52
Repository schema 66
Row 82
    Main 82
    Reject 82
Row connections
    Duplicates 84
    Filter 83
    Lookup 82
    Main 82
    Uniques 84
Rulers 51
Run Job 71, 72, 74, 81, 100, 282

S

Schedular view 110
Scheduler 110
Schema
    Built-in 67
search components 63
Search job 147
Setting
    Context preferences 37
    Designer preferences 25
    Documentation preferences 27, 41
    Preferences 21
    Repository preferences 26
    Stats & Logs preferences 36
    Status preferences 39
Setting preferences 21
Shape 46
Sharing connection 113
SQL queries 102
SQL templates 101
SQL templates management 265
SQLBuilder 102
Start 114
Start component 114

Statistics 75
Stats & Logs 120
StoreSQLQuery 96
Subjobs
    Collapsing 119
    Formatting 119
    Highlighting 119
Sync columns 66

T

Tabs
    Component 282
    Error log, Tabs
        Modules 282
    Job hierarchy 282
    Job View 282
    problems 282
    Properties 282
    Run Job 282
    Scheduler 282
    Talend Exchange 282
Talend and ESB 137
Talend Exchange 106
tFlowMeterCatcher 120, 283
tLogCatcher 120, 283
tMap 84
Toolbar 279
Traces 74
Trigger 84
Trigger connections
    OnComponentError 85
    OnComponentOK 85
    OnSubjobError 85
    OnSubjobOK 85
    Run if 85
tStatCatcher 120, 283

U

Uniques 84
Using queries 102

V

Variable 89
    StoreSQLQuery 96
View tab 70

W

Wizards
    DB connection 182

File delimited schema 196
File Excel schema 217
File LDIF schema 221
File positional schema 200
File Regex schema 203
FTP connection 189
Generic schema 231
JDBC 191
LDAP schema 223

MDM connection 235
Salesforce 228
SAS 194
Web Service Schema 232
XML File Schema 204
Workspace 281

X
Xpath 209

The Talend Community! What else?!

Through the Community utilities, you can learn about Talend solutions, share information with other Talend users, beta-test new versions, submit features requests or code and much more...

Exchange

Ready to develop your own components, jobs and templates?
Want to share them with the community?
Log on to Talend Exchange, and share your extension and maybe they'll be part of a next release of Talend Open Studio.

Forum

Want to talk about Talend Open Studio?
Had any install problems?
Need help with the software? Or maybe you have a suggestion to talk over with the development team. The Talend Forum is the place to go!

Components

Don't know whether your most wanted component is already included in Talend Open Studio? Simply access the exhaustive list of components, and check out the real-time udpates.

Tutorials

Take a quick tour of Talend Open Studio and discover some basic features and popular functionalities.

Wiki

Get all the technical and general information you need to install and best use Talend Open Studio. This includes installation procedures per OS, use cases, component creation support and much more.

Blogs

Behind Talend Open Studio, there's a bunch of guys keen on sharing their experience with you... Here is an open and informal discussion on technical topics related to Talend Open Studio... or not.

Sources

Wonder why this looks so good and works so well? Just browse on your own through all the various files and modules comprising Talend Open Studio and you'll easily see any changes made to any part of the code at any time.

Bugtracker

Looks like Talend Open Studio isn't behaving properly? Report bugs and keep track of them on the issue tracking system. In other words, help us improve the tool to your satisfaction

For more information, please visit the community website: www.talendforge.org

Made in the USA
Lexington, KY
19 July 2011